D1066031

Simon Forman

Simon Forman

Sex and Society in Shakespeare's Age

A.L.Rowse

History is something sacred because it is true.

CERVANTES

Weidenfeld and Nicolson
London

PR2910.R76 c.2

© A.L.Rowse 1974

First published by Weidenfeld and Nicolson
11 St John's Hill, London SW11

All rights reserved. No part of this
publication may be reproduced, stored in
a retrieval system, or transmitted, in
any form or by any means, electronic,
mechanical, photocopying, recording or
otherwise, without the prior permission
of the copyright owner.

ISBN 0 297 76741 0

Printed in Great Britain by
Richard Clay (The Chaucer Press), Ltd.,
Bungay, Suffolk

To
Rebecca West
admirable writer
constant friend

3067342

Contents

Illustrations

Preface

This is a work of research in the exact, and exacting, sense of the word: it is based on original documents throughout, and the result is a mass of new information about Elizabethan society, about people great and small, significant and insignificant. Forman's Case Books take us more intimately into the crevices of society, and of people's lives, than any other documents I know. The main inspiration of my work as an historian has been to penetrate as deeply as possible into the *life* of the past, to recover it and renew it in my own work in accordance with the evidence. From this point of view Forman's papers, waiting all those years in the Bodleian for an explorer, have been a most fortunate find; the only wonder is that no researcher should have got down to them before in depth.

Halliwell-Phillips transcribed the Autobiography for the Camden Society a century ago, but Victorian prudery prevented its publication. It is an advantage of today's open society that so much material can be presented of importance to psychologists, anthropologists and, possibly, medical men.

Most of the book consists of a biography of Forman, drawn from his voluminous papers, especially the Case Books, filled out and checked by all the relevant material elsewhere in print and in manuscript. But in a brief *Part II* I have selected the most interesting and significant of Forman's writings. While adhering precisely to Forman's own words, I have presented them in modern spelling and punctuation. William Lilly observed in his own time that Forman was a repetitive writer; I have omitted a number of 'Ands', with which he frequently began sentences, and I have had to re-arrange a few entries in their proper order of dating. All for the convenience of the modern reader, as with my edition of

Shakespeare's Sonnets: there really is no point in coming between the writer and the modern reader with antique spelling and punctuation. With regard to the text, the matter itself, my usage is essentially conservative. I should add that, with regard to footnotes, unqualified numbers always refer to Ashmole mss.

Though Halliwell-Phillips, an excellent scholar, made a few mistakes in transcribing, the chief difficulty with Forman is that of identifying people. In this field I have had some great strokes of luck, not only in regard to Shakespeare's known landlady and his hitherto unknown mistress and other members of that small circle of Lord Chamberlain Hunsdon and his Company, but even more with regard to Forman's mistress in London, Avis Allen, whom I thought I should never find; she does not occur in any of the parish registers, for the very good reason that she was a Recusant Catholic.

Many more identifications remain to be made – in particular, of the Burbages and Henslowes among Forman's clients – by other and younger scholars than I. But I have, at the least, uncovered a mass of new material, intensely revealing of Shakespeare's age and background, personal and social, and opened up trails for others to follow who have more time than I have left.

I have myself had two spells of intensive work on the Forman papers; the first some fifteen and more years ago, when I retired rather discouraged, finding the people too difficult to unravel – to renew the assault later with a wider knowledge of Elizabethan society and its denizens. It is obvious that my interest in them is historical and social, as living persons, and not at all astrological, as to which I am quite unqualified.

For the opportunity of renewing the attack I am most indebted to All Souls College for renewing my research Fellowship. I regret that, over so many years, I have not kept a record of all the obligations incurred. Miss N. McN. O'Farrell and Miss Joyce Batty have helped me greatly over manuscript material. I am very grateful to the Bodleian Library, whence most of my material has come; to the Librarian of Lambeth Palace Library and the officials of the Library at London County Hall for arranging for me to study the unpublished Lambeth Parish Register; to the Librarian

at the Guildhall, London; to the Master and Clerk of the Iron-
mongers' Company; and to the staff of the Diocesan Record
Office in its delightful quarters in the Close at Salisbury. Sir
George Clark, Mr J. S. G. Simmons, Professor Peter Matthias,
Dr K. R. Andrews, Dr Robert Beddard, and the vicar of Iwerne
Minster are among those who have answered my queries. Dr Roy
Strong, and Major-General E. N. K. Estcourt have kindly helped
over portraits of my characters; even more, I am obliged to the
London collector who came up with an engraving of a portrait
of Forman, which I thought we should never find.

A. L. Rowse.

Part I

Chapter I

An Elizabethan Practitioner: Astrology and Medicine

By an extraordinary chance – the survival of his papers – we can know more about the Elizabethan, Simon Forman, look more intimately into the crevices, the secret passages of a man's life, than perhaps with any man who has ever lived. More even than with Pepys or Boswell, Casanova or Rousseau, André Gide or Henry Miller. This will appear a tall claim; but it can be justified, for Forman recorded his activities, his thoughts and hopes and fears, from day to day and hour to hour, including his sex-life, with veracious accuracy – as it needed to be for astrological purposes. It is probable that there is no other complete record of a man's sex-life with his wife, let alone all the other women who came Forman's way, in the course of his practice or out of it.

Nevertheless, though normally prurient and highly sexed, Forman was no pornographer. We must distinguish between pornography and anthropology. He would have strongly disapproved of the former – we cannot conceive of him writing Thomas Nashe's salacious poem, 'A Choice of Valentines', for example.[1] Forman is simply interested in the facts, every fact about himself and other people, especially women – who were an open book to him, and many laid themselves open to him, for he was abnormally heterosexual: there is not a trace of any other interest, in an age distinguished by the homosexuality (or ambivalence) of Bacon and Marlowe, Oxford and Southampton and Lord Henry Howard, or with the Court of James I.

Forman was simple and straightforward – he would have deeply disapproved of these; abnormally keen and curious – in that like

[1] *The Works of Thomas Nashe*, ed. R.B.McKerrow, III. 403 foll.

Pepys – he was naïve and transparently sincere, again like Pepys, and regarded himself as a moral and even a religious man.

To have left an Autobiography is rare enough in itself for an Elizabethan. Where the few others we have are laconic and extrovert, disappointingly incommunicative, Simon had a natural gift for communication – of all kinds. He is expressive, he takes us into the inside of his personality, his troubles, his suspicions, his loves, his naïve hopes for himself. Naïvety often goes along with genius, or is a condition of it; I am not suggesting that Forman had genius, but his self-revelation is compulsive and obsessive, which are qualities apt to go along with genius, and it is certainly unique.

We can read Simon like a book: his inferiority complex – small in stature as boy and man, he had an obvious sense of inferiority. He thought of himself as a little Joseph in his family, disconsidered among his brethren. His father died when he was but a boy, brought up by an unsympathetic mother, who had no patience with Simon's passion to educate himself and acquire knowledge. One well recognises the pattern: frustrated, picking up scraps of knowledge, largely self-educated, earning his living as an usher and then as an unqualified practitioner – for he longed to go to the university and only managed to get to Oxford as a servant for a year or so – Simon developed regular symptoms of paranoia. And no wonder, considering the persecutions he endured, the shifts he was reduced to for a living, the questionable and sometimes dangerous courses he ran.

The wonder is that he made such a success of life as he did – after years of poverty and insecurity, disrepute and frequent imprisonments, he emerged a substantial citizen, a man of property, independent and respected (by many, if not by all); married to the niece of a Kentish knight, very proud of his wife's armigerous relations; on friendly terms with a number of highly connected persons, a vestryman of his parish at Lambeth, in the registers of which he is always described – so important to an Elizabethan – as 'gentleman'. (In that like his contemporary at Stratford.)

It is evident that Forman is no less interesting as a social than as a psychological case-study. From the point of view of the latter – oppressed by his early circumstances, insecure and undersized, he did not start sexual intercourse until his thirtieth year. Having started late, he seems to have accumulated exceptional reserves of sexual energy and continued with astonishing potency up to the end – in that like Victor Hugo, who, not having dissipated his energy in youth nor having mated until his marriage-night, went on unabated into his seventies.

Forman's education is interesting from both points of view. One sees from his Autobiography that opportunities for elementary education, up to a certain point, were more frequent and available than is usually thought. There was a school on Simon's doorstep in the village at Wilton; there was a free school across the meadows from his home at Quidhampton, in the Close at Salisbury. Simon attended both for a time, at irregular intervals. But the difficulty was to remain on at a grammar school without family support, still more to get to the university as he ardently desired. Simon managed to get to Oxford only in the service of two frolicsome Wiltshire clerics on their way to preferment in the Church, meanwhile spending their time hunting deer on Shotover and chasing wenches in the suburbs.

Simon was naturally chagrined at his lot. I wonder only that he was not more resentful; but that was not the age of social protest, nor did everyone expect to be supported. Virtually alone in the world, he did what he could to get an education for himself. He was largely self-taught; then he learned by teaching others as an usher in country schools (as Shakespeare did for a time). By these means Simon got enough Latin to write it fluently if in elementary style – which was more than most students at the university could with their better chances. We see how passionately attached to his books the poor fellow was – they were a source of power to him, not only as a practitioner. Once they were confiscated from him for years; some were lost; later, he was robbed of others.

No wonder he carried the stigmata of a frustrated man. He wanted above all things to be a scholar: disappointed of this, he never gave up – he certainly had courage, and he believed that there was a Providence; so he did the next best thing, and followed his natural bent as practitioner and astrologer. This worked out better: he would have been lost as a conventional academic, and we should have no cause to remember him. His frustration was fortunate: it banked up his powers as a writer. We see from the mass of papers he has left what abnormal powers of observation and perception he had, what an un-frustrated sense of life, what vivacity and compelling immediacy, what a power of characterisation, what an eye for appearance and personality.

The people he describes live for us – quite as much as in the published pages of Nashe or Greene, more so than in Dekker or Deloney. The whole procession of Elizabethan life goes by, from the top to the bottom of society, from the Queen herself downwards. But we are not seeing them from the outside only, the splendour of their habiliments, costumed for the public gaze; we see them in flesh and blood as they were, in their pleasures and private entertainments, in child-birth and death, in sickness and disease, their fears and suspicions, their credulities, in their underclothes, often with nothing on at all.

Forman became well known in his own day as he came to be successful, of ill-repute and ill-spoken of by some, better thought of by many who placed their confidence in him, while others – and those not the least important in the land, great Court-ladies, peers and knights, leading seamen and City merchants such as Sir William Monson and Nicholas Leate – were completely dependent on his expertise, could not put to sea or lade a ship for abroad without Forman's forecast.

He has his place in the *Dictionary of National Biography* – Sir Sidney Lee wrote it nearly a century ago. In addition to a number of inaccuracies, it is based on a fundamental misconception, which has had its influence on people's thinking of Forman. They think of him as a charlatan and a quack: he was in fact neither.

Forman was absolutely convinced of the truth of astrology – as other people are of the 'truth' of the doctrines they believe in; he relied upon it for guidance in every aspect of his own affairs and for the course he should take daily, as much as in advising others. If many cases did not work out that was because complete accuracy could not be obtained, or something had gone wrong with the calculations, difficult and uncertain in any case; or because he did not know enough, and was anxious to learn more. But, then, everybody believed in astrology, more or less. The Queen had her astrologer, Dr Dee, whom she treated with favour; he had cast the horoscope for the most propitious day for her coronation – and no one can say that that did not turn out well. Leicester's astrologer was the Oxford mathematician – *mathematicus* had also the sense of wizard: Thomas Allen. Allen calculated the nativity of William Herbert, third Earl of Pembroke, to whom the First Folio of Shakespeare was dedicated by its sponsors: Allen said that Herbert would die at fifty; he died unexpectedly, having been perfectly well, within a couple of days of fifty. What was in dispute was *judicial* astrology, i.e. whether enough was known to be able to forecast the future.

As C.H. Josten tells us, astrology provided a 'generally recognised universal law'.[1] Even those scholars who repudiated judicial astrology 'accepted astrological rules as a code linking the eternal and incorruptible celestial spheres to the corruptible sublunar world by an all-pervading system of sympathies and antipathies'. We already see the analogy with sympathetic magic, which has prevailed in all societies until the rise of modern science, and which we shall see in evidence in the medical treatments later in this book. 'The horoscopes, or "figures" which they calculated with the aid of astronomical tables [ephemerides, almanacs etc.] were charts of the heavens, drawn up for a particular time and in relation to a particular place, showing the position of the planets – including sun and moon – in the twelve signs of the Zodiac.'

Exponents of astrology did not fail to make the point that, since the sun and moon had such obvious influences upon the earth, was it not unreasonable to deny that the stars, their conjunctions and emanations, had their influences too? The purpose of astrology was to discover their operation. 'Judgements were based on the supposedly favourable or unfavourable position of the planets in the zodiac . . . on their conjunctions, and on the supposedly harmonious or disharmonious character of certain angles', i.e. 'aspects' in relation to each other. Thus 'it was essen-

[1] *Elias Ashmole (1617–1692)*, ed. C.H. Josten, I. 21 foll.

tial to know the time of birth with great accuracy, because even minor variations would yield widely divergent dates' – hence Forman's constant and conscientious striving after accuracy, or else all the calculations would be thrown out.

The calculations proceeded in accordance with generally recognised rules of interpretation, which varied very little. So that astrologers could help each other with their problems, and did, as we shall see with Forman's pupil and 'brother', Richard Sandy, an Oxford man who was rector of Great Linford, in Buckinghamshire. These two consulted each other over knotty points. Then Forman's papers came into the hands of Sandy's nephew and pupil, Richard Napier; then through the astrologer, William Lilly, to Elias Ashmole. Ashmole's name is held in veneration as the founder of the Ashmolean Museum at Oxford and for his early scientific interests. But he was just as much an astrologer as Forman, whose proficiency in the art (or science) both Lilly and Ashmole respected; they made considerable use of Forman's Case-Books in their own practice.

Thus there was a universal language of signs for the planets, and the Zodiac, i.e. the belt of stars on either side of the path the sun appears to trace annually around the earth – regarded from the point of view of the earth. (It is the relative positions of sun, moon and stars *vis-à-vis* the earth that matter in astrology.) This strip of constellations is divided for convenience into twelve compartments, each with its sign. Then there are the signs for the twelve 'houses', i.e. the departments of everyday life, divisions of the earth's surface – hence 'mundane' matters – upon which celestial forces bear.[1] And so on.

It was all a part of knowledge, like theology.

One sees further its relation to, or analogy with, alchemy or the transmutation of metals (which we can now effect). As Sir George Clark says, in his *History of the Royal College of Physicians*, the alchemists and wonder-workers also used experiment and observation; it was not only the conventional academics who were forerunners of the scientific spirit.[2] Alchemy made its contribu-

---

[1] cf. Christopher McIntosh, *Astrology*, 11 foll., 54.
[2] cf. Sir George Clark, *A History of the Royal College of Physicians*, I. 110.

tion to chemistry, as the intent curiosity of astrologers, and their observations, made to astronomy.

Similarly Forman was no quack either, for all that he had a running battle with the authorities for many years for practising without a licence – until in 1603 he got a licence from Cambridge University. After that 'Doctor' Forman – he was not, of course, M.D. – was secure.

In his early years at Salisbury, when trying to earn a living by practising medicine, he was persecuted and suffered a long imprisonment at the hands of the J.P.s, instigated by his constant enemy, Giles Estcourt, also a persecutor of Catholics. (Forman's sympathies leaned that way: he certainly was no Puritan.) The J.P.s brought in the Bishop, John Piers, from whom Forman could have got a licence if he had been qualified. Inability to study at the university prevented this, though ultimately the Bishop turned out more sympathetic; Simon says that they were 'reconciled' before his leaving the city. But – imprisonment for over a year! – no wonder Simon developed paranoia.

Transferring himself to London, he was had up before the Barber-Surgeons once for daring to practise their trade. Then he was persistently pursued by the Royal College of Physicians, bent on establishing their monopoly and, incidentally, their ascendancy over the surgeons too.[1] Again and again the R.C.P. – 'the Doctors' in Simon's term – haled him before them, fined him and imprisoned him. In the end Simon moved outside their jurisdiction to Lambeth.

Are we to take the side of the Royal College and assume that authority was right?

Perhaps we should if Forman were a mere impostor, whose ministrations were dangerous. But anyone who knows the treatments prescribed by 'qualified' doctors in the Elizabethan Age will know that theirs were hardly less so; with their addiction to constant bleedings, their application of leeches to suck the patient's blood, their appalling purgings, the concoctions they supplied – the toads, newts, snakeskin, snailslime, their dreadful powders.

[1] 'Altogether the College handled over a hundred cases of illicit practice from 1572 to 1603.' Clark, I. 145.

We may well conclude that we should be better off treated by Forman. For one thing, he disapproved of persistent bleeding – he prescribed it infrequently; I have never come across him applying leeches. For another, he set not much store by urinology as the Doctors did, though he had to test the urine of his patients when they sent it to him. In diagnosis he did not go simply by facial tokens and he thought pulse-taking overdone – in which he may have been wrong. He evidently attached more importance to the use of herbs, of which he had knowledge, and the new Paracelsan use of minerals, which the Royal College was long in catching up with.

If a large part of Forman's diagnoses was astrological, the Doctors did not disagree with that in principle; they believed in astrology too: they examined him in it and faulted him for not knowing enough of it. We must reflect that along with this there went an ever-widening experience of all sorts and conditions of men and women, sharp perceptions and abnormal intuitive powers. In sum, it is fairly certain that Forman did less harm and more good by his practice; this no doubt was why his *clientèle* remained faithful to him over the years and he achieved an increasing measure of success to the end.

Since Forman was something of a psychological case himself, he undoubtedly had the psychic gifts, the telepathic experiences and intuitive insights that are apt to go with this. There is a penumbra of such experiences which we must not deny, because it is still not understood or explained, nor is it under conscious control. His unconscious was very active and revealing – hence the fascination of his dream-life.

He ardently desired, like many Renaissance people, to explore this penumbra and to gain control over its phenomena – in Elizabethan language, power over the spirits. If he thought that he could summon them up, so did the eminent scientist, Dr Dee; Forman at least tells us honestly that he did not *see* them, merely heard or sensed them. To such purposes were the sigils, the lamina, the engraved rings, the charms and tokens and amulets – like the crosses so many young people wear on their chests or breasts today, though they do not seem to keep evil spirits away. For an analogous purpose were the love philtres, the figurines, the sexual symbols to compel love. Anyone might want to compel the love of a much desired person or body – as Frances Howard wished to compel the love of Shakespeare's Southampton or the Earl of Hertford (she got him); or as her desperate cousin, Lady Frances Howard, wished to compel the love of King James's boy-friend, Robin Carr (she got him). Both ladies were clients of Forman's, the former for years.

This desire to penetrate the region of the unknown, the unconscious, the subconscious, the suggestible, is what was so exciting to the Elizabethan imagination. Living on the borders of a mental world expanding into the unknown, they did not know what might not be possible. Of course they believed in the ghost in *Hamlet* – and so would its creator. This was the element that excited Forman in Shakespeare's plays and moved him to record it. How much more exciting such a world was to the imagination! – invisible, intangible, yet capable of being sensed, felt along the nerves and in the roots of the brain, themselves possessed by the desire to know, to attain power through knowledge.

This was the leading motive of Forman's life, what gives consistency and unity to all his activities, as much as with Dr Faustus's. Marlowe's *Dr Faustus* is the key-play of the Elizabethan Age, as it was the most popular, with its calling up of the spirits, its Latin formulas for the purpose, Mephistopheles its familiar, its devils – and the anguish of the desire for knowledge for ever unsatisfied, of the frustrated passion to know, the penalties for penetrating into the forbidden.

Something of this *Angst* recurs all through later Elizabethan, or Jacobean, drama. Because of this climate of the spirit I have attempted to diagnose, Shakespeare intuited a great deal of the findings of modern psychology. I am myself so much affected by it that often I cannot bear to look at it laid bare on the stage, it reaches into such crevices of guilt, remorse, anxiety, suspicion, fear. In *Hamlet* there is the whole of the Oedipus complex – the sensitive son's too great attachment to the mother, his horror of the guilt he sees in her, the unbearable bitterness of his reproaches; the cutting edge to his dialogue with Ophelia precisely *because* he loves her. In *Macbeth* the fear and the terror, the retribution of the conscience upon the human spirit for the crime the will has forced upon it, searches similar depths: one can hardly bear to look at the sleep-walking scene, the washing of the hands, the agony of a soul in despair.

King Lear, Othello, The Winter's Tale uncover similar senses of the diseased psyche; we might regard them as type-patterns of psychological cases worked out before us. No wonder these are among the most powerful plays ever written, though we may link with them *The Duchess of Malfi* and *The White Devil* for such searching of the depths.

Even in details, in sudden insights, Shakespeare intuited the findings of modern psychology. When Desdemona at last perceives the horror of Othello's alienation from her, and the reason why, her woman asks her in concern at her state:

How do you, madam? How do you, my good lady?

Desdemona answers, what is surprising:

Faith, half asleep.

This is no casualness: this is what is liable to happen when a woman receives a profound shock; she is numbed, she wants to go to sleep (in fact, Desdemona is half-way to death).[1]

I have noticed a similar instance in *Coriolanus*. Coriolanus is in love with Rome: Rome is all the world to him, yet has rejected him. What he wants to do in revenge is to set Rome on fire. This is profoundly right: there are plenty of cases of people who, rejected, want to kill what they love, but Shakespeare knew intuitively that there are those who want to do it by fire: love is a flame.

The modern study of the psychological significance of Shakespeare's imagery is perhaps the most rewarding aspect of Shakespearean scholarship in our time. With a true poet the imagery is largely subconscious and comes from greater depths than the conscious and the cerebral. With Shakespeare, I have noticed – besides what we all know of him as a clever craftsman – that

[1] I owe this point to the perceptiveness of Miss Elizabeth Jenkins.

his subconscious worked with him and for him day and night: the images connect up and have a life and consistency of their own like vegetation under water. As a writer, he was the most fortunate who ever lived.

Today Forman is best known as the only person, except for John Manningham earlier, to have left us a record of having seen plays of Shakespeare. Forman records seeing four plays in 1611 – *Macbeth, Cymbeline, Richard II* and *The Winter's Tale* – and his report is consistently in line with his own interests: the story and the moral of it, forecasts and prophecies, how and when fulfilled.[1] He must have seen others, for he was a play-goer. His report is headed: 'The Book of Plays and Notes hereof per Forman – for Common Policy.' And this is the point of it: in Elizabethan parlance 'common policy' means 'practical use'. Forman was interested in what conclusions might be drawn from the story, though there are other things we may learn from his account.

He saw *Macbeth* at the 'Globe' theatre on 20 April 1611, and gives us a summary of the play. He observed that Macbeth is lured on by the prophecies of 'three women fairies or nymphs'. During the night of the murder 'there were many prodigies seen that night and the day before'. Naturally he was impressed by 'the blood that could not be washed off by any means', and the ghost of Banquo 'that sat down in his chair' at the supper Macbeth gave. This is what chiefly interested Forman. Perhaps he saw himself when Lady Macbeth walked in her sleep; for he observed, 'and the Doctor noted her words'.

From Forman's summary of the story of *Cymbeline*, undated, one sympathises with Ben Jonson's strictures upon such an incoherent farrago of fable; but one notes Forman's usual characteristics, the coincidences and details that caught his attention, as well as his verbal usages and spellings. His account of *Richard II*, which he saw at the 'Globe' on 30 April 1611, is far more interesting. It contains a passage which does not now appear in the text – we do not know whether it was subsequently suppressed, or whether alterations were made. We do know that the text when

[1] Ashmole Ms. 208, f. 207 foll.

13

first published had to omit the abdication scene, for political reasons. Forman, characteristically, is interested in the practical moral to be drawn. 'Remember therein how Jack Straw by his overmuch boldness, not being politic or suspecting anything, was suddenly at Smithfield Bars stabbed by Walworth, the mayor of London, and so he and his whole army was overthrown. Therefore, in such a case or the like, never admit any party without a bar between; for a man cannot be too wise, nor keep himself too safe.'

There is the essential Forman: simple, candid, yet suspicious, on the alert for what he can learn – within a few months of the end of his life. Still more evident in the concluding passage. 'Remember also how the Duke of Lancaster asked a wise man whether himself should ever be king; and he told him no, but his son should be a king. When he had told him, he hanged him up for his labour, because he should not bruit it abroad or speak thereof to others. This was a policy in the Commonwealth's opinion [i.e. a clever trick in the popular opinion]. But I say it was a villainous part and a Judas' kiss to hang the man for telling him the truth. Beware by this example of noblemen and of their fair words, and say little to them, lest they do the like by thee for thy good will.'

Here speaks Simon the moralist, who had had to make his own way in the world and had plenty of experience of men's treachery. Naïve as he was, he kept a weather-eye open. He saw *The Winter's Tale* at the 'Globe' on Wednesday, 15 May, recounts the theme of psychotic jealousy, but as usual is more taken with the odd coincidences, how 'the shepherd having showed the letter of the nobleman by whom Leontes sent away that child and the jewels found about her, she was known to be Leontes' daughter and was then sixteen years old.' Naturally Simon was intrigued by Autolycus, 'the rogue that came in all tattered like Coll Pixie, and how he feigned him sick and to have been robbed of all that he had; and how he cozened the poor man of all his money. And after came to the sheep-shear with a pedlar's pack, and there cozened them again of all their money. And how he changed apparel with the King of Bohemia's son, and then how he turned courtier, etc. Beware of trusting feigned beggars or fawning fellows.'

We begin to see what the inside of Forman's mind was like; we must not expect absolute accuracy in detail, if we have the imagination to allow for how difficult it is to remember every passage right after first seeing a play. The remarkable thing is how much he did remember, though, with his own strong bent of interest and working imagination, he may have read details into the play afterwards, mixed a detail from one play with another.

Each of us takes to the theatre his own line of interests: this was Forman's. We see it consistently again in his account of *Cox of Cullompton*, a play of Day and Haughton, which Forman saw at the 'Rose' on 4 March 1600.[1] He notes down what impressed him in the story of Cox and his three sons, Henry, Peter and John. One St Mark's day Cox shot his uncle to get his land, and succeeded. Seven years afterwards one Jarvis slew Cox. On St Mark's day next the eldest son, Henry, was drowned by his brothers, who in turn came to bad ends. Then comes the application: 'Remember how Mr Hammond's son slew his father, who begged for mercy, which was denied him. He foretold that his son should bewray [i.e. reveal] himself by laughing: so he did, and was executed for it.'

Forman's Diaries show him attending the theatre, and sometimes making an assignation or a pick-up there – as the upright (as opposed to the horizontal) loudly complained. His Case-Books show him brushing the fringes of the Shakespeare circle. We shall see that among his clients were Burbages and Henslowes; the printers John and William Jaggard, and Richard Field, Shakespeare's schoolfellow, who printed *Venus and Adonis*. Coming closer, we shall find new and unpublished information about the Mountjoys of Silver Street, wig-makers, the French household in which Shakespeare was lodging about the time he wrote the French scenes in *Henry V*. Most fascinating, we shall make the naughty acquaintance, and learn more than we bargain for, about Emilia Lanier, the beautiful Italian mistress of old Lord Hunsdon, first cousin of the Queen and, as Lord Chamberlain, in control of and responsible for Shakespeare's Company.

It is from the detailed evidence supplied by Forman that we have been able to make the indubitable identification of the Dark

[1] 236.

Lady of Shakespeare's Sonnets. For the preservation of this evidence alone all students of our literature, and of Shakespeare in particular, must be grateful to the old reprobate. Without Forman we should have never known who she was – as before my uncovering of him, and discovery of her, she was the most inscrutable problem in our literature.

Forman makes his appearance in literature, under his own name, several times in Ben Jonson. In *Epicœne, or The Silent Woman*, acted in 1609, Davy assures Truewit, 'I would say thou hadst the best philtre in the world and couldst do more than Madam Medea or Dr Forman.' In *The Devil is an Ass*, acted in 1616 – five years after Forman's death – Jonson describes some of the astrologer's equipment:

> They talked of Gresham and of Doctor Forman,
> Franklin and Fisk and Savory . . .
> But there's not one of these that ever could
> Yet show a man the Devil in true sort.
> They have their crystals, I do know, and rings,
> And virgin parchment[1] and their dead men's skulls,
> Their ravens' wings, their lights, their pentacles
> With characters: I have seen all these. But
> Would I might see the Devil! . . .

This was what (or whom) many Elizabethans were on edge to see: a very real personage to them, the counterpart of the Deity all too familiar.

When a woman returns from Spain to set up a School for Ladies:

> All our women here
> That are of spirit and fashion flock unto her
> As to their President, their Law, their Canon,
> More than they ever did to Oracle Forman.

This was written after his death; but though, as we shall see, he was a favourite with women, he had a large practice among men as

---

[1] Virgin parchment was specially prepared; I do not know whether from human skin, but no doubt with appropriate incantations.

well. It is obvious that *The Alchemist* was inspired by Forman – the bogus practitioner is a 'Doctor' – and all the paraphernalia of the profession are caricatured in it, along with its fringe of dubious tricks of the trade:

> And this Doctor . . . he is the Faustus
> That casteth figures and can conjure, cures
> Plague, piles and pox by the Ephemerides,
> And holds intelligence with all the bawds
> And midwives of three shires.

That is unfair – the doctor disapproved of bawds; but this is a caricature, the play a farce, and Ben Jonson was a rational sort of man who may have been sceptical about astrology, as rarely in that age. As usual, Ben has got up the subject and knows all about the apparatus: the casting for things lost, erecting figures in the houses, calculating from the planets for propitious days for one's business:

> Look over, sir, my almanac
> And cross out my ill days, that I may neither
> Bargain nor trust upon them.

Such thinking is not unknown among businessmen or on stock exchanges today – some of them still employ astrologers, as Hitler did. And in enlightened India, there are now professors of astrology in the universities.

Ben Jonson shows himself familiar with other aspects, the alchemical and medical, the Paracelsan (i.e. mainly mineral) remedies, the demand for love philtres and aphrodisiacs. But the real comedy of *The Alchemist* is in its guying of the Separatists, Ananias and Tribulation, the strait-laced, humourless Puritans who show themselves as avaricious and gullible as anyone else. Jonson actually cites by name the puritanical theologian, Hugh Broughton, and his ponderous tomes. A Scotch divine's sympathetic account of Broughton in the *Dictionary of National Biography* doubts whether he was so avid for preferment as popular rumour said. We shall see that he was a client of Forman and that he was quite as greedy for preferment as popular rumour said he was.

Forman's name has been besmirched for posterity by being cited in connection with the Countess of Somerset's poisoning of Sir Thomas Overbury. But Forman himself was dead two years before this notorious event: he had nothing whatever to do with it. It is true that the Countess had been a client of his for philtres and sexual figurines, to entrap the love of the handsome royal favourite, not otherwise engaged in heterosexual pursuits. In that she succeeded – to the ruin of Carr and the death of his friend. But that had nothing to do with Forman – unless one believes that it was by his art that the love was originally procured.

Forman is also known today in the history of the Royal College of Physicians, for he was much harassed by them. He is cited in the history of education for his account of his time at Magdalen College, Oxford;[1] though brief, it is more vivid and convincing than anything else we have. It comes from the Autobiography, which Halliwell-Phillips intended to print for the Camden Society more than a century ago, but then gave up – a great loss, for it is one of the most revealing documents of the age. But the Victorians' loss is our gain; for, I repeat, Forman's candour is not pornographic, i.e. using the subject to stimulate sexual excitement, it is the factual record of a doctor in the course of his practice. This aspect of it, though the most revealing and perhaps unique, is only one aspect among many – the social and psychological, the historical and biographical, and even the literary, for Forman reveals a greater gift for characterisation than most of the professional writers of the age.

Here is young Mistress Flud or Floyd, a Kentish gentlewoman of good family, if not quite a lady in the Victorian sense: she was born Jane Sondes, daughter of Sir Michael Sondes, married to Edward Flud, son and heir of Sir Thomas Flud, Treasurer at War in the Netherlands.[2] In 1600 she was twenty-seven and had been married six years. But three or four years ago she was the mistress of Sir Calisthenes Brooke, soldier son of Lord Cobham, who wrote her letters which she placed under her head at night, wishing to

---

[1] There is a more perceptive and friendly account of him than usual, as 'a wayward genius', in R.S.Stanier, *Magdalen School* (*Oxford Historical Soc.*), 111-12.

[2] Forman is correct, cf. E.Hasted, *Hist. of Kent*, ed. 1779, II. 764.

sleep with him at Throwley Park, 'and no one with her but Susan Rigden, her maid.' And since, 'she loved Henry Wotton and Sir Thomas Gates and others'. Sir Thomas Gates was another Netherlands soldier, a severe disciplinarian who became governor of Virginia, the wreck of whose flagship on Bermuda in a hurricane sparked off *The Tempest*. Henry Wotton was probably the blameless scholar and diplomat, author of the poem, 'The Character of a Happy Life' in praise of the bachelor condition: he found safety in not departing from it.

'And now,' adds Forman, 'Sir Thomas Walsingham,' of Chislehurst, where one pays one's respects at his tomb, the patron of Christopher Marlowe. Sir Thomas had a longer affair with a Canterbury lady, Mrs Webb, who had a passion for him, a regular client of Forman. Mrs Flud was more promiscuous, less discriminating. 'And loved one Cofield, a priest of Throwley, and Sir Robert Rivington. And Robin Jones, her father's man.' We can check this: one Copell was rector of her parish from 1597 to 1605. (One of the difficulties with Forman is that, his information coming by word of mouth, the rendering of names is apt to be variable.) 'Also Wilmar, Sir Thomas Flud's man, and he is dead. She wears Willow for his sake, and a Bramble for Sir Calisthenes Brooke, and Thyme for Sir Thomas Gates [how Elizabethan, with its alliteration!] Also she loved my Lady Vane's son of Kent, and he took her garter from her leg to wear for her sake.[1] And now there is one Vincent Randall that she supposeth and hopeth will have her.'[2] He did not; but she made a better bargain with Sir Thomas May of Mayfield, father of the Caroline poet, Thomas May, by a previous marriage.

We shall find a fuller and sharper portrait of another Kentish lady, with whom Forman was more intimately acquainted, Mrs Blague, wife of the Dean of Rochester; besides many incisive thumb-nail sketches of men as well as women, some throwing a new light on people known to history.

---

[1] Sir Thomas Vane was Lieutenant of Dover Castle in Elizabeth's reign. Hasted, IV. 76; or the young gallant could have been Henry Vane of Hadlow, ibid, II. 252.

[2] Vincent Randall was the son and heir of Edward Randall of Gayseham Hall, near Eastbury, Essex; he had matriculated from Jesus College, Cambridge in 1589. J. & J. A. Venn, *Alumni Cantab.*, Pt. I, III. 420.

The psycho-analyst Jung put a high value upon Elias Ashmole's notes of his dreams, 'especially as no comparable seventeenth-century series of dreams is known to be extant'.[1] But Forman's dream-life was at least as active; his collection of dreams must be even more to be prized, coming from the sixteenth century – is there any other? Forman interpreted dreams as having objectivity, conveying warnings or giving forecasts of events to come; but he had some idea of the subjective element in their causation, their connotation and what they meant for him.

Here is his dream of Elizabeth I that has a wider, an anthropological, significance: it throws a shaft of light, as nothing else that I know, into the erotic stimulus that the menfolk derived from having a Virgin Queen upon the throne – far more convincingly than Ralegh's 'love' poems. In January 1597 Forman

dreamt that I was with the Queen, and that she was a little elderly woman in a coarse white petticoat all unready. She and I walked up and down through lanes and closes, talking and reasoning. At last we came over a great close where were many people, and there were two men at hard words. One of them was a weaver, a tall man with a reddish beard, distract of his wits. She talked to him and he spoke very merrily unto her, and at last did take her and kiss her. So I took her by the arm and did put her away; and told her the fellow was frantic. So we went from him and I led her by the arm still, and then we went through a dirty lane. She had a long white smock very clean and fair, and it trailed in the dirt and her coat behind. I took her coat and did carry it up a good way, and then it hung too low before. I told her she should do me a favour to let me wait on her, and she said I should. Then said I, 'I mean to wait *upon* you and not under you, that I might make this belly a little bigger to carry up this smock and coat out of the dirt.' And so we talked merrily; then she began to lean upon me, when we were past the dirt and to be very familiar with me, and methought she began to love me. When we were alone, out of sight, methought she would have kissed me.[2]

A month later Forman dreamed of her again, coming to him all in black, with a French hood. One hardly needs to be a Freud to spot the symbolism in Forman's dreams: in these the Virgin

[1] Josten, I. 29.
[2] 226.

Queen in white, 'all unready', then trailing in the dirt, and finally appearing in black, with a French hood. He would remember the apprehension in the country – of an almost primitive character – at the threat of a French marriage, people's hatred at the thought of her marrying Catherine de Medici's son, Anjou. As for the tall man with the reddish beard bandying words with her, that is just what Essex – tall and red-bearded – was doing at the time.

What a perceptive psychologist Forman was, and what a writer he would have made! – however, it is all in his writings, unpublished as they are, for a better understanding of him today. His profession made him exceptionally observant of every quirk of personality, every detail of appearance, especially of women, suspicious of every change in their attitude, every move. And there was more to it than that – some gift of extra-sensory perception at work in the telepathic experiences, the curious coincidences, the corroboration of forecasts. Forman is perfectly candid in noting when they did not work out, usually in regard to himself.

Today we can be as open-minded with regard to these phenomena we do not understand, as with regard to the phenomena of sex – we do not have to subscribe to Victorian inhibitions on these matters, or accept their prohibitions. We want to understand everything we can, like Renaissance people, and that means probing to find out.

We shall find many coincidences and odd corroborations. Frances Howard, daughter of Lord Howard of Bindon, came to Forman in 1597, when she was nineteen, to cast her horoscope: his information about her birth and circumstances is all corroborated by external documents. He found that, in spite of the early death of both father and mother, she was born in a fortunate conjunction. 'She shall change her estate three times. She hath a woman enemy, tall, long visage, ruddy. She is melancholic', i.e. temperamental.

Frances Howard first married beneath her, a rich vintner, Henry Pranell, who died. She next is after the Earl of Southampton, some three years after Shakespeare's Sonnets to his young patron have terminated. She has Forman put the question whether Southampton will love her better or not, and what will eventuate.

Again, 'whether he doth bear her any good will, or did tell of the letter, and whether she shall speed in the country.' The answer comes: 'he bears her little good will and she will do ill in the country.' Forman notes that at the end of the year Southampton married Elizabeth Vernon, who was pregnant by him: persuaded to it – if the truth be told – by her cousin, his leader and mentor, Essex.

So the beautiful Howard widow next pursued the widower Earl of Hertford, whom she captured and with whom she jogged along unhappily, until he died in 1621. She then changed her estate a third time – to enter the royal family as wife of the Stuart Duke of Richmond and Lennox, and lies with him in all their glory in Henry vii's chapel in Westminster Abbey.

This Frances Howard – there were three altogether at this time – was certainly born in a fortunate conjunction. We shall hear more of her.

Forman's Autobiography and Diaries are fascinating in their transparent honesty; his Case-Books give us the widest spectrum of Elizabethan society. There are Court-ladies at the top, like these two Howard countesses, or the daughters of Lord Chamberlain Hunsdon, Lady Scrope and Lady Hoby; or Forman is consulted by Lady Hawkins, second wife of the great seaman. It is not only the ladies who are faithful to him – as Ben Jonson insinuated; we have seen that the most constant client, over the longest period, from 1587 to Forman's death in 1611, was the naval commander, Sir William Monson. Several knights appear in Forman's books, Sir Barington Mullins is a regular, Sir William Eure, the soldier son of Lord Eure, Sir Clement Heigham, Sir William and Sir Thomas Cornwallis, the celebrated Sir Thomas Shirley before setting to sea on one or other of his voyages. Mr Leate was not the only client among leading City merchants, there were Mr Richard Staper and Mr Hawes among others. Plenty of gentlemen, from town or country, Wottons and St Legers; a Stafford or Lumley, a Fermor or Tregonwell; James Fitzgerald, the Queen's Earl of Desmond; or a friend of Ben Jonson – it is ironical to think – in Sylvanus Scory: we learn some very unsavoury details about that lascivious son of a bishop. We come upon respectable government officials: Mr Cuthbert Stillingfleet, messenger of Her Majesty's Chamber, is a regular; so is Mr Auditor Conyers of the Exchequer. Forman's most devoted clients – they can do nothing without him – are a clerical couple: Dr Blague, Dean of Rochester, and his wife. There is also their son-in-law, Dr John Dove, the theologian; the well-known Hugh Broughton, or Dean Wood, Mrs Blague's lover.

More important than these elect persons, about whom it is easier for the historian to learn some particulars, is the common run of ordinary folk who appear in the Case-Books, about whom we should otherwise know nothing. It is riveting to peer into the intimate lives of forgotten men and women, the vanished dust of history – so often regarded as its passive material – and to read their hearts. No poets and few prostitutes appear to consult him, though there are a great many women no better than they should be; women come to the doctor concerning their menstrual troubles, hence we learn also about their sex-life – as nowhere else – but the approach is medical. One third of the cases are astrological: numbers of seamen's wives or girl-friends come with inquiries when or whether their menfolk will return from overseas. Hence much information about the sea-life of the Age, the voyages, conditions, privateering, about ships otherwise lost to history or ships about which the historian is glad to know more. Then there is the ordinary practice of an Elizabethan astrologer – such as we find in Dr Dee's Diaries – for finding things lost, stolen or mislaid. In the course of these searches we learn much about Elizabethan social life and the underworld – quite as insecure and squalid as our own. A small number of servants appear: they are as liable to be robbing their masters, as their masters are liable to be giving the women babies. We hear, infrequently, about procuring abortions; we learn immensely more about disease, most of all about states of mind.

Altogether a vast mass of Forman's papers has come down to us. Not only the autobiographical material, but the books he wrote on the Plague, on astrological and alchemical subjects, even one on the creation of the world. They have all remained in manuscript – only once did Forman succeed in getting a little pamphlet in print, *The Grounds of the Longitude*, 1591. (He didn't know how to find the longitude, but neither did anyone else.) Halliwell-Phillips wished to publish the Autobiography, but after printing only some sixteen copies, found that he could not publish in his time.

Perhaps it was as well; for though he was an excellent scholar, and Forman's handwriting in the Autobiography is not really difficult, Halliwell-Phillips made some absurd mistakes in transcription. The entry for 1 January 1595 which he reads, 'I was cosoned by on Osgre a witch', should read, 'I was cosoned by one of Grenewich'. In 1579 'that cursed villain Gilles Estcourte' is misread as 'that cursed William Gilles Estcourte'. (People did not have two Christian names then, by the way.) There are many similar small misreadings, not very important. In any case, unless there is some special purpose in retaining the original spelling, it is far better to render ancient spelling in modern English, not only for the benefit of the reader but also aesthetically.

The real difficulty of interpreting Forman's manuscripts is otherwise. They *are* difficult to read when they are medical diagnoses and prescriptions scribbled in abbreviated Latin. Along with that, on nearly every page, are astrological and, occasionally, geomantical calculations – Forman knew both: these mean nothing to me. The historian is interested only in facts, hardly at all in forecasts, except where they have some point. For the rest, we have an enormous mass of relevant, detailed, microscopic information: a microscope on Elizabethan society.

Here, perhaps, comes the greatest difficulty of all. To interpret the papers, to know who is being referred to, one needs to have an Elizabethan *Who's Who* in one's head. With all the aids of modern research one often cannot find out the person one is after; usually it doesn't matter when people are too obscure and flit briefly once across the page. But there are some people whom I should dearly like to know more about, who have defeated me. After prolonged search I have at last managed to identify Avis Allen, a cheese-monger's wife, a recusant Catholic, with whom Forman was in love: they were hopelessly entangled, not only emotionally and physically but medically – for they both distilled. Their relations make a troubled and pathetic story: one observes the poor woman struggling to free herself from the inextricable entanglement, until she dies on 13 June 1597.[1] It is like a Jacobean melodrama.

Perhaps it is because of these difficulties that the papers have never been estimated at their true worth, let alone been properly explored or made use of by scholars. There is also the question of the climate of opinion. It is not only in regard to sexual life that the atmosphere is freer, the Victorian miasma – so hypocritical too – has cleared away. The most profound revolution in our time is probably psychological; we can now interpret more sympathetically the experience Forman uncovers for us, and we are more open-minded with regard to the margins of the psyche, the penumbra of curious phenomena we still cannot explain.[2] Forman's evidence is of the utmost value here; we do not exclude because we cannot explain.

It has been a stroke of great good fortune that here, on my doorstep, have lain these papers unexplored – except for an occasional citation of Forman on Shakespeare's plays. I have worked at them intensively during two periods, at an interval of some fifteen or twenty years. After my first attack upon them, I retired from the fray somewhat discouraged. Now, towards the end of a life-time of sixteenth-century research, I have returned with renewed zest and a further knowledge of the denizens of the Age, who they were, what they were like, and what they were up to, in the most intimate concerns of their lives.

It is a revelation of what humans are really like, in all times and places, naked and without illusions.

Why, then, should we entertain illusions, especially in this time of social disintegration? It is a much stronger frame of mind with which to confront it, not to entertain illusions. As a philosopher–theologian of the eighteenth century wrote: 'Things and actions are what they are, and the consequences of them will be what they will be: why then should we desire to be deceived?'

[1] 208.
[2] cf. Arthur Koestler, *The Roots of Coincidence*.

Chapter II

A Wiltshire Lad

My purpose here is not to duplicate Forman's account of himself in his Autobiography, but to place it in its setting, check it from external sources and fill it out from other records: to make the picture as complete as possible.

Simon was born 30 December 1552 in the village of Quidhampton, in the parish of Fugglestone (till this century pronounced Foulston) between Wilton and Salisbury. It lies just outside the eastern pale of magnificent Wilton Park, to which the Herberts had been only recently brought by Henry VIII, to that landscape which they have dominated ever since. Henry granted the soldierly first Herbert of this line – one sees his armour now in the Metropolitan Museum and what he looked like in it – the nunnery of Wilton and all its pleasant pastures. John Aubrey, who came from those parts, has a story which, though not strictly true, has a point in it: to the effect that the Earl was glad enough, when Queen Mary came in, to cry 'Peccavi' to the nuns; but when Mary died, he rounded on them with 'Out, ye whores, to work, to work! Ye whores, go spin!' This military language was complemented more properly on his death-bed, when he was said to have expired with the words on his lips, 'They would have Wilton – they would have Wilton.'[1]

The old road from Devizes into Salisbury runs along a field or two to the north of Quidhampton: the village had its own road to the city across the water-meadows and marshes, along river and stream, dominated to the south-east, then as now, by the most beautiful spire in England, the cathedral a couple of miles away. At the east end of the parish is George Herbert's Bemerton. Along the upper Salisbury road is the little parish church of Fugglestone

[1] John Aubrey, *Brief Lives*, ed. A.Clark, I. 316–17.

St Peter, in which Simon would have been baptised – he would still recognise it under the changes of four centuries. Nothing of his time remains in the nondescript huddle that is Quidhampton today, perhaps not even the two or three timber-frame houses disguised under subsequent rebuilding that existed up to our time.

Years later in London, in 1597, Simon dreamed that he was back among the streams and meadows 'at my mother's bridge in Quidhampton and many men had wrought a new double bridge, wonderful strong.'[1] He toiled across it and over the other bridge into a close, where there was much wood and many carts. Many of the men were Queen's men, among them Peter Sefton – his enemy at the time, with whom he was entangled financially and in law-suits. Two men drew their daggers, when Sefton said, 'Put them up, for he is able to master a hundred of you,' meaning by magic. After that Simon dreamt that his man William came at him with a cudgel. Nothing much happened to him that day, 'but I heard of a play'.

When Simon was a boy Quidhampton was a free village with fifteen free tenants, of whom his father was one.[2] This was important in his make-up. The Formans were good yeoman stock, of higher than average standing – though we need pay no attention to the pedigree Simon invented for them beyond his grandfather. That was common form with Elizabethans and even much later – we remember how the Churchills fabricated theirs at the Restoration, and the tart comment of Duchess Sarah upon it: 'it is no matter whether it be true or not, in my opinion; for I value nobody for another's merit.'[3] Simon's education and chances in the world were frustrated by his father's early death, when he was a boy of eleven; he much resented the shifts to which he was put to scramble together an education, and having to work with his hands as a carpenter or looking after cattle. He wanted to enter one of the professions and thought of himself, as such, a gentleman with man-servant in attendance. In time he achieved it – but after many humiliating experiences.

[1] 226.
[2] *V.C.H., Wilts.,* VI. 37 foll.
[3] cf. my *The Early Churchills,* 1.

There was a small free school at Wilton, in what had been, until the Dissolution of the chantries, a lepers' hospital of St Giles.[1] This would have been equivalent to an elementary school, where boys (and girls) learned their A.B.C. It brings home to us that the chances of education at this level were wider in the Elizabethan Age than they were to be again until the end of the 19th century – they were one of the many casualties of the Civil War. But the important thing for the middle classes, and to become a professional man, was to have a grammar-school education – as Richard Field and William Shakespeare had at Stratford. We see how intermittent and brief Simon's schooling was when he went to lodge in the city, to go to the grammar school in the Close kept by the 'furious' Dr Bowles. He was at the grammar school only a couple of years when his father died; it gave him a foundation of Latin, which he subsequently improved for himself. But his mother would not or, with other children to fend for, could not continue him at school. Simon was thrown upon the labour-market and apprenticed himself to Matthew Commin, a general mercer and grocer in the city.

Life was always a struggle to Simon – as to a great many others; the difference was that he minded, knew that he was meant for better things, was exceptionally impressionable, and recorded it all. His dreams tell us everything about him: they are often anxiety dreams, eloquent of his inferiority complex, his constant sense of struggling against odds, his feelings of persecution – all quite understandable. On the other hand, he never gave up; his dreams are evidence of the struggle, his life of his success.

Salisbury was not in a prosperous condition at this time, through the decline of its local cloth industry. There was a good deal of unemployment, which simple folk put down to the influx of immigrants from abroad; in 1568 the town authorities were strenuously expelling vagrants.[2] A few years before, Forman notes, the soldiers returning from the disastrous expedition to Le Havre brought plague into the town. There was another severe outbreak in 1579. Robert Spikernell, landlord of the famous inn, the

[1] *V.C.H., Wilts.*, III. 362.
[2] H. Hatcher, *Old and New Sarum* (in R.C.Hoare, *Hist. of Modern Wilts.*), 281 foll.

'George' – ruined only recently in our time – had to be forgiven his rent.

The Reformation had left its mark upon cathedrals and churches, as if a devastating wind had swept through: destruction of shrines and images, pulling down of roods and roodlofts, removal of altars, whitewashing of paintings; the sale of vestments, sanctus-bells, altar-cloths, the simplification of services. The Reformation left a vacuum in the intuitional, the imaginative, the supernatural area of religion, that which was closest and most consoling to folk-life, cognate with folklore. It is fairly clear that Forman's sympathies were with the old ways, and he was suspected as such; we shall see how he contributed to filling the vacuum in the occult.

Meanwhile, secular customs continued; folklore was very much alive. Still the young men of the parishes went gathering money at Hocktide; still the folk danced at Whitsun, or performed their Whitsun pastorals. Still the bells clattered and clanged from the churches, and in the north-west corner of the Close still stood the squat bell-tower from which boomed the bells of the cathedral. The Bishop with whom Forman had trouble was good John Piers (1577–91). A Magdalen man, when made rector of Quainton in Bucks, he took to tippling in ale-houses with the rustics, for want of better company. Once cured of this, he never looked back: preferment followed preferment; for, though a Protestant, he did not commit the imprudence of marrying and this – in the Queen's conservative eyes – qualified him eventually for the archbishopric of York.[1]

The city's affairs were run by a mayor and corporation of twenty-four, who on feast days and gala occasions wore their scarlet gowns. Such an occasion came in the first week of October 1574, when the Queen visited the city. She had spent the week-end at Wilton, where Simon tells us that he made an oration before her: nothing remarkable in that, it was the regular thing to put on the best scholar of the place who could prate a little Latin. Equally usual was the entertainment the second Earl of Pembroke laid on, a picnic *al fresco* at a hunt in Clarendon Park, where he had constructed a banqueting house of boughs and leaves. But it rained

[1] cf. *D.N.B.*, under John Piers.

hard; so the Queen dined in the Lodge, while the Lords fared as well as they could in their damp quarters.

Leading lights in the city were Giles Estcourt and Thomas Eyre. Estcourt was city clerk[1] and a constant member of the corporation, four times an M.P. for the city. A prosperous lawyer, in 1575 he bought the former college of priests beside St Edmund church; the family lived there in Bedwin Street up to the Restoration. An active J.P., he was a persecutor, as Forman found to his cost; in 1586 he was rounding up Recusants in the city and brought to book the Cornish seminary priest John Hambly, who had the sense to recant rather than be executed.[2] The Eyres were an old landed family who had their representatives in the town: Thomas was mayor in 1587. One sees him and his family on their painted monument in the church of St Thomas.

The Penruddocks, with their Celtic name, had come down from Cumberland in the service of the first Earl of Pembroke, and acquired a delectable estate at Compton Chamberlayne, where they were till this century. The grandson of the first of the family in Wiltshire, Sir John Penruddock, was friendly to Forman and made him tutor to his children. A lawyer of Gray's Inn, John Penruddock was appointed standing counsel for the city; he served as M.P. for Wilton in 1585 and for Southampton in 1586.[3] His son was the Cavalier Colonel of Penruddock's Rising against Cromwell in 1653.

After five years of apprenticeship Simon revolted from it, hoping to get a chance to go on with his education. In the Maytime of 1573 it came with his attendance upon two Wiltshire bachelors of arts, who were cousins: a couple of sportive young clerics, John Thornborough and Robert Pinckney. This episode in Forman's life is already known for the light it throws on the Oxford of the day, and we can check it from outside sources.

John Thornborough was a Salisbury lad who had gone up to

---

[1] Estcourt had been at Lincoln's Inn. cf. *The Black Books of Lincoln's Inn*, I. 404.

[2] *Cal. S.P. Dom., 1581–1590*, 346.

[3] *The Pension Book of Gray's Inn, 1569–1669*, ed. R. J. Fletcher, I. 54, 63; Hatcher, 296.

Magdalen in 1569 and remained there seven years, taking his B.A. in 1573, when Simon accompanied him to Oxford.[1] Robert Pinckney had taken his B.A. from St Mary Hall, now part of Oriel College, the year before.[2] As Bachelors they sat very lightly to their books, spending their time, according to Simon, hunting from morning to night, coursing, fencing, dancing and chasing wenches, particularly the two daughters of Dr Lawrence of Cowley. He was a Fellow of All Souls, Regius Professor of Greek and Archdeacon of Wilts. Since Thornborough and Pinckney were sons of gentlemen, preferment came easily their way.

Pinckney married one daughter and shortly got a living, becoming rector of Lydiard Millicent in 1577; to this Berwick St John in 1579, and Rushall in 1580 were added unto him. These three Wiltshire livings enabled him to found a family, also provided for by Church livings,[3] which raised itself into the county gentry in the next century and stayed there. In the church of Rushall today there is a pretty Elizabethan monument, arabesques and shields, with the initials W.P., one of the family. Years later, in the summer of 1595, when Simon went back to Salisbury to put an end to his long-standing relations with A.Y. (Anne Young), he paid a visit to Berwick St John – no doubt to his old acquaintance.

John Thornborough jilted Dr Lawrence's daughter, and became a much more important ecclesiastic. With the patronage of the second Earl of Pembroke, to whom he was chaplain, he got a nice bunch of livings, in the three years, 1575–8, two in Wiltshire and Marnhull in Dorset.[4] When Simon, on an April day in 1584, rode with Anne Parsons to 'Marlock', I suggest that this is Marnhull near Shaftesbury. This place is, curiously enough, the 'Marlott' of *Tess of the D'Urbervilles* – perhaps Hardy was recalling an earlier pronunciation. A literate cleric who could write books, Thornborough became a chaplain to the Queen and a canon of Salisbury. In 1589 he was made Dean of York in order to forward the work of the Council of the North. He was rewarded with a

---

[1] J. Foster, *Alumni Oxon.*, IV. 1479.

[2] ibid., III. 1166.

[3] Philip Pinckney was rector of Bemerton and Fugglestone in 1648, *V.C.H. Wilts.*, VI.

[4] Foster, IV. 1479.

mass of preferments, and in 1593 with the bishopric of Limerick. In 1603 he was promoted to the see of Bristol, and in 1617 to the better bet of Worcester. He was immensely tenacious and long-lived, holding out there until he was ninety, dying in 1641 just in time to avoid the depredations of the Civil War.[1]

No doubt Simon picked up what he could in the way of learning at Oxford; but he was only a servant, not even a servitor in college, employed in fetching and carrying for these two bright sparks. Dissatisfied and frustrated as ever, Simon, now twenty-one, went back to teach school at Quidhampton and Wilton. At this time he made the acquaintance of a 'Mr Cox', with whom he had much trouble; 'he brought Parson Bref to see my books, and himself was like to kill me'. These people are not identified; but, when Forman was first had up before the Royal College of Physicians, the one medical book he had studied was Cox's on the making of oils, unguents, plasters, etc.[2] This was the direction that Forman's first practice took at Salisbury, after he gave up school-teaching. Cox also dabbled in astrology, magic and necromancy, i.e. the conjuration of spirits from the dead. It looks as if this is where Forman got it from: this is the first we hear of it in the Diary, 1574–5, and the troubled acquaintance lasted some time before it ended in a quarrel.

Simon went on to teach the sons of Mr Duke of Ashgrove, in which family we can locate him. The Dukes were prosperous clothiers out in the countryside, beside the streams with their water-power, as opposed to the decaying industry of the towns. This family owned property in the parish of Wilsford near Amesbury; in 1578 they bought the Lake estate there, and in the next two years built the lovely house of chequered flint and dove-grey stone we see beside the road today.

During these same years Simon wandered about uneasily, tutoring and teaching school, at Iwerne Minster in Dorset, in its delectable situation sheltered under the downs. Here he lay awhile at the vicar's, then had much ado with him, 'lived poorly

---

[1] cf. *D.N.B.* under John Thornborough.

[2] Sir George Clark drew my attention to Francis Cox, who published his *De oleis, unguentis, emplastris, etc conficiendis* in 1575. cf. *D.N.B.* for him.

and did hunt much privily'. Simon must have become familiar with this beautiful hilly country that is part of Cranborne Chase. In 1578 he went back to Salisbury to teach school in the Close for a few months, thence to teach at Devizes and on to Oxford – he must have been as unsatisfactory as he was unsatisfied at being dependent on others. At New Year 1579 he came to a resolution to be no longer dependent but to strike out on his own; for on 17 January 1579 he took the parsonage of Fisherton Anger, then outside the bounds of the city – there is still a Fisherton Street in the western suburbs leading out to Quidhampton, with Fisherton Mill on the Avon.

Here at last he found his vocation – one might say, his dual vocation, in practising both physic and magic. He tells us, 'this year I did prophesy the truth of many things which afterwards came to pass. The very spirits were subject unto me . . . and I had a great name; yet I could do nothing but at adventure.' He was becoming too well known. In June he was laid by the heels by Giles Estcourt, who managed to get at him though living outside the city bounds. Simon was imprisoned for more than a year, despoiled of all his goods and – what he valued most – his books; 'I had much sickness and could have no justice nor law.'

Some years later he wrote some verses rehearsing his former troubles, a thanksgiving to God for his delivery, to the tune of 'Ye children which do serve the Lord.'[1] Though doggerel, they are not more so than the versified Psalms of Sternhold and Hopkins of the tune:

> Though in my youth I was forlorn
> And no man carèd then for me,
> The Lord of me took great regard
> And with his grace did me reward
> For meekness and simplicity.

What we learn factually from the verses is that during his confinement Simon got his keepers on his side, who allowed him out at times to walk abroad with his friends. Meanwhile he appealed to

[1] 802.

the Privy Council. His appeal ultimately got through and on 14 July 1580 he was released. The day after, 'poor and bare, with little money', he departed out of the city, shaking off the dust of his feet, and made for London.

In London Forman was without friends or connections, except for one Henry Johnson whom he treated medically and with whom he spent a month in the Low Countries. In the autumn he came home to Quidhampton, treating sick folk, sometimes sick himself, for the most part forced to thresh and dig for his living – which he thought beneath him. Next year, in spite of being bound over at assizes, he took a house on the ditch, which ran along the eastern side of the city, boldly 'practising physic and surgery. And I began again to live.'

Next year 1582 marked a new departure: sex-life began for him, thus belatedly at thirty: 'the first time in sum that ever I did halek cum muher' – halek is his code-word for intercourse, to become so frequent in the Diaries, and 'muher' is his shortened form, probably representing common pronunciation, for 'women'. He notes that he became first acquainted with A.Y. this year. It was not until 29 February 1584 – Leap Year – that A.Y. became his mistress, and remained so through many vicissitudes.

Meanwhile he had become schoolmaster to John Penruddock's children, and on All Souls day 1582, 2 November, accompanied his wife to London. Simon moved about a good deal, partly with the family, partly on business, but kept up his practice in the vacations in Salisbury, for which purpose he took a house in New Street 'among mine enemies'. There was little profit in tutoring the Penruddock children, so he returned to his practice in Salisbury – changing house to St Thomas's churchyard – and to the love of his mistress. 'I thrived reasonable well: profit by a woman's friendship both in meat, money, and apparel, for healing the sick . . . many things given me, many new friends and much good of the woman whom I loved.'

A predictable consequence came on 27 March 1585, 'when A.Y. was delivered at 7.10 a.m. of Joshua'. There followed too a Chancery suit, initiated by Forman, which throws a shaft of light

from outside upon people mentioned in the Diary.[1] From Elizabethan law-suits it is often hard to tell on which side truth lies.
Simon's former employer, Mrs Commin, pops up again out of the
surrounding darkness, with her kinswoman, Mrs Samways.
Forman claimed that he had healed a wound in Mrs Samways's leg,
which had been maltreated by others; when healed, the family
would pay neither his fee nor his expenses. In his absences he had
had to pay out at least 20 marks to the person who had dressed the
wound. This turns out to have been Robin Grey, with whom
Forman had gone on an adventure to Studland three summers
before – then a haunt of pirates – when the two of them fell into
'the men-of-war's hands'. Mrs Commin deposed that the cure of
Mrs Samways was owing to Grey, who 'had some skill in surgery';
this was unfair to Forman, who would have had more.

What the case reveals is a more tangled background of relations
among these citizens. In the absence of banks there was a great
deal more lending of money among people in those days, and
consequently more disputes. Simon had become acquainted with
the patient's sister, Jane Cole, to whom he had lent money and
who kept possession of his account books. Because of his long
acquaintance with the Commins he often made over to them the
debts people owed him, and gave them his accounts to keep for
him as well as 'his books of art and surgery'. We have a glimpse of
him 'busied in dressing of certain hurt persons in his chamber' so
that he could not go forth when his opponents sent someone to
beat him, himself a small fellow and weak. One morning when
Forman was coming away from sermon at the cathedral, Samways
and another beat him up, threatening to drive him out of the
town. They put it about that he had bewitched Mrs Samways –
always a dangerous charge.

For her part Mrs Commin had been to the Mayor to swear the
peace against Simon, 'who never brake it nor intendeth to do in all
his life'. She rejoined that Forman had no licence to practise from
the Bishop or any other authority, and that the Bishop had pro-
hibited him from practising; this was true enough. She added for
good measure that he had never been worth the twenty marks he

[1] C 2 Eliz. F10/53.

claimed in all his life, and that 'his life and conversation appeared to be such as requireth reformation in these defendants' opinion'.

That was not the point: the fact remained that Mrs Samways's leg was cured. For all his pains, and the flurry of writs he sued out against one and the other of them, Simon was brought before the Bishop and J.P.s and sent to prison again – no doubt for operating without a licence; his house was entered and his goods annexed.

Next year, 1586, Simon had better luck: he shook off his persecutors and was discharged from assizes. 'The Bishop and I were made friends by my Lord Anderson and Sir John Danvers.' This is a grand way of saying that the Bench interceded for him – he always had friends on his side, to offset the enemies. Anderson was the Lord Chief Justice on circuit, said to be a harsh judge – but all Elizabethan judges were severe. Sir John Danvers was a charming man, 'a most beautiful and good and even-tempered person', says Aubrey.[1] 'He was of a mild and peaceable nature, and his sons' sad accident brake his heart.' There was a feud between two of the leading families of Wiltshire, and Sir John's two sons were responsible for killing Henry Long, heir to the family of Wraxall.[2] It was Henry Danvers's hand that shot Long – and Danvers was an intimate friend of Shakespeare's Southampton. His brother Charles perished on the scaffold for Essex, as Southampton nearly did. They were spirited, gifted and cultivated young men: Aubrey says, with county patriotism, 'with all their failings, Wilts cannot show two such brothers'.[3] Aubrey himself calculated the nativities of a number of the family seventy years later – these pursuits still had their following.

In 1587 Simon's troubles thickened upon him. On New Year's day 'A.Y. and I were like to have been betrayed.' In March the city authorities cracked down upon him again. His inveterate enemy Giles Estcourt and the mayor, Thomas Eyre, arrested him and reported to the Privy Council that he had been taken at morning prayer 'with a book in his hand wherein are contained

[1] Aubrey, I. 195.
[2] v. for the whole story, my *Shakespeare's Southampton*, c.vi.
[3] Aubrey, I. 192, 197.

divers bad and fond prayers and devices'.[1] They had thereupon searched his house and seized the residue of his books, which they sent up to their honours, meanwhile detaining Forman in prison.

They also sent up Simon's signed deposition, witnessed by his enemies, one of them Thomas Mompesson, whose family later built the splendid house still in the Close. Simon deposed that the four manuscript books were his, but that the quotations and marginal notes were not of his hand; three parchment rolls were taken from his chest.

The Privy Council discharged him, but, at the request of Estcourt, bound him over to the next assizes.[2] There Simon had no sureties, but two unknown men came forward to stand bail for him. He tells us later that his great enemy was sent to the Fleet for 'falsehood done in fellowship' (some collusive action?). At any rate Forman received his discharge, while Estcourt got a bad name for his inhumanity. Shortly he passed beyond persecuting Simon any more, who tells us that within three weeks Estcourt, his son and son-in-law all died. True it is that in April this year Estcourt made his elaborate will, disposing of properties in several directions, a mourning ring for his friend the Mayor, witnessed by Mompesson.[3]

Fortified by this judgement upon his old enemy, Simon took further steps forward in magic. His books were sent back to John Penruddock's to be investigated, where they lay a long time and some were lost. He took to himself a medium, who served him as Kelly did Dr Dee: this was John Goodridge, 'a gelded man' – perhaps this gave him queer insight, for 'he *saw* first 4 November 1587'. In May 1588 Goodridge came to dwell with him, but Simon put him away in June; later on he returned to his service in London. In August Stephen took Goodridge's place and 'did see first the 21st of September' – this was, I think, Simon's half-brother, of whom we hear much more later. In August too 'Susan Farwell became my daughter': she came from Poole and is the first of the women-devotees who came to include the two Howard

[1] S.P. 12, 199, 21 and 21 (1).
[2] 802.
[3] Prob/11/71, f. 47.

countesses. Already in December 1587 he was visiting Sir George Carey, probably in the Isle of Wight of which he was Governor: he became the second Lord Hunsdon, following his father as Lord Chamberlain, while his daughter consulted the 'Doctor'.

Annus mirabilis 1588 – the Armada passed without a mention in the Diary. What Simon noticed was the strife going on around him, especially with his friends; in November 'the constable came for A.Y., and there followed much sorrow after it'. On the other hand, he was beginning to thrive; 'this year I began to practice necromancy, and to call angels and spirits'.

In 1589 contemporary events caught up with him: he was impressed to serve in the Lisbon expedition under Drake and Norris, which was the English reply to the Armada, and ended in a fiasco. Simon had no intention of wasting time and energy, possibly his life, on that sort of thing. Though forced to accompany the soldiers to Southampton, he was put in prison a couple of days rather than go. Thereafter we find him moving about the country, ill at ease, back to Salisbury, then to Newbury and into Surrey; at last to London, where he arrived 'very poor, and without any penny'. He took a chamber in the Barbican at first, outside the City bounds on the north – beyond Cripplegate out along Red Cross Street; not far from Cripplegate was Silver Street where the Mountjoys lived, whom Simon came to know, and with whom Shakespeare came to lodge.

This year Simon was to settle permanently in London, to make or to mar. It had been 'a wonderful troublesome year. I went from place to place. I got little; I spent and consumed all till Michaelmas. Then it began to mend with me. I practiced again necromancy, magic and physic.'

We shall see how he fared in the new sphere, with larger opportunities opening before him.

Chapter III

Early London Life and Troubles

Forman's move to London was the decisive step in his career: he could not have become the well-known figure he did if he had remained in Salisbury. In spite of the hardships he endured in the first years and the disadvantage of having no connections, the opportunities that opened out were immensely greater. And on both fronts, in magic as well as physic and surgery. The opportunities of practising the former were restricted in a provincial town; in Elizabethan London they were unlimited.

Again, as with astrology, everybody believed in magic, to some extent. The *Encyclopedia Britannica* sagely observes that 'there is no general agreement as to the proper definition of "magic", which depends on the view taken of "religion".'[1] Precisely. This authority goes on to observe that it is impossible to draw an exact line between magic and religion. The word 'religio' probably meant in origin a magical spell. The two are twin ways of putting oneself in touch with the unknown, the supernormal or supernatural powers – though religion, the more sophisticated a society becomes, tries to separate itself out more respectably from the common origin.

Magic is endemic in all societies, as institutional and traditional as religion, not the creation of an individual. Its rites and practices have also the object of propitiating the powers of the unknown, averting evil, persuading or even compelling favours, advancing one's interests, to some extent forecasting the future. Such rites only become magic in the pejorative sense 'when public recognition is withdrawn from them'; and of course 'the religion of alien races is regarded as magic' by other human groups. The anthropo-

[1] *Encyclopedia Britannica*, 11th edition, under Magic.

logist Marett thought that its difference from religion is largely that religion is respectable.

The rites and practices of magic being traditional, there is a body of knowledge with regard to them. This is where the magician, or *magus*, comes in: he needs to know them in order to operate, as with the complicated lore of astrology. One could never learn enough – this is very much Forman's attitude. These practices were based on obvious correspondences, laws of sympathy and contiguity. We see it at work in all human groups, from the primitive hunters who painted the bison they were going to kill, as an aid, upon the walls of the caves at Lascaux, to the old women still sticking pins into wax images, with evil intent, and not only in country villages, today. Sir J.G.Frazer tells us that the idea of sympathy upon which so much of magic rests is that of 'a secret link for things at a distance from each other'. The idea of such links is today more persuasive than it was to Victorian rationalists – with the unexplained, but recognised, phenomena of telepathy and coincidence.

Some minds are more sensitive to and receptive of these than others: hence again the curious powers of mediums like Edward Kelly, as to which there is evidence. It is obvious that abnormal psychology is bound up with this. Our own age has been characterised by remarkable developments in psychological knowledge; we can appreciate the enormous power of *suggestion*, the corresponding importance of *suggestibility*, in bringing things about. We all can witness it at work, with regard to marriage, for instance; it is no wonder that this played a part in Forman's practice. We shall observe, too, the part played by the traditional paraphernalia of the subject – the amulets to avert evil, the sigils or engraved seals, incised or lettered rings, charms or sexual figurines to suggest or compel love.

Black magic was for the purpose of inflicting evil, and this was an indictable offence. In the whole of Forman's practice, of which the documentation is immense, I know of no single instance of his practising magic to hurt anyone. He thought of himself as an upright citizen, as he certainly was an orthodox conforming Christian – rather more religious than most, if not positively pious as Dr Dee was. (Even so, Dr Dee, though somewhat shocked, practised communion of wives, when the spirits told Kelly that they should do so.)

Forman spent Armada year learning necromancy; from Easter to Whitsun 1590, in London alone, with time on his hands, he wrote his book on the subject. We possess this book in Ashmole Ms 244, written on stiff virgin parchment, with its formulas – and also forms of prayer – for calling spirits good and evil, and how to draw out the names of the angels. (We must remember that there was a magic of Names: the Old Testament would not cite the real name of Jah, or Jehovah; ancient Rome had a secret name, etc.). The book includes a section on the heavens, based on the eminent and highly respected mathematician, Jerome Cardan – witness to Forman's scientific interests. There are practical directions on how to find out about thefts, the age of the thief, whether man or woman. No less characteristic of the Elizabethan mind is a section devoted to a 'Book of the Giants' – in whom again everyone believed.

Necromancy meant the art of divination, seeking advice, by getting in touch with the spirits of the departed. The *locus classicus* for it in the Old Testament is King Saul's seeking out the Witch of Endor to raise up the Prophet Samuel for the benefit of his counsel.[1] Since people were long instructed by authority to regard the Bible as written by the inspired hand of God and to venerate it as such, can we condemn Forman and his like for practices which had its warrant, if not altogether its approval?

Nor do we need to defend Forman by recalling that the sciences have developed out of these non-scientific beginnings. Lord Keynes was rather naïve in his excitement at finding that Isaac Newton spent as much time in these pursuits as on mathematics and in regarding him as 'the last of the magicians'.[2] Elias Ashmole, with all his scientific interests, was more intensely interested in

---

[1] cf. Sir J. G. Frazer, *Folk-Lore in the Old Testament*, abridged edn., 291 foll.

[2] Lord Keynes, 'Newton the Man', in *Newton Tercentenary Celebrations* (*Royal Society*, 1946), 27 foll. But note Keynes's view that Newton was 'profoundly neurotic – a most extreme example. His deepest instincts were occult, esoteric, semantic . . . "Of the most fearful, cautious and suspicious temper that I ever knew", said Whiston, his successor.'

magical practices to make spirits appear; he spent much of his time in casting horoscopes, engraving sigils and, when he gathered peony roots and dittany for his purposes, he did so at the full moon with the proper rites, according to Forman's rule.[1]

Once more, I do not wish to duplicate the Diary but to clarify its references, where possible, to fill it out where necessary, and provide it with some external framework. A Star Chamber case of June 1590 gives us a glimpse of Forman in a tavern, 'The Bull', in Lambeth Marsh.[2] An old widow, Mrs Sweyland, was to be persuaded to sign a general release of debts, which she subsequently claimed, from one John Bawd. The persuasion was apparently left to Forman, who was also brought in, as a literate person, because another party to the document, one Henry Milton, could not read. Mrs Milton took the old lady to an upper chamber, where Forman and Milton 'welcomed her and desired her to sit down by the fire and drink with them'.

This she did, and Simon told her 'she were best regard her own quietness, for it would be greatly to her discredit when it should appear before the Lords of the Council that she should sue Bawd and he never owed her anything'. Whereupon Simon read her the general release, and explained it; she willingly sealed it, promising him a reward. Such were the uses of literacy in those days. But it is doubtful whether Simon got his reward, for she went back on her word, to accuse him and Milton of living 'by shifting and lewd practices, cozening and deceiving the Queen's Majesty's good subjects'. This is Mrs Commin over again, and again we do not know what to make of it. A gentleman in the next room viewed the proceedings through a hole in the wall, made for the purpose, and observed nothing untoward.

At All Hallow-tide – a propitious time, when ghosts and spirits walked the earth – Forman 'entered the circle for necromantical spells'. In March 'we heard music at circle'. But he was no less interested in the question of the longitude, which was exercising scientific and practical seamen's minds at the time. In April he

---

[1] Josten, I. 162, 245; II. 1664, 1680.
[2] Star Chamber 5/579/33.

came up from Sussex, where he had been staying with a patron, one Cumber – who had also been a client of Dr Dee[1] – and 'lay at Molyneux' to teach him the longitude. This is Emery Molyneux, the well known compass-maker of Lambeth, who made the splendid globes, both of the earth and of the heavens, of which examples remain to us in the British Museum and elsewhere.[2]

In July Forman put forth his pamphlet, *The Grounds of the Longitude*, the only one of his many writings to reach print, garnished with several Latin mottoes to vouch for its author's respectability.[3] He assures us that he never thought of such a thing until entreated by Mr Robert Parkes, the merchant of Pudding Lane who had befriended him in his necessity. Many men had shot at the problem by cross-staff and instruments; it was not thus to be found 'but by a secret mean . . . unknown except to those to whom myself have showed it. They that do know it are sworn by a sacred oath not to manifest the same without leave of the Author.' There follow sentences from Genesis, Ptolemy, Aristotle and – did not Mercury Trismegistus find the tables engraved with the seven liberal arts?

Then 'divers proffers made in the absence of the Author by Mr Emery Molyneux and others for trial hereof hath not been accepted hitherto because some have thought it either to be done upon presumption or on a bravado . . . But I, the Author, am ready at all times to prefer the same, God willing.' If he can have peace and quiet he is ready to rectify the true places of the fixed stars and correct the inaccurate ephemerides in circulation with tables to be printed shortly, with other books of astronomy and astrology.

Forman's explanation would, of course, be astrological – valueless; but so were everybody else's suggestions until the exact chronometers of the 18th century regulated the matter. Even so Forman was interested in calculations of latitude and longitude: one finds among his notes distances calculated from Quidhampton

---

[1] *The Private Diary of Dr John Dee*, ed. J.O.Halliwell (*Camden Soc.*), 36.

[2] cf. E. G. R. Taylor, *The Mathematical Practitioners of Tudor and Stuart England*, 188.

[3] Printed by Thomas Dawson, 1591, there is a copy of this extremely rare tract in Ms Ashmole 802.

to London, Antwerp, Tübingen, Venice, along with all the calculations of nativities.[1]

With his manic energy and megalomaniac intellectual ambition Forman continued all through his life to write his books on various subjects, medical, astrological, magical and religious, several of which remain in manuscript. And constantly he is writing notes to assist him in his studies – at this time how to make figures to find thieves and things lost or stolen, under the influence of the Peregrine planet.[2] He gives a case of his insistence that a theft of money and rings from a chest was known to three persons, one of them a brother. Upon Forman's description of the culprit, the victim examined his own son and brother, and the theft was confessed. One sees how Forman enjoyed an increasing practice – there went along with the horoscope and his gifts of telepathy, insight into human nature, a constantly widening experience of medical and psychological cases. Underneath was his ardent desire to know and learn; it was useful, if not essential, to learn all he could about his clients – this is why his notes tell us so much about them and so intimately.

For himself he notes from time to time his progress in physic and astronomy. Somewhat later we find him writing a book on astrology, *De Revolutione Mundi*, with the effects of the planets on dearth and scarcity, on plague and sickness; with observations on eclipses of sun and moon, with their influences. He gives us the prices of those things that are cheaper than they were – blissful age of stable value of the currency![3] He constantly notes strange events that stimulated the imagination of the time. 'In Kent there removed a piece of ground of nine acres, trees and all, in the beginning of 1596' – evidently a landslide. In December Dr Rogers was preaching in Wells cathedral on the Wonders of Egypt, when suddenly a tongue of fire shot up the church, followed by exceeding darkness and a noise like thunder. Many were marked with stars on their bodies and other strange things occur-

[1] 208.

[2] 205.

[3] 384. For those interested I quote the prices he gives: currants 25*s* a cwt; grains 12*d* a lb; ginger 12*d* a lb; 'castell [Castile] soap was dear', black soap 23*s* a cwt; hops 40*s* a cwt; pease 8 groats; butter 4*d* a lb.

red at the time. One sees how convincing the portents that foretold the death of Julius Caesar were to Elizabethan beholders of the play.

The year 1592 was a turning point in Forman's life, as it was for the rising dramatist from Stratford. Both years 1592 and 1593 were plague years, and this made for a crisis in Shakespeare's life as in Forman's. For the one the theatres were closed and that meant his means of subsistence – he might well have gone under, as he tells us in the Sonnets, if it had not been for Southampton's support. For Forman the crisis was more desperate, for he and all his household got the plague. But he cured himself and them – at least they all recovered – and at the next visitation he effected many cures and began to come into credit. From 1594, when Shakespeare achieved security with the formation of the Lord Chamberlain's company, Forman also began to prosper.

In the Diary he tells us that at the height of the plague, in July 1592, he sickened with plague-sores in both his groins, and the red tokens on his feet a month after. It was some five months before he fully recovered – a terrible setback for him. In his Notes he tells us how he cured himself, when people had given him up: by lancing his sores and drinking the strong water he had distilled.[1] On his recovery he gave others the same treatment, with success such that his name was made. For his enemies, the Doctors of the Royal College of Physicians, were glad to make their escape into the country. Thomas Lodge, who was one of them, defended them for doing so, on the ground of their value to the community.[2] But Simon sang his song of triumph over them:

> And in the time of pestilent plague
> When Doctors all did fly,
> And got them into places far
> from out the City,
> The Lord appointed me to stay
> To cure the sick and sore,
> but not the rich and mighty ones
> but the distressèd poor.[3]

[1] 802.
[2] v. Thomas Lodge, *A Treatise of the Plague*, 1603.
[3] cf. F. P. Wilson, *The Plague in Shakespeare's London*, 102.

On the basis of his experience he wrote his 'Discourse of the Plague' in 1593.[1] His approach was astrological, as was that of many others. One notes the element of sympathy in his opening, 'As Saturn doth cause the black plague, so Mars doth cause the red plague, especially when he is in Leo or in Sagittary . . .' But there follows a clear description of the symptoms, the sores under the armpits, in flank or groin. Those of Saturn are long in rising and seldom break: 'I have often lanced them or cut them – little matter and much water.' Those of Mars come to a head quickly and often break of themselves – 'be careful about dressing of these sores, they are dangerous and very infective'. If black spots appear on one with the black plague he dies without remedy; if red spots on one with black plague he may escape – 'take care to know these tokens from flea-bitings'. He was in favour of moderate bleeding, and next day strong purges.

As a good Christian Forman subscribed to current orthodoxy as to causation. The plagues sent by devils were allowed by the licence of God. But the plagues sent by God were the most severe of all – and Forman cites the authority of Holy Writ – even though in England there is no Potiphar's wife desiring Joseph to lie with her, no David to number the inhabitants, no wicked Saul. 'Neither is there any lascivious and adulterous Jezebel that, with her painted face and whoredom, enticeth men to come in to her to fulfil the lusts of the flesh, provoking the Lord to wrath and indignation.' Evidently God is a jealous God, and Simon is very strong against whoredom. 'The laws of England are good, the country fertile and good, but the people very bad. And never worse than now.'

Thus the censorious Simon. He gives as signs of God's judgement the blazing stars that have been seen within these twenty years – i.e. the super-nova of 1572 and the great comet of 1577[2] – the earthquake of 1576, the famine of 1584–5, the Spanish Armada, and now this general plague of 1592 and 1593. The courtiers cannot now repent and seek after God; the clergy talk – but a late Bishop of Wells, who lived like a miser, left his wife £30,000 by

[1] 208.
[2] cf. my *The Elizabethan Renaissance. The Cultural Achievement*, 215–16.

report: a nice example! So Simon goes through all estates and degrees and winds up with a long religious exhortation praying that we may find mercy 'in the last day when we shall all come before Him to give account of all our lives and deeds past. Amen.' We shall see what kind of account Simon would be able to make, for no one has left a more particular and detailed one.

The first reward of Forman's services during the plague, and a sign of his increase in reputation and financial success, was the beginning of his long and persistent persecution by the Royal College of Physicians. In February 1593 the Barber-Surgeons called him in question, but that was all; they did not proceed to persecute him, for they were themselves engaged in a running fight with the Physicians. The College was determined to exercise an overriding jurisdiction over surgeons and apothecaries, who flouted it, as well as over empirics and unqualified practitioners who were at their mercy – except for the occasional protection they got from the Privy Council or grandees at Court. The Doctors were all the more determined because their own livelihood was involved; the more successful an unlicensed practitioner the less work there was for them.

But they were not a satisfactory body in themselves. The College was corporately bound to the orthodoxy of Galen in anatomy – who had been put out of date by Vesalius; and with regard to medicines and treatment they took no notice of the doctrines of Paracelsus which, heterodox and experimental as they were, had something new to offer. Sir George Clark tells us, in his history of the College, 'the high hopes of the Renaissance humanists had not been fulfilled. The closer knowledge of Galen had led to no improvements in the physician's art.'[1] This is the perspective in which to see Simon's long battle with the Doctors. Hitherto it has been assumed that he was just a quack and authority must be right. But Forman was no fool; he had a case against the Doctors, and he fought back.

We have a 17th-century account of the College's proceedings against the Empirics, from which we see the determined stand of the College for its jurisdiction against surgeons and empirics

[1] Clark, I. 166.

alike, and also the intervention of personages like Secretary Walsingham or Lord Chamberlain Hunsdon, Lord Admiral Howard or Essex, on behalf of harmless midwives or simple herbalists.[1]

Let us first look at their proceedings from the Doctors' point of view. They first called Forman before them in February 1594 – when they had returned to the City *after* the plague, Simon reminds us. He had been practising for sixteen years, for two in London. He had cured many 'hectical and tabid' (i.e. consumptive) people with an electuary of sweet roses in wormwood water. He boasted that his diagnoses were by ephemerides (i.e. astronomical almanacs) and aspects of the planets – in which they too believed; but when examined in the principles of astronomy he answered absurdly to 'great mirth and sport among the auditors'. He was interdicted from practice and fined £5.[2] On 30 March Simon paid it at the house of the great Dr William Gilbert, President of the College and author of the classic work on the magnet, who lived in Knightrider Street.[3]

A couple of years later the College haled him before them again. They examined him and found him 'very ignorant'; he had learned his physic from the obscure Cox, and in astrology was found ignorant of its common principles.[4] This is improbable; but they fined him £10 and sent him to prison. After a month or so he was released by order of Lord Keeper Egerton. (We find an Egerton among his clients.) Dr Smith and the four Censors of the College thereupon waited on the Lord Keeper to recommit 'so notorious an impostor'. Had up before them again nine months later, he admitted that he had prescribed a compound water – perhaps the 'strong water' he distilled – to a gentleman in a burning fever, who then died. (Might he not have died in any event?) Examined a third time by the Queen's physician he was found wanting in both astrology and physic. He was again committed to prison; but his

[1] Charles Goodall, *The Royal College of Physicians of London*, 1684: Appdx, 'An Historical Account of the College's Proceedings against Empirics.'

[2] ibid., 337 foll.

[3] 208.

[4] Goodall, loc. cit.

close friend and client, the Dean of Rochester, procured a letter from the Archbishop which freed him. After that he took refuge in Lambeth, outside their jurisdiction, where people sought him out as much as ever.

Sir George Clark comments that it was not for his use of astrology as such that the College objected to Forman: their very next President was a doctor whose only publication was astrological.[1] They next attempted to interfere with him at Lambeth by protesting to the Archbishop against 'this intruder into the profession of physic . . . depending upon the speculation and insight of nativities and astrology . . . thereby miserably deceiving the innocency of such simple-minded people as resort unto him for counsel'. As we have seen, Forman's clients included not only simple people but among the highest in the land, among them scholarly clerics, deans and would-be bishops.

Archbishop Whitgift replied disclaiming that he had given Forman any countenance, and hinting that he might be a more suitable subject for investigation by the Ecclesiastical Commission on account of his morals – 'if any man would have taken upon him the prosecution of the cause against him'. But no man did – and the women, as we shall see, were exceptionally obliging. After this the Censors served Forman with another citation; but, entrenched in privileged Lambeth, he refused to obey. The College prosecuted him at law, but Forman at length felt strong enough to counter-charge them before the courts. In the end, by obtaining a licence to practice from Cambridge, he won his battle.

His autobiographical notes and verses give us his point of view against the Doctors.[2] He had remained in London throughout the plague to serve the poor. When the Doctors returned from the country they sent for him to their Hall to demand 'by what authority I meddled in their precinct', casting in his teeth that he had 'learned his skill under a hedge'. Simon replied that he had indeed not learned it in the Schools and that he did not hold with Galen:

[1] Clark, I. 168.
[2] 802.

> For I did judge according to
> The course of heaven and nature;
> And they did judge by the false pulse
> And the deceitful water.

Nor did he agree with the Doctors' constantly prescribing blood-letting when patients were cold, and glisters (enemas) for 'diseases pectoral', i.e. chest complaints. Their urinology Forman called judging by 'paltry piss'. We might well consider that he had the right of it, or at least that he did less harm than they did, who 'oft cure one and kill ten'. For his part, he thought they were pretty ignorant 'in spite of Cambridge and Oxford both' – here, again, the old complaint raises its head, Simon's understandable inferiority complex.

Nevertheless they had attempted to suppress him with fines, and often sent him to the Counter in Wood Street. At last, when they took him to law, they found they could not prevail. He was now independent and free. A later note tells us that, after his imprisonment by the Doctors in November 1595, 'I began to thrive well and, I thank God, I got with half a year almost £150 and great credit.'[1] This was a considerable sum in those days: to earn at the rate of £300 a year put him into the gentlemanly class to which he felt he belonged. And, indeed, after his persecution by the Doctors he never looked back, materially speaking: he began to prosper.

He added, thankfully, 'and had much good by a woman whom I after loved well: A.A'. We shall see who this was and trace the course of the affair.

[1] 240.

Chapter IV

A Love Story and Dream-Life

In his Diary Forman is completely informative about his affairs
with women, which show a marked increase with the extension of
his practice in London and his constant exposure to their charms.
Again we do not wish to duplicate what the Diary tells us; but if
we conflate it with his Case-Books, we gain another dimension.
We learn about the women, their physical and mental condition,
their circumstances, their husbands and friends, and we learn how
Simon made and pursued their acquaintance.

In his profession he was constantly exposed, and Elizabethans
were much more free and easy in these matters than we are: they
were, for the most part, medievals in their behaviour as in their
beliefs. Already in London he had been offered several women to
wife – it was high time he was married. Evidently Mrs Braddedge
thought so, as soon as he began to prosper in 1594: 'But I
intended it not, and she disliked me much till St John's tide.'

Forman gives us a thumb-nail sketch of John Braddedge, who
served him for four years – a rarity in its way, for no one but he
bothered to portray the characters of lower-class people.[1] Born in
1582, he was the son of Elizabeth and John Braddedge in Cheapside; an apprentice at twelve, he was stubborn and self-willed,
gave himself to idleness and would not learn to live in any good
sort but delighted in play and gambling. In September 1597, on
Forman's return from Stourbridge Fair, he put the question for
himself whether 'my boy John in my absence hath spent my
money and deceived me or no'.[2] Grown to filch and consume –
Braddedge was free-hearted – Forman put him away in 1600 and
he went to serve as a lieutenant in the Low Countries. We must

[1] 206.
[2] 226.

add that, since they all believed, Braddedge had his horoscope cast to know what good fortune he should have on taking leave.[1] He came back poor and naked after a couple of years, and in 1603 returned to Ostend. He had begun to be bawdy and lie with wenches at sixteen. In 1607 he married a lame wench in Flanders and next year brought her over great with child and very poor. They came to lodge at Lambeth. He had had a bastard by another that he was contracted to before in Flanders. He came over from the Cardinal-Archduke's camp.

An Elizabethan soldier rises up before us.

We see how one thing was apt to lead to another in the case of a seaman's wife, Ellen Flower of Ratcliff, who became a regular client whenever her husband was at sea. She was interested in other things too. Early in her acquaintance with Simon she attempted to inveigle him: on 5 February 1595 'there came an old quent merchant [the word is Chaucerian] unto me, that was the confederate with Mrs Flower'. This did not appeal: Simon regarded himself as above such things, though not one to neglect such opportunities as the ladies offered. In 1596 Mrs Flower is anxious for news of her husband who went to Stade, but the ship came away leaving him behind.[2] What is become of him? Will he return or no? The answer came that he was on his way homeward. A week later, she wants to know in 'what state he is or whether he will forsake her?' At the end of the month Simon notes, 'he came home 20 April following, in health'. In June next year, 1597, the husband wants to know whether it were best to go on his intended voyage.[3] The answer was that it would be better than to go to his brother, where he would have no money. So he goes; and in July his wife is inquiring after her absent husband, and Simon notes 'halek first at this time'. Her husband returned, for in March 1599 he is away on another voyage about the Cape, i.e. the north-west of Spain.[4] In 1600 he himself again inquires how he shall speed in the *Reuben* to Bordeaux.[5]

[1] 236.
[2] 208.
[3] 226.
[4] 219.
[5] 236.

Simon took the opportunities that presented themselves in the course of his profession. This was the case in regard to the great affair of his life, that with Avis Allen, the wife of one William Allen, and a Catholic. Forman has a note of 2 July 1595: 'A. that now lives obscure for religion's sake, without company, shall – when thirty-six years be come and gone – be constrained to live more obscure, and be in peril of imprisonment and forced by law and go to the church. And then she shall die and be buried out of Christian burial in the thirty-seventh year of her age.'[1] That she was a Catholic Recusant is corroborated from the Recusant Roll of 1594: 'Avisa Allen of London, spinster, alias Avisa Allen, wife of William Allen of the parish of St Botolph in the ward of Billingsgate, London.'[2] She is already liable for the large sum of £100 for refusing to go to church, from the date of conviction to the April following. It is not likely that this sum was extracted, but she lived under threat of it and the danger of pursuit by the law. Such was her horoscope. Avis Allen *was* thirty-six in 1596, and she died in 1597. I can find no record of her burial in any of the registers of the London parish churches.

All the signs are that this was a love affair, not only sex; there was the obsession with each other, the mutual jealousies, vows, quarrels, reconciliations; then there were breaches and renewals, the stimulus of *redintegratio amoris*. It was an Elizabethan poet, Richard Edwardes, who wrote:

> Then did she say, 'Now have I found this proverb
> true to prove:
> The falling out of faithful friends renewing
> is of love.'

There was plenty of this in their troubled relationship: several times she tried to break it off, sometimes specifically on account of sex. Forman and she wished to get married, and that the way would be cleared by Allen dying. This he did not do; it was Avis who died, and Simon was forced to look for a wife elsewhere.

The relationship began in the course of treatment in the year

[1] 234.
[2] *Recusant Roll No. 2 (1593–1594)*, ed. H. Bowler, (*Catholic Record Society*), 94.

1593: 29 November they first kissed, and a fortnight later, 'she rose and came to me, et halek Avis Allen prius 15 December'. Forman cured her of whatever it was that ailed her – later she suffered from a variety of ailments and Simon became indispensable. They had another bond in that they both distilled waters. Simon became a friend of the Allens, for sometimes Mr Allen would bid him home, at another time write him 'a note of discourtesy for lifting up the cup', which points to some practice of magic together. Mr Allen may have been a *mari complaisant*, or something of an invalid, for we hear of his infirmity, for which he consults Forman. Simon was in love with Avis; as early as July 1594 he was casting a figure to know what would become between them, 'whether she would continue the friendship and be faithful to him, and whether she would become a widow and marry him'.[1] Meanwhile Avis was dreaming of him and that he was married to Sybil Chelsam. Years later he added the note that 'it was not so, for he married another'.

At one point in 1594 Avis broke off relations with Simon and later in the year renewed them. In February 1595 Mr Allen – who must have been a person of standing, for he is always referred to respectfully as Mr – sent for Simon to supper; when he didn't go Avis was aggrieved and fell sick. She thereupon sent to him. In March he accompanied her aboard the Earl of Cumberland's splendid new ship, which the Queen characteristically named *The Scourge of Malice*.[2] This fine vessel cost the spendthrift Earl a fortune; he ultimately sold her to the East India Company, for which she made several prosperous voyages. Avis was not appeased, however; Allen made a steadier friend and sheltered Simon when he feared to go home on account of pursuers – apparently the widow Sweyland on the warpath again.

May was full of tiffs with Avis, who was jealous of Joan Wild leaving her apron at Simon's – if she had read his Diary she would see that she had reason to be. In mid-May she broke off sexual relations with him, though patching up the friendship at the end of the month. In June, when Simon was coming from the garden

[1] 354.
[2] G. C. Williamson, *George, Third Earl of Cumberland, 1558–1605*, 142.

with the Allens, Avis saw Joan Wild at 'our gate' and was furious. The 'garden' plays quite a part in their lives; it was evidently a private garden to which there was a key – we hear of that. Contemporary City maps show how numerous these gardens and closes were, and the puritanical, but observant, Philip Stubbes can inform us as to the uses they served.

In the fields and suburbs of the cities they have gardens, either paled or walled round about very high, with their arbours and bowers fit for the purpose . . . And for that their gardens are locked, some of them have three or four keys a-piece, whereof one they keep for themselves, the other their paramours have to go in before them, lest haply they should be perceived, for then were all their sport dashed . . . These gardens are excellent places, and for the purpose; for if they can speak with their darlings nowhere else, yet there they may be sure to meet them and to receive the guerdon [reward] of their pains: they know best what I mean.[1]

Once more we see how intimately informative Forman is as to the social habits of the time, and how completely borne out by external sources.

The Allens lived somewhere in Thames Street, near the river, so that visits to ships offered an amusement. They seem to have had a trading and shipping interest of their own. For the present Mrs Allen went off into the country, and on her return wrote to him breaking off relations. Distilling brought them together again; Simon arrived at a propitious hour to see her at the good work. They renewed their intercourse and made a covenant 'for ever to endure: God grant it may, and never break again.' Upon this Simon rode down to Salisbury to make an end of relations with his old mistress, Anne Young, and take back his rings and tokens.

Simon returned from his visit to Wiltshire at the end of July. In August Mr Allen was not well, and taking physic; he 'sent hastily to have his bill of reckoning drawn out'.[2] He took some offence over something, then made friends again. On 23 September Simon gave a supper-party for the Allens, and for 'Mrs Allen of the Ship'. This may be the wife of John Allen of the inn in

---

[1] Philip Stubbes, *Anatomy of Abuses*, ed. F. J. Furnivall, (*New Shakespeare Soc.*) I. 88.
[2] 205.

Thames Street. The result of the supper-party was that Avis became jealous of Bridget Allen, and broke with Simon, who for his part was dreaming of his old flame, Anne Young, whom he had not yet given up hope of one day marrying. At the end of that month Avis conceived a child – one does not know whether Allen's or Simon's.

Simon was as jealous over Avis, as she was over him. In October he sets a figure 'to know where thy love is and where gone'; and whether 'a woman had any man that lay with her that night'. Where was she on 6 October? – 'Mother Chep' said she had been there and left; actually she had gone to the tailor's and to buy things; she was with Simon at 11.30. For the rest of October she kept away from him, and he was 'marvellously fretted' by it. The breach was over sexual intercourse, which he desired and which she wished she could end. At this juncture, in November he was imprisoned by the Doctors again. When he came out he talked it over with her and 'ended the matter never to use her more'. But she could not hold to that resolution any more than he could: at the end of December they resumed their intercourse.

In January 1596 they both fell sick in the midst of it. This did not check their ardour; after an attempt at breaking off on Avis's part, they were friends again, 'Deo gracias'. There follow details of her physical condition in the Diary in cipher: Avis was now pregnant. In February she desired him 'to leave her company for ever'. In March they renewed their relations, but once she hit him in the mouth and another time scratched his face. She must have been becoming hysterical.

From this point we can follow their relations in depth from the Case-Books; we see from his frequent notes and figures that he is obsessed with her. On 12 March he casts to know when Allen would be out. 'They were both at garden – I went back to the house to see how long he would stay there. When he was gone she stayed there and I spake with her.'[1] This was presumably to make a date; for, three days later, when Allen went out at 4 p.m. 'then I went to her and halek'. In April he is casting to know whether Mr Allen is at home, and whether and when he will go forth; ten

[1] 205.

days later, whether to go after her.[1] He went and found her in the garden, she asked him which of two girls it would be best to take for a servant. There follow notes on 'Women being with child'. If she be heavy and wants to sit or lie about, it is a sign the child will have the falling sickness. If she longs to drink hippocras, i.e. spiced wine, the child will be witty and pleasant. If she wants to travel, especially by water, he will be a traveller; if she is given to reading on her book, the child will be a priest – Forman always uses the Catholic word 'priest' – or a learned man. One sees that the whole thing is based on sympathy, as Frazer says. So much for much of human thinking.

What happens to them is more interesting than what they think. Several times in May Simon casts a figure whether to go to the Allens or no. Once, 'he was at home at work'. A week later both were at home, but there was company so that Simon could not speak with her. William Allen was consulting Forman too; who found that he had an imposthume, i.e. an abscess, in the liver and melancholy infecting the blood. John Allen lived at the 'Ship' in the same street; on 12 June his wife, Bridget, has pains in head and stomach: 'she hath surfeited with sturgeon and Rhenish wine'. (We remember that Robert Greene died after a surfeit of pickled herring and Rhenish wine.) A fortnight later, 26 June, Avis gave birth to a boy, named Alexander.

Simon was now much in and out of the Allens' house. On 3 July, 'I being at Mr Allen's, Bridget Allen was there and I promised her she should be with child and have a son or daughter in the latter end of May next. And that night her husband, being out of town, came home and colted her.' Bridget was twenty-four, and a fortnight later she inquires whether she is pregnant; the answer was not, but shortly likely to be. 'Next day she and her mistress went to a hot-house [i.e. a brothel] – afterwards both were exceeding sick and like to die.' What a flood of light that throws on the manners of the time! – for these were not lower-class, but respectable middle-class people. One observes Simon's disapproval of their going to such a place: throughout the whole of his so

[1] 234. The material for the rest of this chapter is from this source, unless otherwise specified.

well-documented life there is no evidence that he ever went to a brothel. He was an amateur of sex, in both senses of the word.

Meanwhile Avis had a dream of her child and put the question whether the boy would live or die. From a note elsewhere we learn the fate of this child: he was conceived 27 September 1595 at 5.30.[1] From 20 September, being St Matthew's eve, to 26 June would be just forty weeks. 'There lacked two days of forty weeks by my reckoning. The child died 9 July – the nurse had overput the mould of the head with striking it up too hard.' Avis herself was far from well and constantly resorting to Simon for advice. She had pains in head, reins, and heart. 'She seeks her own death voluntarily' – evidently a neurotic. Her figure signified 'life and health to her, if she would be ruled', and also that 'the party desireth much company of Venus'. No doubt – and one sees why he had such an influence over her. The psychological pattern is familiar: she wanted to free herself from sex with him, but could not help herself: he must have been more satisfactory than her husband.

On 19 July Bridget Allen wants to know whether she is pregnant and whether to take horse or no – two days later she rode into the country. Next day Simon 'sent to Vulcan for his garden-keys; he would not lend them me', then, in Latin, whether because he wants to use them for intercourse or because Simon wants to. Two days later Mr Allen, then forty, came with pains in his stomach; he had caught cold at the Royal Exchange and took to bed. Simon gave him cordials and ointments, and he was up again the next day. Meanwhile William Allen from the White Horse in Thames Street is troubled in mind and body, and wants to know whether he will live or die.

All through August there were jars and reconciliations, breaches and renewals of intercourse between Simon and his love – it is surprising what a man will put up with for what he wants. On 15 August Avis wants to know whether it is best to go to Dr Stanhope or no. This must be the ecclesiastical lawyer, a member of the Archbishop's commission, who dealt with recusant Catholics, and confirms that Mrs Allen was one.[2] The answer given is:

[1] 206.
[2] cf. *D.N.B.*, under Sir Edward Stanhope.

'Go not – if she go she will fall into her enemies' hands, she would go to prison or commit adultery [as if she were not already doing that!], add to her sickness and be put in peril of her life.' It would seem that persecution was another bond that Simon had with his lady-love. Next day, 'she sent me word I had broke her heart . . . and she would not come at me.'

Three days later Simon inquires whether she will come or whether it is 'best to send to garden or no . . . I went forth at 5.10 and when I came there he was not within. I went up and found her with Kate and we were friends. He came while I was there and said little.' This was Kate Alison, her maid, who would know what was going on. Next, Simon casts to know whether Kate keeps faith, or dissembles with him. 'It seems not – bears a fair face, but not with a good heart.' Later he added: 'it proved after that she dissembled much and spake ill of me behind my back.' What he wanted to know was whether he would ever marry Avis, and what would be between them – there follow elaborate calculations.

On 23 August he is inquiring whether she will come to him and what is the cause she comes not. Next day: is she at home or is she at the Clink? – that is the gaol in Southwark, where also the brothels were. Simon found that she was at home, 'not at the place suspected, as it proved' – it would seem he suspected the latter. On 26 August, not bearing the suspense – or perhaps deprivation – any longer, he went to the Allens: nobody there to speak to, 'but presently before I returned there came one from thence to me'.

His anxiety is reflected in his dreams in August. He dreams of Jane Cole, with whom he had had relations, looking ill-favoured and out of fashion, and talking 'as if mine enemy'. The same day Avis sent him 'a script containing vile words, being enemy to me without cause'. Next day he dreamed that he felt Avis's venter (i.e. belly) and she was very fat. She asked how she might capture pigeons; Simon said with peason (peas) and salt cate (food). Simon took a fair white pigeon and tied her by the leg; her mate came and wanted to tread her. She was willing enough, but 'they would not because we were looking on'. Simon awoke, very glad of his dream: he thought it propitious. He then dreamed he was in a garden with Avis and her friend: they both 'strove which should call me to the garden with them'. That day he 'went to Avis Allen and halek, and had news from Sir William Monson and Steven, my man'.

Of interest to the psychologist, it hardly needs a psychologist to read these dreams; their interpretation is crystal clear, with their elements of desire, the need for secrecy, and male vanity.

In September Mr Allen was seriously ill – this was what kept them in hope; for on 1 September their servant Kate put the question whether he would live or die. The discouraging answer came: 'he will not die yet'. Forman was on edge to marry: on 2 September he casts a figure to know whether 'best to go to Appelina Fairfax and whether to marry if agreed'. Two days later he casts his horoscope, all in Latin: the indications are that he will be loved by women and honoured by great persons. (He was.) He is engaged in preparing and engraving his magical stones, evidently for sexual purposes: 'at this time the man with the cock was engraved and washed from 4 to 7. 8 September all the image names and characters were engraven and to what content, but it was not shadowed until the next morning. And then we did very little to it but set it out a little and cut it off.' To what intent was this?

Meanwhile Mrs Allen was suffering pain and faintness at heart and in her womb, and 'seems to be with child'. She herself brought her water to be tested. Simon casts to know whether 'Avis Allen is pregnant by me'; the answer was: she appears to be. Thereupon he wants to know what Allen thinks; and also what he will do concerning Kate's pregnancy. For Kate, too, has her troubles. At thirty-six she inquires after her sweetheart, Robert Barnes, twenty-two – whether he be fled, and whether he will marry her or no. Kate got her reward for service from her friends, evidently Avis and Simon; for 'he did marry her by the help of her friends'. But 'he bears a mind to some other poor wench; and she is in love with some other man she is quick of'.

What a vulnerable world for these women without birth-control! – but it is the world as it is, or as it was, uncovered.

Meanwhile, Forman was in trouble again with the Doctors; they carried him before the Lord Mayor on 15 September, who committed him to the Counter for a week, when he was bailed, evidently seeking to get him to promise to move out of the City. On 30 September they imprisoned him again for a fortnight, making him an offer to be bound over. Simon cast a figure to know whether it would be best to agree; the answer indicated, 'do it not but stand to the law and trial thereof, for they also are weak and have as little power as myself. The end of the law will be on my side. If they do go to law with thee, they will not continue it.' However, for the time he decided to give way: 'I agreed with them and am bound in £40 not to meddle again in London after Mayday next.' When that time came he steeled himself in accordance with the advice from the higher powers, took the Doctors to law and silenced them for a full year and a half. Beside the celestial advice he did not as yet feel strong enough to take, he added later, bringing himself up to date, 'All which things came to pass.'

During the interval between his confinements Avis wanted to know whether there was any ill towards her. This is a fairly frequent interrogation with these people – one sees the atmosphere of helplessness, suspicion and fear in which they lived. 'There is no evil towards her till eighteen days hence.' He added later, 'at eighteen days' end she was sick'. She was weak in the reins and suffering from a flux. Early in November Avis wants to know whether her husband has any other lover, in particular Elizabeth Forman, Simon's sister-in-law. He was treating Kate's young man, and found that he 'hath *gonorrhea passio* and a great smarting of his urine'. Robert was telling tales of Simon to Kate, who of course passed them on to Mrs Allen. The atmosphere is reflected in his dream in December, of being laid out on the ground as if dead, surrounded by straw which they set alight. It burned all round him, but did not touch him. Such is it to be pure of heart.

Jealousy is an index of love, and in October Simon puts the question, what is occurring between Avis Allen and his man? Answer: 'There is nothing between them, but he is in love with an

old widow – and she in love with another.' This suspicion gave
Simon an anxiety-dream the same night. He was sitting by the fire
with Mr Allen, who got behind Simon and struck him on the head
with Simon's own truncheon. (The symbol is obviously phallic.)
Simon called out, 'Thou *peasant*' – an insult to an Elizabethan, and
an indication of Simon's sense of superiority over the husband;
'what meanest thou to kill me privily with my own weapon?' So
they quarrelled, and got weapons, Allen calling companions to his
aid and went out into the fields.

That day Avis sent to Simon's man to come to the garden and
speak with her, without telling Simon. So Simon went himself,
and she was very angry: she had wanted to find out secretly if he
had relations with Kate and was prepared to pay the manservant
to find out. She would not believe Simon on oath, upon which he
left her. At this time he was in the midst of law-suits and troubles
with a troublesome cleric, Peter Sefton. When Sefton and his
companions sued out a warrant against Forman, he forsook his
house for a time – so that it could not be served on him.

This is the background of his dream at the end of October; that
he was in a close of green trees, as it were in a pound enclosed
with boards, with many people shooting arrows at him. John
Davies came by, looked over, and at last spied him; Peter Sefton
in a white waistcoat looking as if he would be hanged. That day
Avis sent for Simon to dinner and Mr Allen told him that Davies
had gone to Stade. Simon's right ear began to burn; immediately
his man arrived to tell him that Sefton and Atkins were in collu-
sion against him and had gone to the Queen's Attorney, the
redoubtable Sir Edward Coke, to procure a warrant. William, his
man, reported that 'the constable had been twice to seek me'.
Simon himself gives the obvious interpretation of the arrows being
shot at him, and adds that he left his house till mid-December –
the evasive action Elizabethans frequently took in that excessively
litigious age. With everybody going to law against everybody
else, it made fortunes for the lawyers. No wonder many of the
great Elizabethan fortunes were founded on the law – but we owe
beautiful Blickling to it, and Attorney-General Coke's own
immense fortune, the foundation of Holkham.

With all these troubles on his doorstep, Forman wondered whether it would not be as well to go to sea in Alderman Watts's ship, the *Centaur*, bound for the West Indies. But there was Avis at home, dependent on him. Several times he put the question whether she was pregnant. Off and on she was ill. At the end of November 'I dressed her throat first: all did no good, but did draw down the humour so that it swells very much and did pimple very much.' Simon's anxiety about her is vividly expressed in a dream he had while absent from her at Sandwich. He dreamed that Kate and Mr Allen wrapped her in a white sheet and laid her beside Simon in bed, and she was exceeding cold like one dead. (Unknown to Simon the poor young woman was on her way to her death; this must have been his unconscious realisation of it.) He asked, 'Do you not heat clothes and lay to her to warm her?' Kate said, 'Let her lie; she will be hot enough anon.' Simon began to creep near to her and to warm her body. While he was away she was very sick, and 'so cold she supposed they had poisoned her'.

When Simon returned he was still afflicted with the pangs of jealousy, apparently of his man-servant, William. On 2 December 1596 'she confessed unto me she bore him a good mind; that he had almost overcome her and was somewhat bold with her. She fancied him much and desired to see him. I knew her mind did run much on him and I had great suspicion that he had lain with her and she with him. But she denied it absolutely.'

Two days later Avis put the question whether it was best to continue their love or no. The figure showed that it was

better to continue than to leave off, for fear of a further inconvenience that may follow. They two shall be more together, or die; or else then the woman shall cleave only to her husband. She is unfortunate to herself, forward and overthwart, and hurteth herself – works against her own quiet and will not be ruled by good counsel. She hath a marvellous distempered body that is soon well and soon ill, and she is loth to take physic and anything that will do her good – follows the counsel of those that will do her hurt.

His medical diagnosis follows: most pain is in her throat and head; her matrix (i.e. womb) is cold – let her be her own physician

fifteen days, then give her physic. The advice to himself came –
'meddle not with her for a time, for thou shalt have ill will for
thy pain.'

Such were the pains and penalties of love.

This was on 4 December. Two days later he went and meddled.
After casting to know, he went and found that Allen was abroad
'and the way clear and she abed. I went up and spake with her
without any let.' He put questions whether there was any dead
foetus in her womb, whether going to bed with him were unfortunate and concerning her husband's love towards Kate. The
answers were that the foetus was not dead but in peril of death,
that her husband loved Kate and would be consorting with her in
a week, 'but not halek with her, because there is no reception
between them. Her husband loves her not.'

Next day, 5 December, Simon dreamed that he was in the
Counter and saw many of his old fellow-prisoners. Because of his
dreams he went not out of door but to Mr Allen's at night, who
was abed; and 'Edward and we supped together and that night he
went away to sea.' Next day Simon paid a visit; Allen was out, but
'non halek because she would not for fear'. The day after,
7 December, he dreamed he sat at 'a long stall of mercery with a
white apron and very white sleeves and was all in white and a
black doublet under'. The imagery reflects the position he was in:
relations that were innocent on the surface, black guilt underneath. Many country maids came to buy his wares – as it might be
at Matthew Commin's years before; one big wench came and
chatted freely with him. At evening tide Mrs Allen sent her maid
to him, and at night Avis herself 'knocked at my window to
speak with me'.

Two days later followed a dream of familiar male jealousy: that
'his man sent a message to Avis, and she and her maid took boat
and went over the water to him in Southwark. I dogged her and at
last she deceived me; I lost her and sought after her, but could not
find her for she was in black . . . And again that Avis Allen was
with my man and they lay together, and I was sorely vexed'; then
that she was gone out of town. The same day he was with her, but
she was sick on account of the foetus and 'non halek'. She fulfilled

the dream, however, by telling him that if she were well she would go into the country shortly.

The same day he had a vivid dream of Quidhampton. Dick Howes and he were by the water's side, Dick looking for a trout, the water no faster nor deeper than before. Simon dipped water in a bucket and set it under Mother Moody's hedge at the bridge. He found a book in a wall beside a pond, at the beginning was an illuminated page of Christ in colours, the water black and dark. (Again the contrasting colours of his life.) There came two children of the gentlemen's sons – as it might be Penruddock's – one of them given to divination. That night Avis dreamed that she was in prison, and heard a man say that he was sorry for bringing Mr Forman to prison, but was compelled to. 'That day I was at Allen's from 10 a.m. to 8 p.m. and halek twice, in the morning and at 6 p.m.'

Next morning he was before the Queen's Attorney and discharged; before him again at Sefton's procurement and again discharged: Deo gracias. Simon was able to go back to his home, to receive a visit from the excellent Dr Roger Dodd to inquire whether he would be made Bishop of London. He also received visits from Mr Allen, and from Mrs Allen, whose prognosis was that she would be better: Simon gave her 'the potion' to drink. After a visit from the respectable Mr Auditor Conyers of the Exchequer, a regular who suffered from an appalling variety of complaints, here was Avis again.

This time the figure said that she was pregnant and would quicken in eighteen days. 'She takes thought of one she loved whom she hath forsaken, or that hath forsaken her.' Simon dreamed again of Quidhampton. In October he had dreamed twice of his old love, Anne Young, and a little before the first dream her father died: she must have been thinking of him and the thought reached him. Now he dreamed he was riding home to Sarum behind Thomas Cumber, after visiting a sick person in the country. A woman was wimbing, i.e. winnowing, corn in the farm close. All the meadows were covered with water, as he must often have seen them. A maid wanted 'to go to Sarum with us, but would go over the water with us'. Simon said she could not, but must go by the highway. That day Mrs Allen kept a feast and had company. She wanted to know whether it were best to trust or ride with Mrs Suckling. Answer: 'the good man of the house will give her but bad entertainment – cause jealousy and strife.'

On 3 January 1597 Simon had a dream which clearly reveals his unconscious sense of guilt, of which consciously he was unaware. He was passing over a mixen, i.e. dunghill, which shook under him. In the midst of it someone thrust at him with a dung-fork and Simon fell into the water; someone held him up, but he emerged much dirtied and stinking of the mixen. That day Mr Conyers came for consultation and gave him a French crown. 'And Avis Allen sent me a hot pie to dinner for she had many strangers to dinner; she came to me p.m. at 3 et halek.'

On 9 January he dreamed that he and Mr and Mrs Allen each sent a letter by a blackamoor to a certain man. Mr Allen wrote against the blackamoor in his letter, who attacked him with a knife; Simon defended Allen and saved his life. Next day Mr Allen was bound for his friend in £30,000 – a purely formal sum. Allen thereupon seeks Forman's advice whether he will suffer damage by this. The answer is: he is likely to, unless he discharge himself of it.

A few days later Simon had a vivid dream, of which the motivation at least is clear. He was in a place where many boys and maids were condemned to die, himself with them. He devised a means to save them by flying away. 'I flew to a plum-tree and did see green plums, and ate of great red plums.' When the persecutor came after them, Simon made them all hold hands; some of them could fly but low, but with much ado they flew up on a house, and thence over a field and hedges and water. Thence 'up into a wild down, a desolate place on the side of a hill, and there we rested' – as it might be the high downs of old Sarum that loom down on Salisbury.

That morning Forman arrested Sefton for the money he had lent him, 'and I had a silver bowl for my money'. When Forman went to the Queen's Attorney, 'he entreated me to stay the matter. And after I went to Avis Allen.' He was with her again next day, and on the 20th, 'but did not halek but spake with her'. He himself put the question whether it were best to leave her or no, 'and not to continue her love in hope', i.e. of marriage.

It was at this time, 23 January 1597, that he had his suggestive dream of the Queen, which I have quoted. 'That morning, so soon as I was up, came Mr Sefton unto me to entreat me to forgive him and to end this matter.' But he would not pay Forman's charges at law, 'so with much ado we parted'. (We see how familiar the phrase 'much ado' is – it is often at the tip of Simon's pen.) In the afternoon he went to Avis 'and halek, because shortly she will be sick for a time'; there follows elaborate calculations whether she is pregnant.[1]

Simon's obsession with Avis did not prevent him from casting to know whether Anne Young would be a widow and what mind she bore him – men are naturally polygamous and perhaps what was biting him was the urge to marry. By now, however, Anne loved another – perhaps her husband, one Walworth. On 2 February 1597 Simon is inquiring if Avis is in the garden with Kate and whether he might halek or no. Ten days later, is Avis at home and he out? Disappointingly he was at home, she at her mother's.

This month he dreamed that he was sowing in a field, when three maids came and would sing him a song. When they began it snowed, he took shelter under a big green tree; a child ran before him and fell into a ditch full of water. One sees how much his dreams reflect his early years amid the waters and channels of the Avon. Another dream was of a field full of folk, when someone came and thrust them through the belly with a sword. That day Sefton appeared before arbitrators and 'said that I stood in a white sheet in Sarum [i.e. for fornication] and that I occupied a wench on a stool, with many other false villanies for the which I could have killed him with a good will'. Simon regarded himself – as we all are apt to do – as an innocent, maligned person.

Early in March Forman puts the question whether to bring Sefton before a J.P. to make him swear the peace. Avis is concerned to know what will happen in the matter; the figure indicated that there would be no end, but the plaintiff in danger of

[1] 226.

imprisonment. Simon a few days later – would Appelina Fairfax be free at this time if he went to call? Meanwhile both Avis and her husband were *souffrant*: he with indigestion, gravel and a flux; she 'has much pricking between her fundament and vulva, which sometimes strikes up into her stomach and breast'.

This month he was dreaming that he was among a great many young maids, 'and that I lay my head in one of their laps, and she took me by the hand. And that I saw the Cardinal [Archduke] coming with a band of soldiers.' He dreamed again of Quidhampton, and once more of his old love at Salisbury, as we shall see.

In April Avis puts the question whether her maid, Kate Alison, intends evil against her. Answer: she does, and Avis is in peril of being robbed. This state of mind was not very restful for a neurotic, and next day she inquires again as to her state. The answer is: she is an enemy to herself – has taken some evil drink or medicine. Simon added that in fact 'she had done so'. Several times he casts to know whether she is at home, whether she will come to him, or wishes him to come to her. On 25 April she had gone that morning, with her friend and Mrs Roberts, 'to see their ship which was going into Ireland'; when Simon put the question they were on the water almost at Woolwich.[1]

As for Simon, the barber came to trim and wash him, washing arms, breast and legs – a rarity for Elizabethans. Perhaps this entered into a dream where there were many people and Simon made folk say that he was dead. 'They brought my coffin and a great long piece of broadcloth to lay – Mr Keale the elder was there. [Probably Hugh Keale, jeweller to the Queen.]'[2] People said Forman was dead and he bade them bury him. 'And I was forsaken of all the company and they kept a solemn obit for me' – once more he uses the old Catholic phrase for a requiem. Mr Keale spread a green cloth over two tables and put the coffin under – as for a requiem. The dream was between 3 and 4 a.m.; next morning he heard that Mr Keale's son had died at 2 a.m.: a pure case of telepathy.

[1] 205.
[2] cf. my *The Elizabethan Renaissance. The Cultural Achievement*, 193, 200.

In June Avis was seriously ill. She herself sent to him on 6 June; the answer was that 'she will be sick through her own occasion by some conceipt told'.[1] The sickness would increase. On 10 June her illness was at its height, and Mr Allen sent on behalf of his wife, without her consent. The prognostication was that there was 'some unfortunate body about her that gives her ill counsel'. On the 11 June she was let blood – an extreme measure with Forman – 'and I ministered my dram to her first'.

The Diary for this year is practically empty: Simon must have been worried and miserable. It has only the one entry: – like Swift's 'Only a woman's hair' – in a line to itself:

1597. Avis Allen died 13th June.

Away at Stourbridge Fair that autumn he has a touching little note to say that he saw 'a gentlewoman much like Avis Allen, for whose sake I have a good affection to her'.

There can be no doubt that he loved her.

[1] 226.

Chapter V

The Pursuit of Women; Marriage

The very day after Avis Allen's death, 14 June 1597, Forman came
to some kind of understanding with Anne Waller of Ashby in the
forest of West Bere – presumably Bere in Dorset – by which she
bound herself in £500 not to marry without his consent.[1] If she
did she was to give him £500 for that silver groat he gave her. A
marginal note tells us that William Waller was aged sixty, and
his land was to pass to two daughters. Nothing came of this,
but again and again Simon casts figures to know whether some
woman or other will make a suitable wife: he was desperate to
marry.

For years he had been faithful after his fashion – i.e. in mind, not
in body – to his old love Anne Young. But she was married to
another, Ralph Walworth. In 1590 Simon was casting to know
whether he would ever marry her; five years later, whether she
would continue faithful to him. In October 1596 he dreamed of
her twice, and shortly before the first dream her father died – no
doubt in her trouble she was thinking of Simon.[2] In January 1597
he wants to know whether she will be a widow.[3] In March he
dreamed that he saw her and her mother; he went in at the back
door and knocked. She came dressed all in white and unready, i.e.
in her nightdress; catching at her mother she said, 'Stay till this
strange man be gone out of the house', and Simon heard someone
preparing to come down the stairs. The house was strewn with
flags and rushes, and set out with green boughs, for it was holiday
and fair time. Anne looked very white and pale, and stood in a
half-loft; 'I came here to borrow a broom to sweep a busk,' i.e.

[1] 226.
[2] 234.
[3] 226.

coarse cloth. A week before she had sent for him, and 'I spake with her.'

On 14 May Hugh Fort, an old Wiltshire acquaintance, came with a message from Anne. Simon puts the question whether she was ill and best to go to her; after again putting the question, he decided to do so. 'I rode forth Monday 5.30 p.m.; Wednesday at 10 p.m., I came to her and spake with her. I rode alone almost all the way, and homeward I had no company at all. I came home 28 May 9.10 a.m.' People were more gregarious then; it was safer to travel in company, and they got up earlier in the morning, with the dawn.

In December that year she sent a messenger to him: she wanted help, for he cast to know whether best to do so or no. On New Year's day 1598 Simon dreamt 'I met Ralph Walworth against Mr Cofferer's door' – this was the Cofferer of the Queen's Household, Sir Henry Cock. Walworth drew his dagger on Simon, and 'I had a bush hanged on my back to fling at him and drew my dagger.' In these dreams we see the character of Simon's involvement with Anne. Joshua was his child; there is the feeling of guilt, even if unconscious – consciously Simon was all innocence; and there is the hostility towards Anne's husband. Later he added a note to his inquiry whether she would be a widow and what mind she bore him: 'she loved another, and 7 March 1600 her husband lay sick of a tympany', i.e. dropsy. Simon then cast to know whether he would live or die.

In July 1598 there came a letter from Anne; was it best to send to her or help her?[1] The answer came, 'go not nor send'. However, in October he made the journey into Wiltshire, wondering how he should speed and whether he would be able to speak with her. He managed this 'without any let or hindrance, or making any privy thereof more than my brother, and was entertained friendly'.[2] But it was an unlucky journey:

1. I lost my rapier, cost 13*s*. 2. My man's horse tired – much ado to get another, but he was naught. 3. I sounded [i.e. fainted] at supper at

[1] 195.
[2] 354.

Hartley Row and was very sick. 4. My horse limped and was like to throw me over his head. 5. I was glad to change my own horse, for he trotted so hard I could not sit him. 6. I bought a new rapier by the way, and my man was like to burst [break] him – he spoilt him. 7. I never slept till I returned.

At any rate, we see from this Forman travelling like a gentleman in style, sword at his side, man-servant in attendance.

The next thing we hear is that in April Anne is mortally ill of dropsy. She sent John Evans of Wilton with a letter asking for a prescription 'for her sickness, life or death'.[1] Forman sent her one made of 'sage, marjoram, elderbuds, ashbuds, berberis, liquorice, aniseed, aloes and juniper berries'. If it did not do her any good, it probably did little harm – and we see from it how much he was a herbalist. She died on 8 May 1600.

Appropriately before midnight on All Hallows' Eve, 1 November, Simon dreamed of Anne Young.

She was all in black and had a black cypress [i.e. light scarf] on her neck. She told me she lay at Roger Sharp's and there she had left her sucking child; for she gave suck and so came to seek me. We walked together, but I could not have any conference with her because of other company that was with us. It grieved me much, and so she went away I know not how; and with my grief I waked.[2]

This was the end of his first love; again the psychological elements are obvious: there was its secrecy and furtiveness, the screen of other people between them; the child was his, but Anne was all in black – she was dead, his grief awoke him.

He recognised his responsibility for Joshua. When his mother died he was fifteen: he had been born 27 March 1585. A later note says, 'Joshua came to dwell with me 1602, about Midsummer, and he died 8 October 1603, 2 p.m., of an imposthume [ulcer] in his stomach and plague also – and had good tokens on him before and after he died. He lived 18 years 6 months 11 days 7 hours.'[3]

Thus came to an end this long passage, from early days, in Simon's life.

[1] 236.
[2] 236.
[3] 206.

We have seen how anxious he had been to marry either of his two great loves – the early one from Salisbury days, Anne Young, and the later in London, Avis Allen – and his wish that their husbands might clear the way by dying. However, it was the wives who died, leaving him emotionally unsatisfied, more than ever keyed up to get himself married and establish a family. When Avis died in the summer of 1597, Simon was forty-four – this was abnormally late for marriage for an Elizabethan. Circumstances had been against him all the way and made it difficult, if not impossible; but now he was prospering, no longer a *mauvais sujet* but a good citizen – in his own eyes and recognised as such by many, if not by all.

Simon, of course, was an authority on marriage; as an astrological practitioner he was often called on in matrimonial cases. His notes provide directions how to find out whether a man shall obtain the woman he desires; but the examples he gives from his practice are more revealing of the facts of life and society. There was the man who was rich, yet the woman he desired rejected him because he had a sore leg. A certain married woman who was in love with another man who kept her – though this was unknown to Simon – came to him to know whether she should ever marry 'such a man which was in love with her'.[1] (A pretty piece of feminine disingenuousness!) The answer came that 'she shall not marry him because her husband liveth and he loveth another. She hath him at advantage.' Simon added what subsequently happened, as he often did: 'they came not together: much controversy fell out between them and she went home to her husband, and about Michaelmas he [the lover] married another'.

'To tie a man not to meddle with a woman *et contra*' one should proceed as follows:

In the time of matrimony take a point [a lace] and tie three knots thereon. When the priest says 'Whom God hath joined together let no man separate' then they knit the knots naming the party, saying 'Whom God hath joined together those let the Devil separate. *Sara* until these knots be undone.' And he shall never meddle with the said woman. *Probatum*.

The revealing thing is that these people believed in the sacramen-

[1] 205.

tal; we see again that Simon always uses the old word 'priest', never 'minister'. For the rest, it throws a shaft of light, as this whole book does, into ordinary folks, 'thinking'.

Several times we find notes how to find whether a wife, or any other woman, be honest or no. Simon was very keen to know this, and as a complete believer in his science he frequently casts figures on his own behalf – whether Avis was betraying him with his man, for whom she confessed to a fancy; whether, when he ultimately entered into the sacrament of marriage, his wife was playing him false (as he certainly did her); whether there was trouble brewing for him (there often was); what would become of him; whether he would be advanced to some dignity, knight, lord, or earl, or commander in the field – never say die was the Elizabethan motto; whether to voyage to the Indies on one of Alderman Watts's ships.

Several times the figure cast conformed to the pattern of his life. For example, in youth he had wasted his stock and goods, and was driven to depart from his friends. He was then 'made joyful for a time by reason of women' – as he had been at Salisbury. He would be 'hated of my brethren and stand in danger of my life'. Then he would 'get brethren and sistern' – evidently fellow-dabblers in magic – 'have fellowship with women and joy again of my friends'; but, the figure foretold, 'being in honour, shall be imprisoned by the Queen, where I shall die'. Upon this, 'O God have mercy on me for my [sc. thy] son's sake. And turn all evil fortune to good luck. And grant me to die in thy truth. Amen.'[1]

Whether the effect of this prayer or no, Simon's fortune did not turn out ill; he died, if not precisely in the odour of sanctity, at any rate in the full tide of prosperity.

On 7 April 1592 he considered marriage with a girl he met in the street 'whom he liked well of and, by inquiry understanding whose daughter she was and where she dwelt, intended to make some errand unto her father's house to come acquainted as well with her friends, intending to espouse the wench if he could obtain her good will, she being free from all other'.[2] After casting to know

[1] 205.
[2] 354.

74

what entertainment he would have, he went to the house: nobody at home but the girl and another maid. Simon sent out for a quart of wine and made merry with them. A gentleman who knew him came in and politely made off. When the mother arrived she bade Simon welcome with a gammon of bacon and a cheese. Another guest came, who took him into his confidence and opened his secrets to him. Then the father came home and entertained him well. At six in the evening Simon returned home without declaring his purpose but having kissed the girl twice.

We see how these things were done in that age. But Simon never proceeded without casting the horoscope; and the figure showed, 'she will prove a whore and bear outward in her behaviour a fair show, but she will play the whore privily'. Completely ruled by his special source of knowledge, he went no further.

In May 1596, a month after his first treatment of Avis Allen – while the fleet was preparing at Plymouth for Cadiz – Forman is casting to know whether it were better to go to Appellina Fairfax, one Southwick's daughter, and whether he would obtain this appetising widow. In June he cast again, and sent a letter by his man, who brought it back again, for she was not at home. In September he wanted to know whether to go to her and whether to marry her, if it were agreed. Nothing happened; he tried to settle his doubts by inquiring (in Latin) whether he would be loved by women and honoured by great lords. Next he wondered whether to marry Oilman's daughter. In 1597 he was still in quest whether the fair Appellina were free. On 22 August he received a visit from a neighbouring clergyman, Dr Thomas Stallard, who was rector of St Mary at Hill, Billingsgate, as well as of All Hallows, Lombard Street.[1] He was also Archdeacon of Rochester, so perhaps the friendly Dean Blague had told him of Forman's circumstances, and they were neighbours at Billingsgate. He said, 'I was a stranger at his house and willed me come home, he might chance to do me good. The question is whether he means to give me his daughter or no.'[2] The answer came, 'he means it not. These are but fair words, neither is it for any good he will do thee.'

[1] J.Foster, *Alumni Oxon.*, IV. 1405.
[2] 354.

Since Forman abode strictly by the precepts of his faith, he did not
take advantage of the invitation, perhaps to his loss. In October he
queried, 'whether I might obtain Elizabeth Briscot if I laboured
the matter. [Later.] She was at this time promised to another and I
missed my purpose. I came too late.'

So what about the widow Boothby in St Lawrence Lane? This
was the lane running from West Cheap up to St Lawrence Jury at
the north end, which had 'many fair houses' and prosperous resi-
dents.[1] Simon, like most right-thinking Elizabethans, was looking
for a well-to-do widow. A female friend carried Simon's letter to
the widow, who read it with thanks for his good will, but was not
disposed to marry till her troubles were ended. She 'would have
known what I was; but I charged Mrs Jonas not to tell, unless she
would admit me to her presence'.[2] This betrays some lack of
confidence as to the impression his occupation or standing might
make, along with his underlying confidence in himself. This,
where women were concerned, was justified, as we shall see – the
more remarkable when one considers his appearance; small of
stature and, as he describes himself in a marginal note, a redhead,
yellow beard, speckled face. He must, however, have had a charm
for them.

In September 1597 the question is whether he would obtain a
widow Calverley, of Holborn; but he has not forgotten Mrs
Withypoll's daughter whom he had seen at Stourbridge Fair and
liked for her resemblance to Avis.[3] Unfortunately the astrological
signs indicated an addiction to sodomy, of which the very normal
Simon disapproved: no progress here. In April 1598 should he
marry Katherine Gittens, who dwelt with Mr Bede in the Strand?[4]
On 19 April he reduced the question whether they would marry,
on her behalf, 'she being with me'; two days later he put the
question for her again. On 24 April he put the question for himself (in Latin) whether she was a virgin – he apparently thought
that important – and what would be her disposition. 'Further,

[1] Stow, I. 270.
[2] 354.
[3] 226.
[4] 354.

whether I shall obtain the said Kate if I make love to her, and whether she shall be a profitable wife or no.' There must have been some impediment: the affair did not proceed. This was not the end of Miss Gittens' prospects, for in April 1598 the Archbishop's man, George, at Lambeth sent two figures to be put whether to proceed with her, and the event. In October the question is 'if I go to Barnsley's daughter behind the Change a-wooing – if I shall speed, or wed?'[1] The 'Change' was Sir Thomas Gresham's magnificent Royal Exchange upon Cornhill. A note adds, 'I never went to her.'

A closer pursuit was that of Sarah Archdell, a maiden of twenty. He met her at six o'clock of an April evening, 17 April 1599; she lived in Budge Row, which was continuous with Watling Street, 'on the right going to St Antholin's church, right against the Rose at the stonning steps,' i.e. standing steps for marketing wares.[2] Two days later Simon cast to know if she conceived well of him and would marry him if he put the question. 'The 19 April I was at the Curtain' – the well-known playhouse in Shoreditch owned by James Burbage, where Shakespeare's earlier plays were performed and where he would have played as well as at the neighbouring Theatre. 'There she came, and her uncle and friends, and sat before me. After the play we went into the fields together, and so I had some parley with her, but nothing of anything touching the matter. She seemed very kind and courteous and I led her by the hand all the way almost.' On 22 April he put the question whether her uncle would assist or be against him in his suit. 'This day he and I met at the Curtain again, and after walked in the fields; but I never moved the matter to him.' That evening he was supping with the Condwells when he looked out of the window and saw Sarah passing by with her uncle. Simon overtook them in the fields beyond Moorgate, where they stayed till ten o'clock. He had some talk with her, but could not say his mind for the presence of other persons. Two days later he again put the question, and whether he would meet Sarah again. 'I met with her uncle the same afternoon in Coleman Street, coming out of the fields where he had been to walk.'

[1] 354.
[2] 219.

Nothing came of it, and Simon cast about for other possibilities. Would Anne Eglesfield do? or Mistress Lee, Captain Monson's sister? At last, on edge to marry, he made a sudden decision in July 1599 and forthwith married a young girl of good family. He was in his forty-seventh year, she was nineteen.

Forman's frustrations in the field of matrimony were no discouragement to his appetite for women; whenever he had an opportunity, he took it. The interesting thing is that they so rarely refused it. When one of them did, he noted it down along with all the rest: Isabella Webb would have nothing to do with him in that way. But others did, respectable as well as unrespectable, married and single, patients as well as maidservants. What a free-for-all Elizabethan sex-life was!

One difference was that Simon had the advantage of astrology to aid him in his quest. A note 'De Amore illegitimo' displays the figure to 'show whether he shall ever halek with her, whether she is honest or a harlot, etc.'.[1] After a certain figure he provides an example: 'He went presently after and found her in her chamber sewing and her husband teaching below. He stayed with her, kissed her, felt her, did anything with her, but yet she would not halekekeros hariscum tauro; and so in great kindness left her.'

Forman recognised that 'illegitimate love' was immoral; but, like almost all humans, kept his principles and his conduct in separate compartments, and did not allow precepts to impede practice.

At the height of his affair with Avis Allen, a breach between them was patched up on 26 January 1596, 'Deo gracias'. Three days later, '2.20 p.m. halek Julian in Seething Lane'.[2] This was the lane that ran from Tower Street up to Hart Street, and the parish church of St Olave where Forman's kindred spirit, Samuel Pepys, was laid to rest. Julian was a married woman, and 18 February 'halek Julian Clark'. On 28 February – 1596 was a Leap Year – 'Halek Anne Nurse at 3, Ankers 6 p.m., and Judith' – a probable miswriting for Julian. (Forman, who is so careful as an astrologer to note dates and times – in case of consequences – is apt to be free

[1] 392.
[2] 208.

and easy about names, as well as with their owners.) '2 March, halek Joan West.' There followed a rapprochement with Avis, whom he found at the garden on the evening of 12 March and 'I did halek etc. cum illa' (with her).

The Allens were respectable well-to-do folk. Not so the Hipwells. 'Halek prius Elizabeth Hipwell 15 June 1596, 4.20 p.m. studio [in the study]. He is a lewd fellow . . . spends all and keeps ill company and theft, like to have been hanged for robbing. A faint-hearted fellow, a yellowish beard and brown head. Fovit prius pro peccato inter anum et sodomy; illa halek cum duobus del Finchley et habet 4 or pueros et fuit filia Stars.'[1] There is little enough information about sexual variations in Elizabethan life, and naturally Simon disapproved of deviations. He continued to carry on, however, with Mrs Hipwell.

Sometimes the presence of the husband frustrated Simon of his intentions. On 20 August 1597, he inquires whether 'best to go forthwith to Mrs Cooley or no'?[2] Cooley is the old and proper pronunciation of Cowley, and this is fairly certainly the wife of the actor in the Lord Chamberlain's Company. Augustine Phillips, Cowley's fellow in the Company, appears as well as a Cowley among Forman's clients. In this year 1597 Cowley would be playing in the two parts of *Henry IV*; we know that in *Much Ado About Nothing* he played Verges. He lived and died in Shoreditch, in the parish registers of which are noticed the baptisms and burials of the family.[3] His wife Elizabeth died in the same year as the Company's dramatist, 1616. This August evening at 6 Simon 'went and spake with her, but he [the husband] was then newly come in. If I had gone presently [i.e. immediately] I had found her alone: it had been best to have gone presently.' Early evening would be the time an Elizabethan actor would return from performances, which took place in the afternoon.

In October 1598 Forman became friendly with another respectable couple, John and Anne (or Agnes) Condwell, who lived in the Old Jewry, the street leading up from the Poultry through its

[1] 234.
[2] 226.
[3] E. K. Chambers, *The Elizabethan Stage*, II. 312–13.

continuation in Coleman Street to the open fields beyond Moorgate. Mr Condwell suffered from stone and gravel – as many did, and no wonder, considering the sediment and impurities in what they drank. Mrs Condwell, aged thirty-seven, Forman diagnosed to suffer from 'languishing sickness; her time draws on to die, she cannot live long'.[1] Month after month she seeks Simon: he diagnoses catarrh in the stomach, jaundice indicated, then she is sick of melancholy. Time and again she wants to know whether she is pregnant; the answer was that she was, and 'ex duobus formis' (presumably twins). Apparently this was not so, for Mrs Condwell continued to inquire whether she was not pregnant. Until Simon took steps to make her so, along with his wife. '1601. 16 January, 9 a.m. halek Anne Condwell; at 12 noon, Frances Hill [his maidservant]. The 26 January, at night towards Monday, my wife dreamed that she was with child, and Mrs Condwell the same night dreamed so also.'[2] There appears a certain impartiality in these observations.

At Easter 1598 Forman took Bess Parker into his household as nurse to help professionally in his practice; but her more intimate services led to complications, from which Simon extricated himself with some difficulty and at some cost. It is, however, consoling to reflect what light the story throws into the recesses of Elizabethan life. By 14 July we learn, 'halek Elizabeth Parker p.m. at 10, et eo tempore fugit matrix virgam virilem' and she felt herself to be pregnant. The same day 'p.m. a pain took me in my left thigh in the sinews under the buttocks, like a scald or cramp . . . and troubled me that same night and the day following that I could not sleep nor scant stand the next day'. We need hardly wonder after his exertions; nevertheless, four days later, 'halek Elizabeth Parker a.m. at 1 bis, et ultimo sanguinata est'. On 29 July the strait-laced Simon casts to inquire whether Bess is a harlot or no. That night he dreamed that she was a month or six weeks pregnant.

In November Bess herself put the question whether she was pregnant; the answer was that she was with child some five days

[1] 219.
[2] *Autobiography*, below p. 297.

or so. This was hardly surprising. For Simon, who noted down everything – one never knew when it would come in handy – observed that on 8 November at 10 p.m. when his half-brother Stephen Michell 'lay here, Elizabeth Parker was on the bed kissing with him and the boys, I being abed. I stayed with them till almost 11 at night. The next morning my boy Ted told Stephen I watched her everywhere, and of the bag of stones. Eustace said, if she were disposed to pleasure any other good fellow, what had I to do with it?' At the month's end Bess was disposed to pleasure Simon, for '24 November halek E. Parker 9.15 p.m., et seminavi per multum semen at matrix hausit multum virgam adhuc tempusque'. Two days later, where had Bess been while Simon was at Lambeth, for 'she went forth . . . and then I warned her away'. At Christmas Bess Parker left Simon's service.

On 30 December Simon 'heard piping of the fairies, as I was wont before trouble. Questo, whether there be any trouble towards me or no . . . It seemeth there is some trouble or imprisonment towards and it will fall out' next week.[1] It did not, but Bess sent him a token. 'It seems by this figure that she is with child and that her Master hath put her to some other place and that she will come shortly to her mother.'

In March Bess's brothers wanted to know who was responsible for her condition. Simon said that on 22 August she had been 'sent to Mary Fardell that lay in childbed, and Nicholas Fardell did occupy her before she came away'. When her child was born on 9 June he argued that that made nine months, 'and so it seemeth to be Nicholas Fardell's child'. Evidently action was threatened, for Simon noted:

In this action remember these that follow: Whitfield, how he had her. The smith that used her. William Casson, how he had her. Old Westley, how he did use her. Captain Ruddlesdon at Mr Bragg's. Fardell of Southwark when I sent her to his wife's lying-in. The time that she went to Hackney, and she went not thither but to Lambeth. The time that she went to Fleet Street, when I went to Lambeth in an afternoon and forbade her to go out. The time that she stayed so long at market.[2]

[1] 195.
[2] 219.

It is an Elizabethan Sarah Gamp that Simon would conjure up. All to no avail, when Bess was delivered of a daughter on 9 June, 'she sent to know my mind'. Simon was now in a position to pay up; there follow various payments, altogether several pounds, to Bess's nurse and presumably the nurse's brother. This may be the man who had been prevailed upon to marry Bess two months before the birth of the child. Bess brought her to Simon, himself now married; it was called by the strange name of Fennena: there could hardly be a more authentic recognition of paternity.

One might suppose from this recital that sex took up a lot of Forman's time; but not so, he took it in his stride. It is true that his practice opened to him many opportunities, of which he made the most; but in fact sex was only a small portion of his activities – it was his energy that was phenomenal. Here we should confine ourselves to those activities which chiefly concerned himself; and even these self-regarding occupations and amusements are to be seen against the background of his regular practice, astrological and medical, in which he was increasingly engaged from morning till night. He was a very hard worker; in the intervals of work he wrote and wrote, his 'books' as well as writing up his cases.

His notes are like pieces of mosaic – it is a very laborious job to fit them together to form a picture. But we do get snippets of information to indicate something of his background; very much more, of course, about himself and what he is up to, not only his occupations but his fears and superstitions. Then there are his dreams. A perceptive historian of late classical antiquity points out that 'the historian is in danger of forgetting that his subjects spent much of their time asleep and that, when asleep, they had dreams'.[1] He observes that Aristides' dreams helped him through the 'breakdowns' that might have threatened his successful career. This is one of the therapeutic rôles of dreams, and we can see that Simon's helped him at various junctures to surmount his psychological difficulties and his troubles. He thought that they were warnings – as in a sense they were – and foretellings of what would come about. He regarded them as objective rather than

[1] Peter Brown, *Late Antiquity*, 49.

subjective. In any case, they were part of his activity as a whole, of the warp and woof of this life so singularly exposed, and all of one piece by night as well as day.

Sometimes a tantalising vista opens, of the dangers to which he was earlier exposed and out of which he had so laboriously climbed to a prosperous status. In October 1595 he was inquiring whether he would suffer injury from some deed and words spoken by the mother of one unspecified. 'No harm happened, but he was imprisoned for half a year, then hanged for his villainy. But I was in continual fear of it till he was hanged. And sometimes it cost me money; I fed him with hope and fair words, as others did, till he was hanged.'[1] Who was this unfortunate? It looks as if Forman had been under some threat of blackmail.

On the other hand, there were always friends to help him in his troubles – we shall see who some of them were. In 1593, when he was called before the Barber-Surgeons, 'I was like to have had great trouble, had I not made good friends to save me from them.' The Physicians, however, continued to persecute.

Life was packed with interest and avocations for someone of so alert a mind and gregarious a nature – in addition to his regular daily practice. His Case-Book for 1598 shows what an extensive practice he had: on 20 February, 6 cases; 22 February, 5; next day, 3; next, 7; 25 February, 5. Each of these necessitated casting a horoscope and working out the calculations, besides the medical side, hearing, diagnosing, prescribing, or practising surgery.

Until 1597 he continued to inhabit the Stone House, in Billingsgate, which was the large re-vestry of the parish church of St Botolph, now secularised and let out as chambers and apartments. It is curious that among all the multifarious writings about London nothing has been written about the idiosyncratic vicinity of Billingsgate. However, with the aid of Stow, we can visualise something of the background of Forman's daily life. It was extremely convenient for the resort to him of all kinds of folk, especially sea-going and their dependents. The harbour of Billingsgate was the largest inlet just east of London Bridge, as Queenhithe was further along to the west. Upon its wharves,

[1] 205.

at this time, was unloaded every kind of ware – especially fish, corn, fruit and vegetables – except groceries. Between it and the Tower stood the new Customs House, which had swept away the old medieval building in which Chaucer had served for a dozen years.[1]

St Botolph's church, in the re-vestry of which Forman resided, lay along Thames Street in a line with St Magnus. Thence one went up Fish Street into the large thoroughfare of Gracechurch Street; one crossed Thames Street to go up Botolph Lane or St Mary Hill into East Cheap, where Falstaff's Boar's Head was, at the western end. To the south were the wharves along the river and, very close, London Bridge leading to Southwark. Forman's practice and *clientèle* led him frequently across the bridge, as did his visits to the Bankside theatres, the 'Rose' and the 'Globe'. These were backed by gardens, the Bear Garden, the Pike Garden and – further afield towards Lambeth – Paris Garden.

Towards the end of the year Forman bought the lease of Mr Wedmester's house at Lambeth, managing to exclude Mr St Leger 'that would have cozened me of all'.[2] Here he lived until Midsummer 1598, made a profit of some £40 by selling the lease for five or six years, and went back to the Stone House.

While at Lambeth his study was rifled with the connivance of his assistant, John Goodridge, 'a gelded fellow', and a number of his astrological books stolen, which he valued above anything.[3] Among them were manuscript treatises, in Latin, of Albubather on nativities, of Alcabitius on the conjunctions of the planets, with the commentary by Thomas of Saxony which Forman would translate a couple of years later; Richard Anglicus on the rules for testing urines, and a book of notes on the astrolabe. There was besides the Geneva Testament that his old love 'A.Y. sent me'. The thieves brought some of the books to Mr Coomy to sell – he was an amateur astrologer to whom the books would be useful: the thieves knew what they were about. Forman notes 'all three

---

[1] H. B. Wheatley, 'Notes upon Norden and his Map of London', *London Topog. Record*, II. 42 foll.
[2] 392.
[3] 219.

Cambridge men'. Thomas Russell was the son of Thomas Russell of Frankfield by Lewes in Sussex. William Grange, 'a Northern man', we can identify as the sizar of St John's who took his B.A. from Trinity in this year 1598: he came to no good.[1] Neither did George Nicholas, sizar of Trinity from 1592,[2] whose 'mother dwells in Westminster; he is gone beyond sea and become a seminary priest'.

Life had never a dull moment with Simon – perhaps herein lay another source of his charm. There was, for example, the calling of spirits from the dead. In 1591 he was inquiring whether he should ever *see*; next year whether the spirits will obey him.[3] Five years later, it is 'whether I shall have that power in necromancy that I desire, or bring it to effect'; in October 1597, for John Good-ridge, 'whether he should obtain his desire in necromancy'; again that month, 'whether the spirit will appear'. Apparently it did, for two days later, 'whether the said spirit will ever appear again this night following, if I should go or send John'.

The said spirit did appear and said that he walked there for killing of his father. He cast out much fire, and kept a wonderful ado; but we could not bring him to human form: he was seen like a great black dog and troubled the folk of the house much and feared them. And between 11 and 12 at night the bed . . . four or five times, and cast out such fire and brimstone that it stank mightily. That night he kept much ado and reared mightily.

The truthful Simon added, 'But I saw him not. I saw the fire and then saw him in a kind of shape, but not perfectly. Salathiel.'

31 October 1597 would be All Hallows' eve, when spirits walked. Was it best to call the spirit this night? 'We went, and it was good that we went, for he came and talked with us. I saw him not, but heard his talk.' 2 November is All Souls day.

> Midnight sounds, and the great Christ Church bell
> And many a lesser bell sound through the room,
> And it is All Souls night . . .
> > A ghost may come . . .

[1] J. A. Venn, *Alumni Cantab.*, Pt. I, 11. 247.
[2] Ibid., III. 254.
[3] 354.

Simon inquired whether he would. 'This night he came according to his wont and raved much; we bound him strongly and kept him till almost four o'clock in the morning.'

One night in 1599 he dreamed that he 'was in the chancel of a church with John Ward, our clerk, calling of spirits'.[1] This would presumably be the parish clerk. Simon thought Ward had the power, but none came. Noticing the church door open, Simon went to shut it, when there entered an old woman with dark hollow eyes and two daughters – one the ugliest creature he had ever seen, and a witch. The air was full of spirits flying. The old woman said she had come to learn Simon's cunning. He said that his power over spirits was of power divine and performed to God's glory; her daughter's was a contract with the Devil, and worked. 'That day came Mrs Riddelsden from Lady Hayward to learn her future life. On 16 August my wife had her bracelet put seven times double on her arm and a scratch on her face in the night.' It was generally recognised that witches scratched.

Three weeks later he was inquiring whether a dream of his being at sea betokened trouble. He was 'in a boat, with others, among rocks on the coast of Cornwall; they came to the very turning beyond the Mount where the water ran swift and the stern of the boat touched the high cliffs'. They landed where the houses were built close down to the water's edge, and lodged in an inn. That night also he was troubled about hiding his paper books of prophecies, i.e. as opposed to his parchment manuscripts.

He was convinced that his prophecies of certain people's deaths had fallen out truly, and noted over a dozen instances. Including that of Lady Buckell who, coming out of the country, died 'the same day that I told her'. No idea that that might have settled the matter for the poor lady.

That year Simon had had much trouble in his household. 'Bess went from me et fuit gravida [and was pregnant]. Alice my maid came home and had much ado with her mistress. Robert Landell I put from me because he deceived me. John, my man, robbed me while I was out of town and played the villain with me many ways, both with his tongue and also with his hands; and with my distil-

[1] 219.

lations was negligent.' We have a glimpse into his chamber when he refers to 'my pots of water on the stills in the corner by the chimney'.[1] Into his 'strong water' there went thyme, angelica, fumitory, saxifrage, wormwood, bugle, ginger, senna, carraway seed, licorice and twenty other things. These herbs had to be collected or bought – we have a rare mention of an apothecary of Bucklersbury. Stow tells us that this street, running up to the Great Conduit in Cheapside, was occupied wholly by grocers and apothecaries, and a ballad recalls how Bucklersbury smelt 'in simple time'. In February 1598 Forman was preparing hazel wands: just between moonrise at 7 p.m. and 9 p.m. 'I did let to be cut eight hazel wands of one year's growth within the day and hour of eight just. Jane did cut them instante [close], being a virgin and in that hour they were whited and written on.'[2]

There was the making of the philosopher's stone. For its making we have a later indication. 'A man digging in the ground found three chests of lead in which were 12 or 16 lb of tawny earthy powder. I bought a dram of it, like brown clay.'[3] Experimental as ever, he found that it had no taste, but after three-quarters of an hour he felt an itching in the roof of his mouth. He then cast to know if it was of any value. Evidently the philosopher's stone was baked out of some such mineral material. In August 1599 Simon notes, with candour, 'to know what will become of my stone, whether ever it will come to good effect, and whether it will be profitable to me, or no. At this time my stone had stood closed in the tripod Attonor twelve weeks, and it was black upon and thin underneath.'[4] Making the stone was a difficult business and involved fire – for the stone in making in 1599 was 'set on fire and spoilt'. Seven years later he is still working at it: he had often made it before, 'yet now deluded [i.e. it eluded] him'. We may regard the word 'deluded' as an appropriate *lapsus linguae*.

We find him regularly making engraved rings, lamina and

[1] 226.
[2] 195.
[3] 392.
[4] 354.

sigils for his clients – usually women for this class of goods. A note on the making of lamina says that on a September day in 1596 'the man with the cock was engraved and washed from 4 to 7. 8 Sept. all the image names and characters were engraven and to what content; but it was not shadowed till the next morning. Then we did very little to it, but set it out a little and cut it off.'[1] Evidently this was a phallic figurine to incite or compel love, such as the Countess of Essex used in her pursuit of Carr, King James's favourite, as we shall see later. On 17 June 1597 he began to make 'my lamina of gold and Daniel to engrave it'; it was made out of a gold angel worth 40s, with a lion engraved.[2] He notes the ring he gave Alice Cheyne in 1599 'with the red coral stone. The sigil of 4 was made the 4 of January, 4 a.m. within the hour of 4. The ring being formed, he began to engrave it at 7, and finished it and set the stone by 8.'[3] We observe the human 'thinking': the significance attached to the coincidental and the sympathetic, the illusory rules with their hallucinatory authority for credulous humans.

Forman continued on his way, ruled by these illusions. If he lost his scissors or a pair of yellow garters, he immediately cast a figure to find them. The fact that the figure was no aid to their discovery, or that the forecasts made did not usually turn out true – as he candidly reported – made no difference: that must be due to an inadequacy or an impediment in the calculations. He attached importance only to those which turned out right – a small minority. This is completely characteristic of ordinary humans' thinking: one studies the varieties of foolery, as Swift and Flaubert did, with fascination and contempt.

'If I sneeze once at the left nostril after sunset, it means an unknown person is coming; if twice at the right nostril before sunrise it means a friend coming speedily for physic or some sick body.' And so on. He then gives examples. But what interest it gave to every minute of the day, in the absence of rational thought or the appreciation of beauty, the only redemption of man!

Of course Simon had opinions – all humans have, whether

[1] 234.
[2] 219.
[3] 195.

qualified to hold them or no. These things he held to be prejudicial to a commonwealth: iron mills, glass houses (i.e. glass manufacture) for spoil of wood, sugar houses for spoil of wood and eggs. The first two were commonplaces at the time – as it might be on the level of the *Daily Express* or the *Daily Mirror*. But Forman added to these, the 'printing of books, because it hindereth scholars and writing, and maintaineth vice'. This is more personally revealing. It shows Forman, as befitted an astrologer and magician, in favour of keeping knowledge esoteric and in manuscript – we have seen that his own 'books', which meant power to him, were mostly manuscripts. On a lower level of motivation, he was against printing because he could not get his own writings printed – also very human. And he was against vice – we have seen what a moralist he was. He was also against 'rich men, lawyers, and judges', for obvious reasons: 'judges that do injustice for reward should be stripped of their skins and hanged up in the place of judgment'. I do not know what he would have thought of a Brady or Myra Hindley – the Elizabethan Age produced no such sophistication of horror.

But we are studying a human being who has exposed himself as no one has done, not even Pepys or Boswell or Rousseau, and with more naïve candour and ingenuous truthfulness than a Henry Miller.

Or there was hunting for hidden treasure, a favourite and not unreasonable sport of the time, for many people hid their valuables, in the insecurity of that age, now returning. Forman had at hand the formulas required to find things hidden in a house or out of it; we have directions 'to know what it is hid there, how deep it is, whether it may be found or no, of what value, whether newly hid, whole or diminished'.[1] Planetary influences and the divisions of the 'houses' governed these matters, but there are also geomantical figures to aid the searcher. There was treasure concealed in William Burnfield's house in Ironmonger Lane; was it in the cellar or above stairs?[2]

[1] 392.
[2] 226.

The figure indicated that 'the treasure was five feet deep in the north-east corner of the cellar, in moist and watery earth'. It was 'kept by the spirit of Tobith Algrade that had it and by other spirits also'. On 2 September 1597 they dug and dug; but 'we digged for treasure in vain'. They did not give up; a week later they returned to it. Again they were frustrated. Why? 'It was drawn away northward when we came to it. And so we had it not for lack of time.' The implication is that it was still there. It reminds one of Pepys at the Restoration digging in the Tower for Cromwellian treasure, supposed to have been deposited in butter-firkins – which turned out to be, rather, a mare's nest.[1]

For light relief there are the usual amenities of housekeeping – and Forman's increasingly successful practice necessitated setting up house and a larger household. In May 1598 he pays Mr Richard Perkins of Lambeth 22*s* 6*d* for beer, strong and small.[2] From the orchard there he proposed to sell all apples, plums, wards (keepers), quinces and pears, reserving the 'apricocks' to himself. (But were these all real, or notional?) All through the impoverished period of his life Forman had been rather careless of money; now that he is beginning to thrive, he becomes more interested. Setting himself up, he wants to make money – he considers making a purchase of wheat in Wiltshire, on which to make a profit: a rational enough activity. He began to accumulate money; but he is never mean about it. We find him frequently making presents among his large circle of friends and acquaintances. In September he paid 20*d* for a pair of stockings for his boy, John Braddedge: a good sum, they must have been of good quality. In the same month he examined some twenty-one fellows – he called them 'cutpurses' – about the theft of his purse, all with the aid of astrology: they were all between seventeen and twenty-four. No indication that he discovered the culprit. Becoming well-to-do, he was becoming a potential victim.

From 1593 to Christmas 1599 Forman occupied chambers in the Stone House, except for the months October 1597 to Midsummer 1598 when he was at Lambeth, but did not give up his chambers,

<hr />

[1] cf. my *The Tower of London,* 189.
[2] 195.

where he had gained his hard-won, modest prosperity. We can now identify the Stone House as the re-vestry of the parish church of St Botolph, Billingsgate, built by a Fishmonger Mayor, John Rainwell, whose epitaph was within. Stow tells us that this was 'a proper church, and hath had many fair monuments within, now defaced and gone . . . all destroyed by bad and greedy men of spoil'.[1] A contemporary inhabitant of London regretted as much as Stow the destruction wrought by Reformation iconoclasts and depredators:

> When I have seen by Time's fell hand defaced
> The rich proud cost of outworn buried age;
> When sometime lofty towers I see down-razed,
> And brass eternal slave to mortal rage . . .

Since Simon's abode was the re-vestry of St Botolph's, the church in which he dreamed he saw spirits flying was right next door. Stow tells us that the parish was 'no great thing', but crowded with immigrants who had streamed in from the Netherlands and paid high prices for houses which were turned into tenement dwellings. He further complained that they did not pay the parish poor rates, 'for the stranger will not contribute to such charges as other citizens do'.

Here then was Forman's background before he moved permanently to Lambeth, after his marriage. For him there was no avoiding the rates and taxes, which his respectable status involved. Along the street from the church, in Thames Street, lived the Allens; Mr Allen was rated for Subsidy at £20, which places him in the ranks of the well-to-do middle class. Forman was rated for £5, to pay 13s 4d. This was the same figure at which William Shakespeare was rated in the parish of St Helen, Bishopsgate – though we must remember that he was only a lodger (like Forman), his real home and his property being at Stratford. In 1599 Forman's rating went up to £8 on which he was assessed to pay 21s 8d.[2] On 2 January 1599, 'two came for 40d for soldiers. The question is whether they will recover it or no, because I suppose

---

[1] Stow, I. 207–8.
[2] P.R.O., E 179/146/394.

I ought not to pay it.'[1] He consulted the auguries whether it was best to do it, but there was no avoiding it. Next day he paid a special levy to equip Essex's army for the emergency in Ireland; the following day, 13*s* 4*d* for subsidy 'at £5 in the Queen's book'. It took some time for the tax collectors to catch up. He noted that one-fifteenth throughout England came to £38,000.6.9¾; in Billingsgate ward, some £39 odd.

Prosperity facilitated, if it did not positively enforce, marriage. It seems that the girl, Jane Baker, of seventeen or eighteen, was a newcomer to his household, when he thought of marrying her. The event was rather sudden, in the end. '5 July, 1599, best to marry Jane Baker: whether she will prove an honest good wife, and what her friends will do for her.'[2] Next day, 'best to keep Jane and marry her or not?' 13 July, he inquires again whether to marry her. Evidently her friends were willing, and Forman's great friend and client, Mrs Blague, wife of the Dean of Rochester and Rector of Lambeth, helped in the matter. For young Miss Baker was a Kent girl – her name was really Anne – her father John Baker, 'civilian of Canterbury', who had been a proctor in the ecclesiastical court there. But her mother, Forman tells us, was Dorothy Munnings, sister of Sir Edward Munnings of Waldershare.[3] This was a matter of great pride to Forman, and settled the issue so long in debate. He had indeed arrived.

The marriage took place on Sunday 22 July, 1599, at 7 a.m. in Lambeth church and was performed by the curate. At 3 a.m. it began to thunder and lighten, and rained exceedingly to 5, when they went forth to Lambeth. There accompanied Simon, Mr Best and his wife, Dick Cook, friend Condwell and 'my boy John [Braddedge] and my mother Waller' – this must mean Anne Baker's mother, who was attended by her man, and Mrs Cure of Southwark.[4] There followed Mr Cure, and Mr and Mrs Gudging of the Strand. 'One Fratells gave my wife at church' – her father was dead, her mother remarried and glad to see her become mis-

[1] 195.
[2] 354.
[3] 802.
[4] 219.

tress of the house instead of a servant. 'Mrs Blague, Mrs Apple-yard and others went to church with us.' Simon distributed 8*s* 2*d* among curate and attendants. 'We dined at Mrs Blague's and came home between 1 and 2 p.m.'

Marriage did not make much difference to Forman's way of life, except that he had an inexperienced girl now as mistress of the house; he continued to be master, however. Both wife and her mother now consulted him for his expertise. The girl came to him a virgin, and in the months after marriage at once wanted the figure cast to know if she were pregnant: in August, 'much pain in her stomach and vomiteth oft'. But on 7 September, 'I did halek cum uxore mea et eo tempore fuit illa valde cupida de halek et matrix fugit virgam.' Sexually awakened, the question was put whether she conceived then. The same day 'I did bethong my boy with a rope-end, and the night following he was out of the door after I went to bed.' Marriage brought an increased recognition of status. Forman left his old chamber and took all the little house for himself. 'This year two offices were laid on me – sidesman [in church] and gatherer for the poor.'

A rise in status, for an Elizabethan, at once expressed itself in clothes. Simon had a purple gown made for himself, velvet cap, coat and breeches, a taffeta cloak, a hat and much besides. Then he had his picture drawn. It is very fortunate that an 18th-century engraving of this shows us what he looked like in his later forties. Very convincing it is: a small face underneath the bushy beard and beetling brows; small sensitive mouth, large exploratory nose; broad, lined forehead; above all, the magnetic, obsessive look in the large eyes with their piercing stare. Here is our man, sure enough.

He bought himself a fencing sword and had the belt garnished with silver, besides a broadsword to wear by his side. Altogether he laid out almost £50 in apparel for himself and his wife; seemingly the knight's niece brought with her no dowry, but Simon did not need to look for the endowment of a widow now. He could afford to spend money on pictures, linen and household equipment, besides lending out sums on the security of plate or jewels. His brother John came to batten on him; aged thirty-eight, he had raw humours in head, stomach and limbs. His half-brother, Stephen Michell, stays with him from time to time and regularly has the horoscope cast before going to sea.

His mother-in-law was no less dependent on him for advice. She and her husband had some suit in hand over a piece of property; she puts questions to him through Mrs Cure, of that well-known Southwark family of whom the head had been Saddler to Henry VIII and has his monument in St Mary Overy. Next she wants to know whether best to go to Denshire – the old pronunciation of Devonshire – to see her mother. The answer came, not this month. In November 1600 he found that she was a very sick person, her 'disease more than natural, is contra naturam.'[1] The horoscope was ominous. Later that month, was she dead? Was it best to ride to her or no? She died on 1 December 1600.

Meanwhile, how was married life with a young girl proceeding?

In September Simon is putting the question (in Latin, in case anyone looks into his Case-Books) whether his wife has a lover and is false to him. In January 1601 he himself was sharing his favours among his wife, Mrs Condwell, and Frances Hill, his new maidservant. On 15 March 1600 he went to see the play *Sir John Oldcastle*. This would be the second part of the play put together by Drayton, Hathway and Munday, to cash in on the success of Shakespeare's Falstaff. It was produced by the rival company, the Admiral's, for Henslowe. There Simon picked up a woman whose address he wrote down: Ann Sedgwick alias Catlyn in Aldersgate Street, right against the Cock.

Four days later 'Ledsome went up privily to my privy unknown to me. Nota de uxore, and four days afore of the conversation had cum uxore mea' (with my wife – Simon always writes inaccurately, 'cum uxore meo'). On 9 April, he casts

to know what my wife made at Mr Bestow's, when I went to the Royal Exchange and she bid the maid say she was above when I came in. And while I went up she went to call her. Because I liked not her lies and excuses she began to talk peremptory to me with howling and weeping, and would not be quiet till I gave her two or three boxes [blows]. She

[1] 236.

upbraid me with her friends. It seems that she will be meretrix [a whore] and went with some other intent. But as yet there is no fact done.

Evidently not, for on 30 October 'my wife's course came down and it was the first time that ever she had them'.

However, married life had set in with its usual severity.

It was a question now of settling for good, and it was best to do so out of the range of the persecuting Physicians. Forman consulted the auspices with regard to several houses; but everything pointed to Lambeth, where he had already spent several profitable months, and would enjoy the shelter of the Archbishop's peculiar and the proximity of his invaluable friends, the Dean of Rochester and his wife, when in residence there.

Just before Whitsun 1601 he made his final move. We have the charges for removal: two loads of stuff by water, 2s; 32 yards of dornix, a coarse kind of woollen material for curtains and carpets; payment to carpenters, 5 days apiece at 16d – 13s 4d; to a joiner and a tiler; for boards, laths, nails, etc.[1] At the Stone House, he left in the great chamber 12 yards of wainscot, worth 12s; a joined door and partition; 72 yards of painted cloth in two lower rooms, with buttery doors and wainscot. It gives one a glimpse of what his accommodation there had grown to: he left it for good and 'gave up London quite' at Midsummer.

Henceforth his name would grow in inseparable association with Lambeth.

[1] 411.

Chapter VI

Shakespeare's Landlady, and the Dark Lady

Forman has long been known to Shakespeare scholars for his accounts of four performances of the plays at the 'Globe' in 1611. He was a playgoer and, since he wrote notes about everything that occurred to him, it is not surprising that he should have done so – he jotted down things that struck him in other plays too. Everything that throws light on Shakespeare's background, that gives us factual information about those who lived with him and knew him, is of value; for it helps us to place him firmly, with historical actuality, as an Elizabethan among Elizabethans.

In addition Forman gives us some new information about the Mountjoys, who kept the shop in Silver Street where, we know, the dramatist was lodging about 1600.

Most valuable of all, Forman provides information which points strongly to Shakespeare's Dark Lady of the Sonnets, who gave him such anguish in those years, 1592–3, for Forman had relations which follow a strikingly similar pattern with a strikingly similar woman a few years later. Of all people, Forman is the likeliest source in which she might turn up – his papers are such a mine of information about all sorts and conditions of people at the time. Nor is it surprising that Shakespeare's mistress should come to consult Forman, since his known landlady, Mrs Mountjoy, did so.

Mrs Mountjoy's husband was a French wig- or headdress-maker. It is a little ironical that Shakespeare should come to lodge with them, when only a few years previously he had expressed distaste for the habit of shearing locks from the dead to provide false hair for the living, both in the Sonnets and in *The Merchant of Venice*:

So are those crispèd, snaky, golden locks . . .
Upon supposèd fairness often known
To be the dowry of a second head,
The skull that bred them in the sepulchre.

But this was rather a literary conceit of the time, not to be taken too seriously.

Shakespeare was lodging there a little after 1600, as we learn from a law-suit of 1612 that relates to events some ten or so years before.[1] It was brought by Stephen Bellot, a former apprentice of Mountjoy, who had married his daughter. Bellot wanted the promised dowry that went with the girl Mary, their only child.

It came out in evidence that Shakespeare was the intermediary in making the marriage on behalf of Mrs Mountjoy. He deposed that 'the said defendant's wife [Mary Mountjoy] did solicit and entreat this deponent [Shakespeare] to move and persuade the said complainant [Stephen Bellot] to effect the said marriage'. And it was Shakespeare who, on behalf of the Mountjoys, promised the dowry to the young man and made the couple fast: 'they were made sure by Mr Shakespeare, by giving their consent, and agreed to marry'.

Shakespeare could not remember the exact amount after a decade or so, but thought it was about £50 'to his best remembrance'. He must have been on confidential terms with the family to have been entrusted with such a service on their behalf.

The house in Silver Street was not beyond reproach – but we see from the evidence accumulating in this book that the Elizabethans were not disagreeably respectable. A little later the elders of the French Church in London reported Mountjoy as of licentious life, and both he and his son-in-law *débauchés*.

It happens, as so rarely, that we have a depiction of their house in Ralph Agas's pictorial map of London. There it is with its little pentice of a shop-front, at the corner of Silver Street and Mugle Street – like that of the glover's in Henley Street at Stratford originally. Silver Street was obliterated in the German

---

[1] The documents were brought to light by C.W.Wallace, cf. Chambers, *William Shakespeare*, II. 90 foll.

blitz and the 'improvements' after, like so much else of Shake-speare's, and Forman's, London: it was a short cross-street in the area where London Wall turned north to make a right-angle round to Cripplegate. At the other end, it ran into Wood Street, the main thoroughfare going down to Cheapside – thence along to St Paul's Churchyard, where the publishers and booksellers put out their wares.

Now, through Forman, a shaft of light penetrates beyond the shop-front in Silver Street. Mrs Mountjoy came to consult him on 22 November 1597; as she went along Silver Street on 16 September last, she lost out of her purse a gold ring, a hoop ring, and a French crown.[1] We learn that she was then thirty – three and a half years younger than her lodger.

Ten days later she comes to consult Forman medically. She is suffering from pains in head, side and stomach – weakness in the legs and a swimming in her head. Forman diagnosed, 'she seems to be pregnant for eleven weeks – seven weeks more and then it will come from her, or stay hardly'. i.e. with difficulty. Evidently an astrological forecast. In March 1598 she comes to know whether her husband will be sick or no.[2] She had someone else in view, for the next thing is that Mr Wood puts the question on behalf of Mary M. 'whether the love she bears will be altered or not'. We learn later that Mr Wood lived in Swan Alley off Cole-man Street, not far from Silver Street. The next thing is that Mrs Wood wants to know whether to keep shop with Mrs Mountjoy. The answer came, 'they may join, but take heed they trust not out their wares much, or they shall have loss'.

A tantalising marginal note reads: 'Mary Mountjoy alained' – which means concealed. What went on in the house in which Mr Shakespeare was a lodger? Evidently the lady's affections were straying from her husband. In the same month he comes to put questions concerning his apprentices, presumably whether they would make good or no. Forman did not know French, so that his rendering of their names looks odd; they seem to be both French, like Bellot: Gui Asture, and Ufranke de la Coles.

[1] 226.
[2] 195.

above Fugglestone – the church of Forman's childhood

below Salisbury Close – background of Forman's early years

above The London that Forman knew

left Where Shakespeare lodged with the Mountjoys from Agas's map, *c.* 1560. The house is at the corner of Silver Street and Monkswell (Mugle) Street

right Map of London in 1593

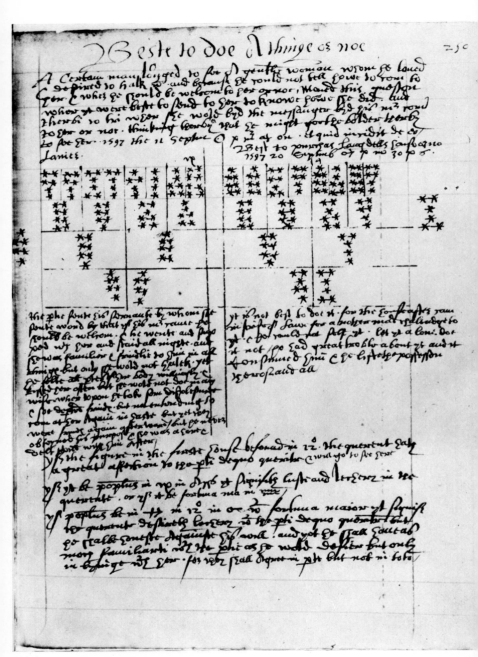

Forman visits Emilia

That was the end of their consulting Forman. But what a loss that their lodger does not figure in Forman's papers as a client, though he does as a dramatist!

However, we come tantalisingly closer to Shakespeare with a client who came to consult Forman first in May 1597. On 17 May there appeared Emilia, the daughter of Baptista Bassano and Margaret Johnson. The Bassanos were a prolific family of royal musicians who had come from Venice in the reign of Henry VIII. Emilia was married to a Lanier, of an equally prolific family of musicians who had come, apparently from Rouen, a generation later. Emilia was now twenty-seven, born therefore about 1569–70. Forman tells us, 'she hath had hard fortune in her youth. Her father died when she was young; the wealth of her father failed before he died, and he began to be miserable in his estate.' We learn further that 'she was paramour to my old Lord Hunsdon that was Lord Chamberlain and was maintained in great pride; being with child she was for colour married to a minstrel', i.e. Lanier. This was four years before, i.e. 1593 – the year in which Shakespeare was writing the Sonnets to his musical dark lady, for whom his love had originated in pity:

If thy unworthiness raised love in me . . .

The very next year, 1594, the Lord Chamberlain's Company was founded, with old Lord Hunsdon its official head. (James Burbage, Shakespeare's lifelong associate in the theatre, had always been Hunsdon's man.)

On 3 June Emilia Lanier came to inquire whether her husband should have the suit he was after. Forman tells us that she was brought up in Kent and had been married four years, but the old Lord Chamberlain had kept her long. 'She was maintained in great pomp. She is high-minded – she hath something in her mind she would have done for her. She hath £40 a year and was wealthy to him that married her, in money and jewels. She can hardly keep secret. She was very brave in youth. She hath many false conceptions. She hath a son, his name is Henry' – evidently after the Lord Chamberlain, the father.

On 16 June she inquires whether her husband shall come to any preferment before he come home again. He had gone to serve, in hope of promotion or gain, in the Islands Voyage of 1597 to the Azores. Commanded by Essex, it was largely his fault that the fleet missed the treasure-flota on its way home to Spain; they came back poor. Southampton was in command of the *Garland* on this expedition.

On 2 September, when she puts the question whether she shall be a lady, i.e. of title, and how she shall speed, we have a fuller character-sketch of her, with all Forman's vividness and perception. 'She hath been favoured much of her Majesty and of many noblemen, hath had great gifts and been much made of – a nobleman that is dead hath loved her well and kept her. But her husband hath dealt hardly with her, hath spent and consumed her goods. She is now very needy, in debt and it seems for lucre's sake will be a good fellow, for necessity doth compel. She hath a wart or mole in the pit of the throat or near it.'[1]

There follows, what is less important, Forman's forecast. 'She shall be a lady or attain to some greater dignity. He [her husband] shall speed well and be knighted hardly [i.e. with difficulty], but shall get little substance. The time shall come she shall rise two degrees, but hardly by this man: it seems he will not live two years after he come home. And yet there shall some good fortune fall on her in short time.'

Simon's interest was aroused by the lady and her circumstances; the absence of her husband provided an opportunity. A note about her expands our information for us: 'whose husband was gone to sea with the Earl of Essex in hope to be knighted – though there was little cause why he should – demanded in his absence whether she should be a lady or no'. Forman added later: 'he was not knighted nor yet worthy thereof', and similarly for her. On 10 September he puts the question, 'if I go to Lanier this night or tomorrow, whether she will receive me and whether I shall be welcome et halek'. An unattached note at this point, difficult to interpret, may relate to her: the figure 'shows the woman hath a mind to the quent, but seems she is or will be a harlot. And

[1] 354.

because . . . she useth sodomy.' We must remember that this is astrological, not necessarily factual.

We are informed what happened next day, 11 September. 'A certain man longed to see a gentle-woman whom he loved and desired to halek with.'[1] He put the question whether it were best to send a messenger to know how she did, and whether she would bid him come to her or no. 'The party sent his servant by whom she sent word that if his master came he should be welcome. He went and supped with her and stayed all night. She was familiar and friendly to him in all things, but only she would not halek. Yet he felt all parts of her body willingly and kissed her often, but she would not do in any wise. Whereupon he took some displeasure, and so departed friends, but not intending to come at her again in haste.' To this he added, 'but yet ready were friends again afterward – but he never obtained his purpose [he meant at that time]. She was a whore and dealt evil with him after.'

Six days later, on 17 September, she simply sent for Forman.[2] He put the question whether it were best to go. The horoscope indicated that she appeared to be afraid, but was not. Another six days passed, when he put the question whether 'best to go to Lanier today or no'.[3] He did not obey her command, but 'next afternoon *she* sent her maid to me and I went with her to her.'

October 29 was a very full day for Simon; living now at Westminster he went to see the state opening of Parliament by the Queen in her robes, the sword of state carried before her. 'A certain man being to see her Majesty go to the Parliament, a gentlewoman stood by him to whom he promised some courtesy, and in conference on further matters to come to him at any time if he did send to her.'[4] Questo – if best to send at this time. 'I sent my man at 4 p.m. by a privy token to her, and she came presently [i.e. immediately] and did halek etc. very friendly.' A marginal note gives us the name of Joan Harington, presumably a lady of that well-known family. Half an hour before he had put

[1] 354.
[2] 226.
[3] 354.
[4] 226.

the question whether 'to go to Lanier's [note the disrespect of the reference simply to 'Lanier'] this night or no'. She sent both her man and maid: 'I went with them and stayed all night.'

His relations with the Italian lady were not exclusively physical: at the end of 1597 he reminds himself to put the question, in Latin, what happens concerning Lanier's tales as to the invocation of spirits – whether not an incuba 'and whether I shall end it or no'. The last we hear of her is on 7 January 1600, when Forman wants 'to know why Mrs Lanier sent for me; what will follow, and whether she intendeth any more villainy'.[1]

And so the questionable Italian lady, of the musical family, passes out of Forman's cynosure; she appears no more in his books.

But there is further information to be gained about her. Her parents were buried in the parish of St Botolph, Bishopsgate, just outside the walls of the City, next to Shoreditch: this was the vicinity where many of the theatre-folk and the foreign Court-musicians lived. The registers are full of them. Baptist Bassano, 'the Queen's musician', was buried on 11 May 1576, when Emilia was a little girl of six.[2] She had a sister Angela, married to a man of decent standing, Joseph Holland. Their mother, Margaret Bassano, as she is named, was buried on 7 July 1587, leaving Emilia at seventeen to take the chances of life.

As Forman said – he must have learned it from her – her father could ill provide for her. His will had left to Emilia, 'daughter of the body of Margaret Bassany alias Margaret Johnson, my reputed wife, the sum of £100 . . . to be paid at her full age of twenty-one years or day of marriage'.[3] The bestowal of the girl in marriage was left to the mother; but she died before she could see to it. Emilia was left on the world, with nothing but her Italian looks and, no doubt, her skill on the virginals.

Not long after the elderly Lord Chamberlain took her and kept her 'long', evidently for some years, as his mistress. Forman tells us that Emilia had been brought up in Kent – her father, as Court musician, would have been much in attendance at Greenwich.

[1] 236.
[2] *Registers of St. Botolph Bishopsgate*, transcr. A. W. C. Hallen, I. 277, 295.
[3] Prerog. Court Cant., Prob/11/58, f. 21.

Lord Chamberlain Hunsdon had the manor of Sevenoaks near by. Henry Carey, 1st Lord Hunsdon, was the Queen's first cousin; he was the son of her mother's sister, Mary Boleyn, Henry VIII's mistress, by William Carey, to whom she was married off when the King discarded her. The son, born about 1524 and loyally named after the royal master, was much in favour with Queen Elizabeth. He was a good servant of the state, a soldier, straightforward, much given to swearing, a very masculine type. The Queen made him Lord Warden of the eastern Marches; he lived much at Berwick, where, in addition to his numerous family, he had a bastard, Valentine, who became Bishop of Exeter.

Lord Hunsdon was no Puritan, and from 1564 he had his own company of players. James Burbage, builder of the first theatres out in Shoreditch – in which Shakespeare played early on – was one. In 1585 Hunsdon was made Lord Chamberlain, and this proved a boon to the players as a profession, in addition to his own Company, for he was able to give them support at Court against the hostile City authorities.

Hunsdon had the keepership of the royal palace of Somerset House, where he resided, but he also had a lease of the buildings within Blackfriars which the Burbages later turned into an indoor theatre. Hunsdon's son, who became Lord Chamberlain in 1597 – the year in which his father's former mistress first came to consult Forman – had his residence in Blackfriars. We shall find his sisters, Lady Scrope and Lady Hoby, later consulting Forman about their brother's health. In fact, Forman had known the second Lord Hunsdon years before, in his old unrespectable Salisbury days, when he had been called on to visit Sir George Carey, as Hunsdon was then.

In the crisis of the Armada, 1588, old Lord Hunsdon was summoned from the North to take command of the Queen's bodyguard, in case of invasion. The stimulus of such an exciting time would have made a propitious moment for picking up an available girl from the musical ambience of the Court.

We do not indeed have to look far for the musical young lady, of easy virtue and difficult temperament, who became Shakespeare's mistress for a time, the Dark Lady of the Sonnets. It is perfectly clear that the Sonnets are autobiographical – that is why they were not published until years after, by Thomas Thorpe: the publisher dedicated them gratefully to Mr W.H., from whom he got them. This is Thorpe's dedicatee, not Shakespeare's – and not at all the young lord of the Sonnets, though scores of books have been written under that misapprehension. The sonnets were written to and for the obvious person, Shakespeare's patron, the young Earl of Southampton, whose personality and circumstances could not be delineated more clearly.

I have said all along that, if ever Shakespeare's mistress did turn up, she would be someone who was known in the Southampton circle. *Love's Labour's Lost*, which is a skit on it by its poet, presents the dark Rosaline in practically identical language with that of the Sonnets. We must remember that Emilia told Forman that she had been 'favoured . . . by many noblemen'. Southampton, whom the dark lady of the Sonnets entangled for a time, could easily have been one. Nor would he have been remote at Court from its Lord Chamberlain.

A number of music-books were dedicated to Hunsdon, so perhaps he appreciated Emilia's playing on the virginals besides other things. It is fascinating to think of the dramatist of the Lord Chamberlain's Company becoming infatuated with his discarded mistress. But who could be closer, or more likely?

In the year of Forman's death, 1611, Emilia Lanier put forth a volume of verse, *Salve Deus Rex Judaeorum*, from which we learn the hitherto unknown fact of her religious conversion. Surprising as this is, it is nevertheless understandable with her experience and background: the book has the consciousness of sin behind it, expresses repentance and pride reduced to humility by conversion. Though there is no doubt about the sincerity of her faith, we may wonder how far the old pride was subjugated: there is no abject humility discernible. Her conversion and the inspiration to write had come about at the hand of a countess, and most of the poems were dedicated to countesses – she had not ceased to be 'high-minded'.

What is more to the point, unique in itself and all the more convincing, is the strongly feminist vein, the distrust of men answering them back for their defaming of women, not only standing up for her own sex but carrying the war into the enemy's quarters – for with her now men had become the enemy. Fascinating as this is in itself – for I know no other such feminist outburst in the literature of the time – it has an illuminating significance for us. Such women, with their experience at men's hands, often enough come to detest them. We know too that Emilia had been humiliatingly married off, and was unhappy with her husband.

But two years before, in 1609, Shakespeare's Sonnets had been published, not by his will – we know that he did not correct the proofs – but by Thomas Thorpe the publisher, who had got the manuscripts from a Mr W.H., to whom he was floridly (and confusingly) grateful. But these Sonnets contained a most defamatory portrait of a woman – no wonder they were not published by Shakespeare. (They had been written years before: those about her, while the affair had been going on, in 1592–3.) Shakespeare's experience with Southampton and Emilia created the deep emotional crisis that great artists often go through; before it he wrote talented, promising work, after it he wrote works of genius fulfilled. Though the experience – with the capability of a man of genius for suffering – tormented him and drove him 'frantic-mad', it is not likely that the experience meant so much to her. It is evident enough from the Sonnets that she had been bored by the infatuation of an older man – he was five years older and that meant more then – that she looked down on the mere player, demeaned him in speech with others and used him to make a pass at Southampton, a better bet. And this apart from her tormenting temperament, refusing then yielding, finally going back on her word; promiscuous, passionate, inconstant; 'proud' and 'tyrannical'. A recognisable Italianate temperament, as to which Shakespeare and Forman are completely agreed and consistent with each other, each having a similar experience at an interval of three or four years.

To be exposed in print is another matter. The Sonnets came out in 1609 – we may assume without Shakespeare's wish; Emilia's volume of verse, with its passionate address against men's defaming of women two years later.

Her book is of the utmost rarity – so feminist a tract cannot have been popular in that world.[1] Four copies are known to exist, only one is said to be complete; neither the Bodleian nor British Museum copy is complete, but one can obtain completeness by conflating the two. It is the more surprising that the book should have been taken no notice of in that, besides the exalted persons to whom it is addressed, the verse is accomplished enough, runs smoothly in professional manner, where so many amateurs faltered. After the Countess of Pembroke, Sidney's sister, Emilia is the best woman-poet of the age – not that there was much competition – the great Queen's antique doggerel being rather derisory.

It is nice to learn that Emilia was a woman of literary, no less than musical, cultivation, an educated person with an easy knowledge of Renaissance classical terms of reference, again understandable with her Italianate background. Though there is familiar acquaintance with the Old Testament stories, there are a few Catholic flecks – a Hail Mary and a tribute to St Peter's power of the keys, appropriate in a Bassano. Here we are not to consider the book as literature but for the light it throws on her personality and background.

Throughout she is conscious of the rarity of a woman-writer in that age, at the outset begging James I's Queen,

> Vouchsafe to view that which is seldom seen,
> A woman's writing of divinest things.

From the first we are presented with a regular theme, her pitiable condition, her consolation only in Christ:

> And since my wealth within his region stands,
> And that his cross my chiefest comfort is,
> Yea in his kingdom only rests my lands,
> Of honour there I hope I shall not miss:
> Though I on earth do live unfortunate,
> Yet there I may attain a better state.

[1] I am indebted for my knowledge of it to Mr Roger Prior.

One cannot but recognise a certain *arrière-pensée* in her several references to her misfortune, lack of wealth, lands and honour, perhaps something of her old unregenerate self.

She told Forman in 1597 of the favour she had received from Queen Elizabeth; now again in 1611,

> So that I live closed up in sorrow's cell
> Since great Eliza's favour blessed my youth,
> And in the confines of all cares do dwell
> Whose grievèd eyes no pleasure ever view'th:
> But in Christ's sufferings such sweet taste they have
> As makes me praise pale sorrow and the grave.

She refers to herself as one

> Whose untuned voice the doleful notes doth sing
> Of sad affliction in an humble strain.

She had been reduced from pride to humility by her conversion, she tells us; whether welcome or no, we need not doubt its sincerity, even if it is contemplation of James I's Queen,

> Whose power may raise my sad dejected Muse
> From this low mansion of a troubled mind . . .

> Not that I learning to myself assume
> Or that I would compare with any man:
> But as they are scholars and by art do write,
> So Nature yields my soul a sad delight.

Nevertheless,

> Why should not She now grace my barren Muse
> And in a woman all defects excuse?

The next poem also contains a tribute to Queen Elizabeth in verses dedicated to her namesake, Princess Elizabeth, who later became celebrated as the Winter Queen. Emilia asks the Princess to accept

> the first-fruits of a woman's wit.

This is followed by a poem 'To all virtuous ladies in general', with the moral:

> Let Virtue be your guide, for she alone
> Can lead you right that you can never fall.

They are adjured to

> avoid the bait
> Of worldly pleasures, living always free
> From sword, from violence, and from ill report.

For herself,

> Yet some of you methinks I hear to call
> Me by my name, and bid me better look
> Lest unawares I in an error fall . . .

She proceeds to call in evidence the Court ladies known to her, beginning with Lady Arabella Stuart:

> Great learnèd lady, whom I long have known,
> And yet not known so much as I desired . . .

No doubt, with what we know of her proud aspiring mind.

Susan, Dowager Countess of Kent, is next addressed:

> Come you that were the mistress of my youth,
> The noble guide of my ungoverned days . . .
> For you possessed those gifts that grace the mind,
> Restraining Youth whom Error oft doth blind.

As it had led Emilia astray. Not so the Countess, who has never yielded to error,

> Nor to those weak enticements of the world
> That have so many thousand souls ensnarled.

(We recall what those are from *All's Well*: 'enticements . . . and all those engines of lust'.)

> Only your noble virtues do incite
> My pen, they are the ground I write upon;
> Nor any future profit is expected.

As to that we may wonder; we shall see.

A longish poem, 'The Author's Dream', is dedicated to Philip Sidney's sister, the Dowager Countess of Pembroke, the foremost woman-writer of the age. It has a stanza devoted to the antithesis between Art and Nature, so frequent with Shakespeare; but this is a commonplace of the time. More to our point is the re-iterated consciousness of sin:

> . . . though our sins in number pass the sand
> They are all purged by his Divinity.

There follow a poem to Lucy, Countess of Bedford, a prose address to Margaret, Dowager Countess of Cumberland, and a poem to the Countess of Suffolk, whom she evidently did not know:

> Although, great lady, it may seem right strange
> That I, a stranger, should presume thus far . . .

A tribute follows to the maritime Earl, better known to us as Lord Thomas Howard, who got away from Flores when Sir Richard Grenville met his fate:

> And rightly that he is descended
> Of honourable Howard's ancient house,
> Whose noble deeds by former times commended
> Do now remain in your most loyal spouse:
> On whom God pours all blessings from above,
> Wealth, honour, children, and a worthy love.

As to these we can only say that the lady was always supposed to be Robert Cecil's mistress – they both were in receipt of Spanish pensions. Even the *Peerage* allows that 'her rapacity was the chief cause of her husband's downfall'. When he became Lord Treasurer he embezzled the enormous sums from the state that enabled him to build vast Audley End. King James said peaceably that it was 'too large for a King, though it might do for a Lord Treasurer'.

In the end they fetched up in the Tower for a spell, with the Somersets, Robin Carr and his wife. So that a Court wag was able to observe that an alternative government could be provided within the Tower, 'with a Lord Treasurer, a Lord Chamberlain, a Captain of the Pensioners, and a Secretary'.[1] As for the Suffolks' children:

> And let your noble daughters likewise read
> This little book that I present to you:
> On heavenly food let them vouchsafe to feed:
> Here they may see a Lover much more true . . .

than Robert Carr, for whose love daughter Frances poisoned his friend, Sir Thomas Overbury.[2]

The opening of the next poem has an ironical ring, when we learn,

> Titles of honour which the world bestows
> To none but to the virtuous doth belong.

Anyway, we know how keen Emilia had been in her unregenerate days to get one; so that we may take the demotic flavouring of the next verse with a pinch of salt:

> All sprang but from one woman and one man,
> Then how did Gentry come to rise and fall?
> Or who is he that very rightly can
> Distinguish of his birth, or tell at all
> In what mean state his ancestors have been
> Before some one of worth did honour win?

We know that she was of illegitimate birth herself and no doubt this gave an edge to her temper, the concern with 'honour,' the itch to acquire a title. Of the one who wins honour she goes on:

> Whose successors, although they bear his name,
> Possessing not the riches of his mind,
> How do we know they spring out of the same
> True stock of honour, being not of that kind?

---

[1] cf. my *The Tower of London*, c. 7.
[2] See below; c. xi.

A pointed question indeed, coming from the mother of Lord Chamberlain Hunsdon's child. If the kind Countess of Dorest will extend her favour,

> So this poor work of mine shall be defended
> From any scandal that the world can frame . . .

> I do but set a candle in the sun
> And add one drop of water to the sea . . .

(We remember from *The Comedy of Errors*,

> I to the world am like a drop of water
> That in the ocean seeks another drop;

but this is, of course, just a commonplace.) She goes on,

> For well you know, this world is but a stage
> Where all do play their parts and must be gone . . .

Where have we heard that before? – In both *As You Like It* and *The Merchant of Venice*. But this is only another commonplace, and I attach no significance to it. More significant to my ear are the lines about Christ as the proper object of love:

> Yet lodge him in the closet of your heart
> Whose worth is more than can be showed by art.

In the accent of that one hears a familiar voice and thought, and remembers the *Sonnets*, with the image of Southampton's picture locked up in Shakespeare's chest.

There follows upon this an address in prose, which defends women against men's defaming them and takes the offensive with a good deal of personal feeling. 'Often have I heard that it is the property of some women not only to emulate the virtues and perfections of the rest but also, by all their powers of ill speaking, to eclipse the brightness of their deserved fame.' This 'men, I hope unjustly, lay to their charge . . . All women deserve not to be blamed, though some, forgetting they are women themselves . . . fall into so great an error as to speak unadvisedly against the rest of their sex.' She then moves over to the offensive against men, regarding 'such points of folly to be practised by evil-disposed men, who – forgetting they were born of women, nourished of women and that if it were not by the means of women they would be quite extinguished out of the world and a final end of them all – do, like vipers, deface the wombs wherein they were bred'. And more to the same effect, against their 'unjust speeches'.

I know no outburst against menfolk from a woman, like this, in the whole of Elizabethan literature. Here is a smouldering passion against them, for all the genuine religious consolation of the poems. The psychology is perfectly clear; but was she reacting to a closer, more intimate resentment? Only a couple of years before, Shakespeare's dark and musical, passionate and temperamental mistress of years ago had been exposed, as few women in literature. Are we to suppose that the unexampled exposure of her character would not be resented by the woman alive to read it?

The longish poem that follows is addressed to the Dowager Countess of Cumberland, widow of the buccaneering Earl, George Clifford, who had neglected her and treated her badly. Emilia knew all about 'her inward cares . . . and sorrows of thy soul.' The Countess had now retired from Court,

> The great enchantress of weak minds admired
> Whose all-bewitching charms so pleasing be
> To worldly wantons, and too much desired
> Of those that care not for eternity,
>> But yield themselves as preys to lust and sin,
>> Losing their hopes of heaven hell-pains to win.

It is women's beauty that is their overthrow:

> That pride of nature which adorns the fair,
> Like blazing comets to allure all eyes,
> Is but the thread that weaves their web of care,
> Who glories most where most their danger lies;
> For greatest perils do attend the fair
> When men do seek, attempt, plot and devise
>> How they may overthrow the chastest dame
>> Whose beauty is the White whereat they aim.

Here again Emilia spoke out of her own embittered experience, and one cannot but recognise personal touches in the poem. The chaste Countess had retired from Court into the country:

> Thou, being rich, no riches dost respect
> Nor dost thou care for any outward show,
> The proud that do fair Virtue's rules neglect
> Desiring place, thou sittest them below.

Here is an Emilia signature-tune, in which she reveals herself and her prepossessions. The Countess gives no countenance

> To foul disorder or licentiousness,
> But in thy modest veil dost sweetly cover
> The stains of other sins to make themselves,
> That by this means thou may'st in time recover
> Those weak lost sheep that did so long transgress –

– Emilia herself being one of them.

We are then treated to a number of famous women whose beauty led to their ruin:

> 'Twas beauty bred in Troy the ten years' strife
> And carried Helen from her lawful lord;
> 'Twas beauty made chaste Lucrece lose her life,
> For which proud Tarquin's fact was so abhorred;
> Beauty the cause Antonius wronged his wife,
> Which could not be decided but by sword:
>   Great Cleopatra's beauty and defects
>   Did work Octavia's wrongs and his neglects.

There follow no less than five stanzas about Antony and Cleopatra, somewhat extraordinary in a poem devoted to the Passion of our Lord.

> Great Cleopatra's love to Antony
> Can no way be comparèd unto thine:
> She left her love in his extremity
> When greatest need should cause her to combine
> Her force with his to get the victory . . .

One would think that she had seen the play, the visual impression is so strong – and indeed *Antony and Cleopatra* had been staged only three or four years before.

> That glorious part of death which last she played,
> To appease the ghost of her deceasèd love,
> Had never needed, if she could have stayed
> When his extremes made trial and did prove
> Her leaden love unconstant and afraid;
> Their wicked wars the wrath of God might move
> > To take revenge for chaste Octavia's wrongs,
> > Because she enjoys what unto *her* belongs.

So much for the 'black Egyptian', as Emilia calls Cleopatra. The Countess, on the other hand, wages fight

> Against that many-headed monster Sin
> Whose mortal sting hath many thousand slain

(With Shakespeare the many-headed monster is always the people.)

> But your chaste breast, guarded with strength of mind
> Hates the embracements of unchaste desires . . .
> Even as the constant laurel always green
> No parching heat of summer can deface,
> Nor pinching winter ever yet was seen,
> Whose nipping frosts could wither or disgrace.

Among the famous women of the past here celebrated appear Deborah, Judith who slew Holofernes, Esther and the Queen of Sheba, inspired

> To come, to see, to hear and to admire

Solomon (we are reminded, inevitably, of Julius Caesar.) Emilia views the Queen of Sheba

> Acting her glorious part upon a Stage
> Of weakness, frailty and infirmity.

And we are back again with the constant theme of the book, 'our charged souls, full of iniquity', 'our sins of blood and wrong', and the no less recognisable themes of how much the poor are richer in spirit than the great – a consoling thought when one has failed of a title –

> A seeming tradesman's son, of none attended
> Save of a few in poverty and need.

Only the love of Christ, not of men, saves us:

> Sweetness that makes our flesh a burden to us,
> Knowing it serves but to undo us.

Poor Emilia! she is left with the thought,

> What pride hath lost humility repairs.

The last poem, wanting in the Bodleian copy,[1] describes with some satisfaction the rural retreat of Cookham, where her conversion had taken place, under the aegis of the virtuous Countess of Cumberland.

> Farewell, sweet Cookham, where I first obtained
> Grace from that Grace where perfect Grace remained;
> And where the Muses gave their full consent
> I should have power the virtuous to content.

So it was here that Emilia took to writing verse, inspired to it by the Countess:

> Yet you, great Lady, mistress of that place,
> From whose desires did spring this work of Grace,
> Vouchsafe to think upon those pleasures past
> As fleeting worldly joys that could not last.

She refers to the espousal of the Countess's daughter Anne to the Earl of Dorset – with whom, as we know, she had an unhappy married life. All three, the two Countesses and Emilia, had that in common, and now they had the consolations of religion.

But we see from her book – virtually as unknown as her life has hitherto been – how much of it had been passed in the musical margins of the Court. So unexampled a feminist manifesto,

---

[1] I am indebted to Mr Dennis Rhodes for a Xerox of it from the British Museum copy, incomplete in the preliminary leaves.

coming from that background needs something very poignant and special to explain it.

With Cookham we are back with the facts of daily life.

In 1604 King James granted Emilia's husband a patent to charge 6*d* upon every load of hay, 3*d* upon every load of straw, sold within London and Westminster.[1] This must have been a useful addition to his salary as one of the King's musicians, together with what remained of the old Lord Chamberlain's annuity of £40, to keep her to maintain life in the style to which she was accustomed. But in 1613, two years after her book, Alfonso died.[2] Whereupon Emilia agreed with his brother Innocent to obtain a new patent and allow her one-half of the profits. The patent came to Clement Lanier, and many years afterwards we find Emilia in 1635 petitioning King Charles I.[3] She *said* that she had received only £8, 'being in great misery and having two grandchildren to provide for' (Henry and Mary). Hearing that a new patent was being sought, she prayed that the new patentee should pay her £50 out of the profits. This was opening her mouth rather wide. She was now an old (for the time) woman of sixty-six.

Clement got the patent; the King ordered him to pay Emilia £20 p.a., and after her decease £10 p.a. to her two grandchildren during the continuance of the grant. But this was by no means the end of the matter: it led to a battery of petitions, threats of lawsuits etc. The tenacious old lady petitioned the Council again and again, making her charges against Clement, until in May 1637 he came back with his side of the case.[4] She had exhibited a bill in Chancery against him, then changed her mind, withdrew it and sued him *in forma pauperis* in the Court of Requests. He was ordered to pay her 20 nobles p.a. until the hearing of the cause, which he paid, but she never procured the cause to be heard. Instead she appealed to the Privy Council, which ordered him to

[1] *Cal. S.P. Dom., 1603–1610*, 146.
[2] *Cal. S.P. Dom., 1611–1618*, 210.
[3] *Cal. S.P. Dom., 1634–5*, 516.
[4] *Cal. S.P. Dom., 1637*, 115–16.

pay £5 in arrears and £10 yearly until he got the full benefit of his grant – part of which was now contested by the Lord Mayor and Court of Aldermen.

Clement obeyed the order, paid £5 and was willing to pay £10 p.a.; but Emilia 'not being satisfied with any of the same orders preferred another petition' to the Council, obtaining £20 p.a. – which he was unable to pay because of the City's opposition to his grant. He now wanted to appear before the Lords with his counsel. Next year, 1638, the poor distracted Privy Council, with a crisis on its hands – nationwide resistance to Ship Money, rebellion threatened in Scotland – threw the matter back to the Lord Mayor, asking him to take order so as 'his Majesty shall not be further troubled to interpose'.[1]

The Civil War was approaching. Still the tough old lady held on her way, and must have held on to something of her annuity; for when she died and was buried, it was as a 'pensioner' in the parish of St. James Clerkenwell.[2]

I am persuaded that we are dealing with one and the same woman, not two, as I had previously thought. The characteristics and circumstances all hang together and point to a recognisable personality, temperamental and passionate, with a literary cultivation now added to her musical background – all the more cogent and compelling, one that enriches our conception of her, bodies her forth and gives her back, as never hitherto, a local habitation and a name.

I am all the more convinced, from the character revealed in the poems, the re-iterated consciousness of sin, the conversion, yet still the remains of the old high-mindedness, the pride, the resentment against men, the snare her own beauty had been to her in her 'ungoverned' days, the small circle to which she belonged, the Court musicians, the Lord Chamberlain, her brief affair with the player-poet of the Company, that here in this Italianate woman we have the Dark Lady.

[1] *Cal. S.P. Dom.*, *1637–8*, 472.
[2] I owe this information to Miss Mary Edmond.

Chapter VII

A Covey of Clerics; the Dean of Rochester and his Wife

We have already observed that clerics were no less responsive to the charms, or dependent on the ministrations, of Forman than other folk. Even the puritanically inclined Hugh Broughton was a client. But Forman's closest devotees were his neighbours, when in residence at Lambeth, the Rector, Dr Blague and his wife. He was also Dean of Rochester; even when away from Forman's proximity, this precious couple were dependent on him, medically and astrologically: they could hardly make a move without having the horoscope cast. The Dean was not otherwise than respectable; this can hardly be said of his wife, who must have constituted the chief obstacle to further preferment and the bishopric the poor Dean yearned for –

> Make me, O sphere-descended Queen,
> A bishop, or at least a dean.

Blague got no further up the ladder than a deanery.

He was otherwise quite comfortably provided for. Born at Gloucester about 1545,[1] he matriculated from Queen's College, Cambridge in 1568, became a Bachelor of Divinity at Oxford in 1574, and a Doctor of the same at Cambridge in 1589.[2] Becoming a member of both universities had the advantage of spreading a wider net for patronage and preferment. The young scholar must have been promising, for he attracted the attention of Burghley, in whose family he matured. Burghley sought to promote scholarly persons in the Church; few Elizabethan clerics were literate, in any aggressive sense of the term. The Queen herself said that

---

[1] This supplements and corrects the *D.N.B.* account of him.
[2] J. and J. A. Venn, *Alumni Cantab.*, Pt. I, vol. 1, 163.

only some five hundred – out of as many thousand – could preach, and fewer still were those who could write a book.

Blague could do both, so he was marked out for preferment. In 1572 he produced *A School of Wise Conceits*. It was only an alphabetical anthology of phrases, pointed and witty, translated from Greek and Latin; but at least it showed that he knew Greek as well as Latin. Later, in 1603, he published one sermon, preached before King James at Charterhouse; and that is all that is known of his works. But, thanks to Forman, we know a great deal more about his life; and, as usual, everything correlates with external sources of information about him. We shall see that he was too much occupied with other things to do any more writing.

In September 1570 he received the rectory of Braxted Magna, Essex, which he held on to for the rest of his life. Next September he got that of St Vedast, Foster Lane; this enabled him to marry his first wife, Mary Holborne, a London resident, in 1572.[1] On acquiring the rectory of Lambeth in 1577, he next year relinquished St Vedast. Lambeth he held on to; we find him regularly present at the making up of the parish accounts every year up to 1587, if only irregularly present at services in church, for he had other chores.[2] In 1584 he was present at a vestry-meeting which decided to collect money for new bells; the well-equipped Rector contributed the exiguous sum of 5s., but we shall see that he had other calls on his funds.[3] In 1580 he had been presented to the delectable country rectory of Ewelme, near Oxford, which he kept till 1596. Meanwhile, in 1591, he was made Dean of Rochester; in 1599 the Queen presented him to the rectory of Crayford in Kent, more convenient a rural retreat than Ewelme. After preaching before King James, and some vicissitudes, he was also provided with the rectory of Bangor; no question of residing in so remote a country, he merely received the emoluments. A chaplain-in-ordinary to the Queen, his private life was hardly

[1] *Marriage Licences of the Bishop of London, 1520–1610*, ed. J. L. Chester and G. J. Armitage, 53.

[2] *Surrey Record Soc. XLIII. Lambeth Churchwardens' Accounts, 1504–1645*, ed. C. Drew, Pt. II. *passim*.

[3] ibid., 151.

ordinary with such a spouse; there is nothing to indicate that he was not a good man, but he had a lot to put up with.

Early in his career, a professional scholar, he appears at Oundle in May 1576, to examine the boys on a Saturday afternoon. He reported 'there be excellent boys for their time, as by two epistles made by two of the scholars doth well appear'.[1] On Sunday he made 'a very good sermon in the church, where was great audience of gentlemen of the county and others, which brought to us great store of good victual and dined with us'. A good preacher was at a premium, but he found the almsmen 'very ignorant, and took order that, if they did not learn the Lord's Prayer, the Belief and Ten Commandments before Whitsuntide, their pensions shall cease'. How very disciplinarian of him! – but in later life he could never keep his second wife in order.

She was a gentlewoman of good family: Alice, daughter of Sigismund Brock and Anne Jerningham, of that old Catholic stock. She had been born on 9 May 1560, and was married to Blague when she was only fifteen, he a widower of thirty. Forman was impressed by his being a Doctor of Divinity, himself frustrated of such things, but he gives us a wonderfully vivid character-sketch of the wife – he was a born writer *manqué*.

She had wit at will [i.e. intelligence enough], but was somewhat proud and wavering [i.e. inconstant], given to lust and to diversity of loves and men; and would many times overshoot herself, was an enemy to herself and stood much on her own conceit. And did, in lewd banqueting, gifts and apparel, consume her husband's wealth, to satisfy her own lust and pleasure, and on idle company. And was always in love with one or another. She loved one Cox, a gentleman on whom she spent much. After that she loved Dean Wood, a Welshman, who cozened her of much: she consumed her husband for love of that man. She did much overrule her husband.[2]

After all, was she not a gentlewoman, and he a mere scholar, years older and less potent than she?

She was of long visage, wide mouth, reddish hair, of good and comely stature; but would never garter her hose, and would go much slipshod.

[1] *V.C.H., Northampton*, II. 247.
[2] 206.

She had four boys, a maid, and a shift [miscarriage]. She loved dancing, singing, and good cheer. She kept company with base fellows, such as she was herself of, of lewd conversation – and yet would seem as holy as a horse. She was never without one bawd, or cunning woman or other, to keep her company, to her great shame, to paint her, etc.

The picture of an Elizabethan Dean's wife rises up before us, with her lascivious mouth and slipshod ways: a slut. Simon knew her through and through: he had tasted of her favours twice, in June and July 1593, while still at the Stone House, a few years before he moved to Lambeth, when she and her husband became his neighbours and clients. After that, not again; but his portrait of her is completely corroborated by their dealings together and the external evidence.

In March 1596 Burghley noted Blague down among those Doctors suitable for further preferment, evidently for a bishopric; in April 1597 the Dean is petitioning him for it.[1] Early in 1598, while Forman was residing conveniently nearby in Lambeth, both the Dean and his wife came to consult him, separately, about their troubles. On 16 January Mrs Blague of thirty-eight (correct), 'hath not her course, gravel and pain in back, like to vomit, in shoulders like to sound [faint], fearfulness and trembling. She hath taken thought', i.e. is a prey to anxiety.[2] She had, indeed, something on her mind. Next day it was her mother, aged fifty-eight: 'she hath a canker in her breast and, some say, a wolf'. What does this mean: some ravening spirit? The day after, Mrs Blague inquires whether her mother will live or die; the figure signified death speedily. On 22 January the Dean demanded to know whether he should come to any greater dignity.

Mrs Blague had more than her mother on her mind: there were her dealings, both amorous and financial, with the deleterious Dean Wood. This predatory cleric from Anglesey had graduated from Jesus College, Oxford, in 1580, becoming Master of Arts in 1584.[3] In 1590 he became (absentee) Dean of Armagh, and in

[1] *Salisbury Mss.*, VI. 122; *Cat. Lansdowne Mss.*, 163.
[2] 226.
[3] J. Foster, *Alumni Oxon.*, IV. 1671.

1596 he acquired a benefice in his native island. Next year he succeeded Dean Blague in the rectory of Ewelme – it would not be improbable to assume that money passed on the occasion. Poor Dean Blague, with such a wife, needed it; Dean Wood did not, for he had married the widow of 'Rich Ballet' of Cheapside. This goldsmith had been a principal creditor of the brilliant, and extravagant, artist Nicholas Hilliard, who had had to mortgage his house in Gutter (or Guthron's) Lane to him.[1] The lease now came, with a lot of other property, to Dean Wood in right of his wife. Gutter Lane, off Cheapside, was next to Foster Lane, with the church of St Vedast rising behind – all very convenient and neighbourly.

Dean Wood, having married an old widow, felt the need to console himself elsewhere. Simon, who kept his ears open and eyes upon everyone, is able to tell us what he had from the Dean's maid, who had seen him 'occupy Wem's wife in her own house in the garret. His wench confessed that her Mr Dean Wood did occupy her against the bedside, her mistress being abed at Tottenham.'[2]

On 22 January 1598 Mrs Blague has her horoscope cast to know 'whether ever Owen Wood will make restitution of that good he hath had from her'.[3] The answer was, no: she must go to law for it.

In February she still wonders whether Owen Wood bears her any love or no; the answer is encouraging, the figure indicating 'he hath done and will do again'. On 24 March she inquires 'whether there will be controversy or no between Owen Wood and Anne Heybourne. And whether Mr Blague shall be bishop.' The next day, obsessed and insatiable, she repeats the questions. (The desirable Anne was the wife of that musical member of the Queen's Household, Sir Ferdinando Heybourne, whom we still can see on his monument in Tottenham parish church.)[4] Next day Dean Blague is reported 'as stuffed in the stomach: give him a dietary and purge'.

---

[1] E. Auerbach, *Nicholas Hilliard*, 23.
[2] 236.
[3] 195.
[4] cf. my *The Elizabethan Renaissance: The Cultural Achievement*, 87.

An episcopal possibility had opened up with the death in 1596 of Bishop Coldwell of Salisbury – of which the Queen had deprived the see of its brightest jewel, Sherborne Castle, for the benefit of Sir Walter Ralegh, and had kept the see vacant for a couple of years to benefit the Crown by its temporalities.[1] This was a provoking situation to aspirants to the Apostolic Succession, and the curious Forman put the question for himself at the end of March whether Dr Blague would obtain the good will of my Lord of Canterbury or no. 'This day he went forth to the Court by my counsel and direction, and moved the matter to the Archbishop [Whitgift]. He granted him his good will and furtherance; all went well with him this day.'

On 6 April Forman put the question whether it was best to make the Lord Treasurer [Burghley] privy to 'our proceedings for Dr Blague'. The answer came, better not to do it. (To those acquainted with the mind of Lord Burghley the oracle was probably right.) Before the end of the month the anxious Dean wrote up from Rochester to know whether he would be bishop of Salisbury, and whether the Archbishop had moved the matter to the Queen or Sir Walter Ralegh. (It was during this interval that George, the Archbishop's man, sent Simon two figures to cast whether to proceed with Kate Gittens, whom Simon had considered for himself.) Early in May Dr Blague sent his waiter from Greenwich – where he would be in attendance as a royal chaplain – to know whether he would be consecrated bishop of Sarum. Again he put the question what good or ill was towards him; at the end of May, whether he would get Salisbury. The horoscope indicated that 'he is such a one as the Archbishop is enemy to'; it signified that he should sue to his Grace.

The Dean was sick with anxiety; his wife inquired for him solicitously. 'He hath a scouring in his belly, and between his neck and head, and in the stomach. And melancholy. There will be some alteration in him some three days hence – and [in Latin] is in peril of death. Give him physic.' The son Nicholas, aged sixteen, was ill too: fever, pains in head and stomach, fearful and melancholy. In June Mrs Blague is inquiring what good or ill is

[1] cf. F. O. White, *Lives of the Elizabethan Bishops*, 320 foll.

toward, and in July for her mother, Anne Scott, for she had married a second time – with her Scott relations the Dean's lady fell out. In August Frances Culpepper of Rochester died; at once Mrs Blague wants to learn, 'what substance she left and where her money is'. Hopefully the Dean brought word that her Majesty had been moved for him: what would come, would he obtain it? A fortnight later he is at it again. The conscientious filer of information added a note later: 'he had it not'. It was not until November that the Queen nominated Henry Cotton to the see of Salisbury; he had nineteen children to provide for: the diocese made good pasture for multifarious preferment.[1] For the Blagues it was all very provoking.

No wonder the Dean's wife was unwell again in October, with 'pain in her right breast, dizziness and stinking rotten phlegm'. In June she had been inquiring what would eventuate with Dean Wood. From a letter of Robert Sackville, son of Lord Buckhurst (to succeed Burghley as Lord Treasurer), we learn that Dean Wood had reported Sackville as intervening in these matters of preferment.[2] The latter rejoined that he had never spoken to Dean Wood except to reprove him for calling Dr Blague's wife 'many evil sorts of names, not seemly to be written'. But that the good Doctor himself 'hath with weeping tears imparted unto me . . . divers filthy discourses and lewd matters of Mr Wood and Mrs Blague'. The point of the letter comes at the end, that Dean Wood and Mrs Blague had plotted 'to invest her husband with a vain conceit and imagination thereof [of the bishopric], of purpose to work him to resign his best benefice over to Wood'.

It is possible that the upright Sackville had had his palm greased to press for the Dean's promotion, but, on learning what his wife was up to, had desisted. Her love for Dean Wood, of the amorous Celtic temperament, was great, and continued. The affair was really the end of the Dean of Rochester's hope of a bishopric, though in June 1599 he is still wondering whether he might not fill the vacancy at Ely,[3] which had been left without a pastor for

[1] White, 397 foll.
[2] S.P. 12/265, no. 80; *Cal. S.P. Dom., 1595-7*, 556-7, calls him Sacheville.
[3] 219; White, 401 foll.

nearly two decades, while the Crown made use of its revenues for secular purposes – supporting Don Antonio, Pretender to the Portuguese throne, among others. Though deemed unworthy of a mitre, the Dean need not give up hope of further tit-bits of preferment. As Shakespeare expresses it, who says almost everything to be said about the age: the Queen of the fairies gallops by night

> O'er ladies' lips, who straight on kisses dream,
> Which oft the angry Mab with blisters plagues
> Because their breaths with sweetmeats tainted are.
> Sometimes she gallops o'er a courtier's nose,
> And then dreams he of smelling out a suit;
> And sometimes comes he with a tithe-pig's tail,
> Tickling a parson's nose as a' lies asleep,
> Then dreams he of another benefice.

How true the picture is all this book goes to show.

At the end of the year Alice Blague wants to know whether Edward Scott is faithful to her and her husband – this is probably her step-brother; for the answer comes that, though there is no good will on either side, he does not make or meddle with his father. At New Year 1599 Edmund Blague inquires for his mother, troubled with much phlegm; then Mrs Blague for her son Edward, now seventeen.[1] A week later she wishes to know what shall ensue between her and Scott, evidently a family dispute; two days later, whether Dean Wood will help her with £30. It seemed he would come or send to her before next week, but no money was to be had. Again in March she is anxious to know whether to send to Dean Wood.

The Blague household must have been worth a pretty penny to Forman; in addition to the family there were the servants. In February the good Doctor is inquiring for Newington, evidently a benefice. At the same time a question is put for Mrs Blague's maid, and again two months later though she has left her lady's service – we can imagine why. The sister of another girl in service with the Blagues was 'much vexed with spirits in her youth, and

[1] 195.

did see them and speak to them. They took her out of her bed when she was eight or nine years old and carried her away up into the town and left her under the market-house, where she was found by the watch.'[1] Humans will believe anything – provided it is silly enough. We are the less surprised when the lady of the house comes running round to consult Forman 'because of the crickets'.[2] Never a dull moment: this is the Elizabethan age after all.

Then, too, she was a complaining woman of a type we all know. In February her 'gall overfloweth and runneth up into the veins of the neck; in her matrix [womb] much wind and choler and water'. In April 'salt phlegm and melancholy mixed in the blood' are indicated; she is to 'purge well, then let blood' – exceptional treatment for this exceptional lady. At the end of the month she is inquiring hopefully as to the infirmity of John Young of Rochester, 'whether he will live or die'. The answer was that he was 'fearful and full of melancholy . . . there will be some alteration in twenty-seven days'. In the margin is a figure for Dean Wood and Alice Blague. In fact John Young lived on till 1605; this was disappointing, since he turns out to have been the too long-lived bishop of Rochester.[3] In May she is checking up (astrologically) on Dean Wood. It is 'no time for them to meet under fifty-two days. Ned Scott proposeth evil and bawdry: ill will come of it; meddle not in it nor speak any more of it till eight days be past.' Nevertheless Forman, who had his periscope on her, found that she had been 'at Mrs Carano's and there met with Dean Wood', on 18 May and again two days later. 'She rode in a chariot to Tottenham [where the Heybournes lived] and he bade her not welcome. He came from church with Ferdinando's wife. It rained Sunday afternoon, and she stayed there all night.'

On 27 March of that year, 1599, Essex set out from Tower Hill on his fateful expedition to Ireland, which achieved nothing but a fiasco and presaged his ultimate end within the walls of the Tower

[1] 206.
[2] 219.
[3] White, 251–2.

two years later. Forman has a vivid account of his departure, with a fascinating forecast of what would come of it – which we shall quote in its place. Mrs Blague was anxious to know what would become of David Wood, son of her beloved Dean Wood, who was accompanying Essex as far as Wales, and what would happen 'ere he return'. The Woods belonged to Essex's following; two years before Essex had sent the Dean to Cecil with a recommendation of him for the archdeaconry of Anglesey.[1]

Earlier Forman had made a sigil for Mrs Blague, a ring with coral, about which we are given details, with verses on love, the element in which she lived and moved and had her being. On 2 July she has her horoscope cast to know whether there will be love between her and James Bennet. On 12 July is there good or evil towards her because of the crickets: and is it best for the Dean to go to Rochester? Nine days later what will come between her and Bennet; in a couple of days she agitates again. Meanwhile she has generously given Forman and his wife their wedding dinner at the rectory, having probably taken a hand in arranging this Kentish marriage.

In August she comes with her usual 'pain between head and neck, in belly and reins'; while her husband pines for Sir Thomas Heigham's benefice. The planets' reply was that 'it will very hardly be effected'; nor was it. However, at the end of the year the Dean was presented to the rectory of Crayford in Kent, which was more convenient for a country residence. Later on, in 1607, his son John was married there.[2]

On the July day on which Mrs Blague was seeking the love of James Bennet, her Canterbury friend, Mrs Webb was closeted with Forman to know if Sir Thomas Walsingham, whose mistress she was, would be faithful to her. This was Christopher Marlowe's patron and friend, of whose mansion at Scadbury only a fragment remains, though we have his tomb in the parish church at neighbouring Chiselhurst. Forman gives us his usual pen-portrait of the lady, born in 1561, married to William Webb at fifteen or sixteen, who died in 1604. She had eight or nine

[1] *Salisbury Mss.*, VII. 263.
[2] 802.

children by this 'tall, slender, very honest man'.[1] She herself was 'very fair, of good stature, plump face, little mouth, kind and loving; desired to go gay, and to have many jewels, to fare well and to keep good company'. After this, we are not surprised by Simon's note: 'halek Martha Webb 15 March 10 past 2 p.m., plene et volenter [fully and freely]'.[2] Next year he rode down to Canterbury to spend Michaelmas with the Webbs; but, though a Michaelmas goose would be present indeed, the visit was not a success.

In 1600 Mrs Blague continues to be emotionally involved with the enchanting Dean Wood, though at New Year she is casting whether Lord Windsor might not be a possibility.[3] This was the 5th Lord, of Stanwell in Middlesex, a couple of years younger than herself; nothing came of it, he died a comparatively young man in 1605.[4] She coupled his name with the alluring Dean Wood, inquiring whether any evil was towards her. The answer came that before the end of the month there would be some mischance to her husband or herself. Nothing happened. Mrs Webb was anxious to know 'whether Sir Thomas Walsingham loves her or not'; or perhaps Mr Hore did? The sage Simon, or the planets speaking through him: 'Neither of them does, trust them not: they dissemble.' Poor, pretty, luscious Mrs Webb, inquiring for Sir Thomas again in March, wants to know 'what will ensue and be the end between them'. The discouraging answer came: 'it seems she loves him better than he loves her. Their love is at highest; it will come to nothing, for it is now at an end.'

Mrs Blague was in somewhat more hopeful case, inquiring 'whether Dean Wood will continue his faithful love to her *only*, or no'. 'He doth now use her wonderful kindly, but it will not continue. His land is now in sale.' In March she sent Forman the names of Dean Wood's lovers, to know what would come of them, and between him and her. The infatuated woman next

[1] 206.
[2] 219.
[3] 236.
[4] *The Complete Peerage*, ed. cit., XII, Pt. II, 799.

wanted advice whether to ride with Dean Wood into the country, to learn whether she should have any child by him and whether the friendship between the receptive Mrs Webb and him were at its highest. Forman noted, 'received at this time 26s 8d, and she will pay me £5 more when he is a full friend to her'. So Simon's supernatural gifts were being pressed into service to incline the Dean's heart towards the other Dean's wife – the kind of occult service he was performing for Frances Howard, to become Countess of Hertford, and was later to perform for her cousin Lady Frances Howard, Countess of Essex, to ensnare the love of King James's boy-friend, Robert Carr.

As for Dean Wood, Simon noted down his words in April that 'he is good for nothing but to kill men's wives and women's husbands'. (He is here adapting to himself what was said of Julius Caesar.) But, when he came to die, he left an extremely generous and very Welsh will.[1] His son David has disappeared, perhaps serving in Ireland with Essex – of whom there is a memento among all the plate bequeathed: a silver ewer 'fashioned like the reindeer, the arms of worthy Essex in whose memory I caused the same to be made'. He left money to the poor of the parishes of Chilmark and Cheveril magna – so well known to Forman – which livings Dean Wood had snapped up at some point. There were numerous bequests to his Welsh kith and kin, with a touching bequest 'for finding a divine service every Sunday and holiday throughout the year for ever in the chapel of Talyllyn, where my mother lieth interred'. To Jesus College, Oxford, he left money for a fellowship and a scholarship, with preference to the kin of his name, 'if any such shall be thought fit'. To the 'late created' Bodleian Library he bequeathed 100 marks. To his wife he left all her jewels for life, all household stuff and napery. Mourning cloaks and remembrances in every direction.

But never a thing to Mrs Blague with whom his relations had been so equivocal.

Dean Blague's horoscope on 16 April shows him 'melancholy and waxeth hot in body. Twenty-two or twenty-three days hence

[1] Prerog. Ct. Cant., Prob. 11/115.

he will stand in danger of life from some enemy under pretence of friendship.' How exciting life was rendered for these credulous humans! The ladies had their usual (monthly) troubles. Mrs Webb felt pain in her stomach and the hinder part of her head; she was suffering from melancholy and fever, and was to purge (she certainly needed a scouring). Mrs Blague 'cannot eat well. It is much in breast and stomach – she is like to have her mother's disease.' This fortunately was not so, though she too might be said to have 'a wolf in the breast'. On 16 April the good Doctor himself came to know on behalf of his wife 'whether she be enchanted by Dean Wood, or no'. They might well wonder.

At the end of the month both Dean Blague and his wife are troubled 'with much sand in their backs and she much pain in the pit of her stomach'. They were both to purge. Anyone who knows the horrors Elizabethans subjected themselves to in purging will appreciate that this was no joke. Mrs Blague was in addition to be put on a strict diet and to be let blood – Forman was very sensibly sparing in the use of the latter; but one might quote Guy Fawkes in justification, 'dangerous diseases require dangerous remedies'. In May the Doctor fell sick with a fever of two fits; Mrs Blague was more concerned to know whether they would recover New Elm or no, some property in dispute. 'It seems they shall, if they follow it, or get some recompense for it.' In June Forman has a memorandum for the Dean's lady: 'remember to make her dietary for her breast and swelling of stomach against choler and pain of her head'. For herself the lady is anxious to learn whether her husband 'will die within two years or whether he be near his time, as Mary Havers saith'. This would open up new possibilities. In the interim she was having to send her plate to pawn, to raise £30.

Mrs Webb continues to pine for Sir Thomas Walsingham; in June she inquires 'what will happen between them after this'. Forman made a carat of Jupiter for her between 4 and 5 a.m., 5 June – presumably when the planet was in the ascendant – 'and I gave it her 7 June, 6.50 a.m.'; attendant upon the planets as they were, they needed to be up early, and Forman frequently was, dedicated as he was to his science (as others to their early devotions). William Webb, ten years older than his wife – *hinc illae lachrymae* – has pains in his buttocks and hips, swells in ankles and feet, and has gonorrhea. Mrs Webb promptly came to quarrel with Simon over her husband's gonorrhea – whether for saying he had it, or for not curing it, we are not told. If a cure was not effected the practitioner was sometimes held responsible and charged, or the patient asked for his money back – though this very rarely happened to Forman. Mrs Webb kept him busy, one way or another – once it is 'remember her forehead for a plaster'. Mr Webb cannot have been very agreeable, and we next find his wife casting to know about Sir George Manwaring, whom she fancies. The lady had her domestic uses: she procured Frances Hill as a maid for Forman's service. At once suspicious, Simon casts to know whether Mrs Webb had any intent in procuring her, and whether the girl would be true and faithful in serving him. (He did not fail to make use of her services in all senses.) Nevertheless in November Mrs Webb is still casting for Sir Thomas Walsingham; Simon notes that he is to 'remember the image', followed by the astrological sign for Jupiter, i.e. to compel Sir Thomas's love.

In October and November Dr Blague consults Forman several times over a law-suit in which he was engaged against his bishop; evidently the Dean had his enemies at Rochester. When it came to a hearing, the Dean 'had the day against his enemies'. Next Mrs Blague wants to know what will happen to her dear Dean Wood, because the Archbishop of Canterbury has sent for him. It does not transpire for what purpose, but hardly to discipline him; for the next query is 'whether Dean Wood shall be bishop of Wales?' The righteous Simon, or rather the planets speaking through him: 'he shall not have it'. Nor did he.

The first half of the year 1601 is covered by the last full Case-Book of Forman's to survive; in it the Blagues and their friends are as much to the fore as ever. Forman's own affairs become a little involved with theirs; through his marriage, in which kindhearted Mrs Blague had taken a hand, he had advanced in social status, almost to that of an equal. In the Registers of

Lambeth he is always designated 'gentleman'; this is the status to which William Shakespeare advanced – neither he nor Forman was ever an esquire. Simon's wife, who was a gentlewoman by birth, goes down to stay at Crayford, no doubt with the Blagues, at their country living. Mrs Blague, as a Jerningham even more than as the wife of a Dean, associates with Court-ladies, and is a familiar acquaintance of old Lord Chamberlain Hunsdon's daughters, Lady Hoby and Lady Scrope, a lady-in-waiting to the Queen.

At New Year Mrs Blague has a cough in her lungs.[1] Mrs Webb is gunning for Charles Montagu: what is she to him? The answer: 'he loves her not. Nothing will come of it.' If anything does, 'it is not he'. In February Mrs Blague, a milch-cow for Forman, had several consultations. Her son Cornwallis is sick – 'he is in danger of plague or pox'. His mother is in controversy with one Parker: what will come of it? Her friend Lady Hoby has fever and rheum in head and stomach – as has Dean Wood. Dr Blague recommends Simon to take Delahay's house at Lambeth: is it best to do so? In March Mrs Blague inquires whether Dean Wood will be a bishop? 'Her mind is gone from him in one respect, yet cleaves to him in another respect. As for the bishop she desireth, he desires her, but is joined to another.' This is what the planets say, not the bishop; but Forman's description of the lady's mind as 'wavering' is confirmed.

In May poor Dr Blague is moved – we can imagine by whom – to make over a lease he had made to Sir James Stonehouse, to Mrs Blague. This led to trouble and a law-suit, and of course further astrological consultations. On 13 April Margaret, Lady Hoby, aged thirty-four, came herself, suffering from melancholy and phlegm. (The stars often have a 'melancholy aspect' in the literature of the time.) Lady Hoby 'went away to Court from Mrs Blague's, 18 April' – so she had been stopping for a week in Lambeth with the Dean's lady. Mrs Blague is curious to know what is the matter with Lady Scrope's husband; 'his grief seems to be some discontent about his father'.

The Dean's wife often has a dream about 'the old man' – this

[1] 411.

means not her husband, but Simon. He is not best pleased by the phrase, and is suspicious of her sending for his wife upon the dream and casts to know what will come of it. It led to no further ill than a visit of Mrs Forman to Crayford for a few days, from which she returned 'well wet'. But Simon himself fell sick in May; 'I shall be more sicker for seven days, melancholy humour and phlegm.'

Mrs Webb kept him very busy. In April he was making a sigil for her under her maiden name, Martha Shackleton. The design is drawn, with names on the sides: Jesus, Emmanuel; Ananelon pax Dayabel (interpret who may). Then, 'Sanctus Philippus, nolo mortem peccatoris, sed ut convertatur et vivat [sic], Martha Shackleton.' Mrs Webb did not desire the death of a sinner, but that it might be turned from her and she might live. Made in the shadow of Lambeth Palace, this is hardly an Anglican inscription. But then the Reformed Church left no place for the numinous and the occult: Protestantism starved these sensibilities for which the Catholic Church had provided cults, with appropriate cult-objects, images and symbols. Forman and his like were filling a felt need – as also that for private confession.

Now Mrs Webb was robbed and of course turned to him over this – one of the things that, everyone agreed, astrologers were for. 'He that stole it his name was Arnold, a gentlemanlike fellow; he was taken abed with two wenches. She heard of the gown and cloak. He is in Bridewell: he hath been burned in the hand afore.' The lady recovered her things with much trouble, but was shortly involved in a law-suit with John Pett of Frittenden, Kent. He was a lawyer of Clifford's Inn. Simon has a very disparaging account of his spiritual pastor, Edward Hargrave, the parson of Frittenden. Evidently derived from pretty Mrs Webb, we must discount some of it. 'He cozened Thomas Bathurst of certain kine. He robbed the poor of the parish. He caused a landscoke or purse to be made to deprive William Webb of his right of certain leases. He did conycatch [cheat] Samuel Sanderson to his utter undoing. He cozened one butcher of Staplehurst for kine, which he had bought before and paid his father.'

Forman sought to know if he would recover some property, if Dr Blague would make it over to him and 'I took law for it' – evidently a property already mortgaged, or with some lien on it. The Dean regularly consults him in business matters, whether to send an important letter or not. In June the matter of the Stonehouse lease is before Lord Keeper Egerton; Forman forbids Dr Blague to go on an unfavourable day, but permits him to go in company with Dr Dove, the cleric who became the Dean's son-in-law. This let the Dean in for trouble with the Lord Keeper.

Mrs Blague recruits clients for Simon, and defends him against the Royal College of Physicians. In June he casts to know whether to take Sir Thomas Cornwallis in cure, on the letter he had written to her. Sir Thomas, now over eighty, was the head of the Suffolk Catholic family, and had been Comptroller of the Household to Queen Mary.[1] Through his marriage to a Jerningham he was a close relation of Mrs Blague.

His horoscope indicated pain under the ribs on the right side of the stomach – 'it seems some imposthume' (ulcer). Mrs Blague regularly took her consultant's medicine: for twenty-one days in May 8*s* for every glass. In Lambeth Forman was becoming quite well-to-do. In July she took her vomit: 'it worked upward and downward'. In return she told him what 'the Doctors intended against me'; the Blagues helped him to approach the Archbishop for protection. Simon drafted a letter to him, but of course consulted the stars before sending it. In the event, he never did remove from Lambeth: there he prospered increasingly. He naturally was interested in the condition of his eminent neighbour; in June he diagnosed Whitgift's disease, pain in the side, much cold, in danger of jaundice. (The Archbishop had no jaundice; however, no matter, to a true believer.)

In June Dr Blague was sent for by the Lord Keeper. Forman bade him not to go: 'it was good that he went not, for the Council all sat there and Stonehouse was there: if he had gone he had been overborne.'[2] This, however, may have given the Lord Keeper

---

[1] cf. *D.N.B.* under Cornwallis; and *The Elizabethan Renaissance: The Life of the Society*, 116.

[2] 411.

a bad impression and been the beginning of the Dean's trouble at his hands.

In July Mrs Blague loses a piece of plate. Urgently Forman has to cast both horoscope and geomantical figure. A later note follows: 'this cup was laid up safe by one of her servants'. Next day she is after a scarcely decipherable knight – probably Sir Henry Bowyer. Then she wants to know what Stonehouse intends, and the outcome of the Dean's suit over the mortgaged property. In August the Dean desires the advice of the stars whether to proceed against Thomas Baker, and whether Dr Dove shall have one of his benefices. The stars say: 'let him not do it'. This seems good advice. In September his wife has much heat in her head, melancholy and gall; in October, 'pain in her left side and hip – like to prove sciatica' (an early use of the word). In November she had another dream of Simon, evidently that he had gone on a voyage. An absolute and convinced believer, he took it very seriously: there are both astrological and geomantical figures to find out how he should speed. He went on no such voyage.

With this the regular Case-Books end, though we have a few further jottings about the family. State papers and legal cases throw some further light on its affairs. In January 1603 Dr Blague was confined prisoner in his house at Lambeth by the Lord Keeper.[1] Evidently his law-suit with Stonehouse, about which the planets had spoken with no certain voice, had turned out badly. Now we hear the Dean in his own person, petitioning Secretary Cecil:

a poor priest brought up in your family and devoted at your feet, I beseech you either command me to attend you or signify by some body what I shall do. For I am unable to bear the threats of her Majesty's heavy despleasure suggested against me, her innocent and faithful servant. My estate is weak and by Mr Stonehouse's unjust vexation made weaker. I have provided a poor portion of £6 a year for my wife and children. This Mr Stonehouse would wring from me. Your father, when I was made Dean by his means and yours, gave me this charge at the Council table: that, seeing I had matched with a gentlewoman well

[1] *Salisbury Mss.*, XII. 616–17.

allied and had by her three sons and a daughter (whereof two are graduates in Cambridge), if now, being made Dean, I did not provide for them, they would all condemn me of gross negligence. This I would honestly perform, but am hindered by indirect courses.

The Dean followed it up with a more eloquent missive – not for nothing had he been preferred as a preacher; but it was his preferments that were now being threatened.

Is it possible an eagle should still pursue a fly? Have I so lost my sovereign lady that neither she, nor the service to her, can be remembered by some? Had any chaplain of twenty-five years' service a poor pittance? Cannot *this* be held? *O me miserum!* The parsonage of Braxted in Essex, of the Earl of Shrewsbury's patronage, is shot at. I have enjoyed it thirty-three years quietly: now a lapse is pretended to it. Whoever heard the like? I hold it with another, by a lawful dispensation, before I served her Majesty. A third benefice I had of you as Master of the Wards, passed under the Privy and Broad Seal by your only means: which third benefice, and more too, the Statute allows to the King's and Queen's chaplains, etc. For the first I only am now sifted. The Lord Keeper is ready to give a presentation of it to vex me. *Quid feci?* [What have I done?] The good Earl of Shrewsbury has somewhat stayed it. Noble patron, pity an old preacher; stop it at the fountain with the Lord Keeper. I am unable any longer to sustain the fury of his wrath. Look to this speedily, and let my grey hairs go quietly to the grave.[1]

That worrying, plague-ridden summer Mrs Blague was afflicted with 'melancholy and much wind. It makes her heavy, sad, faint, unlusty [something new in her experience] and solitary; and will drive her into a melancholy passion.'[2] There follow prescriptions and purges. So also that summer for the sickly Edmund and the Doctor, who 'drank our diet and was well the next day'. The Dean, who could not keep his wife in order, had defended himself like a man. No harm came to this old *protégé* of the Cecils; he hadn't done anything wrong. On James's accession he was renewed as a member of the Ecclesiastical Commission.[3]

[1] *Salisbury Mss.*, XV. 352.
[2] 411.
[3] *Salisbury Mss.*, XVI. 291.

The Lord Keeper was overruled: the Dean was re-presented to his living of Braxted, which he kept to his dying day.[1] To him that hath shall be given: at the end of the year the rectory of Bangor was added unto him.

His family continued to be something of a liability. In 1607 he had to plead with Cecil again, now Lord Salisbury, on behalf of his son Thomas, who had been with Dr Brook when the bailiff served an arrest on the latter in the precincts of Lambeth Palace. The bailiff was killed, but Dr Brook and young Blague claimed that they were innocent and had left the Palace another way than that where the bailiff met his end. Archbishop Bancroft, who had succeeded Whitgift, was angered, and would not be pacified. 'This unkindness of the Archbishop has cast me into a fever, grieving that my observing of him should be thus rewarded.'[2] One sees something of what Archbishops, no less than Deans, had to put up with.

In 1609 Morgan Harris, a sailor of Rochester, brought a suit against Blague as Dean, concerning a cottage leased from the Dean and Chapter, which had been re-granted at the request of one of the prebendaries to a widow, Joan Heath.[3] This was a routine matter, so far as Deans and Chapters were concerned. A couple of years more, and the Dean was beyond such things. He made his will in his last days, 4 October 1611.[4] 'My goods movable and immovable I give to Alice, my beloved wife.' He gave her full use of all his temporal possessions during her life with 'power to sell anything to maintain her in the meantime'. After her death, 'when St Giles comes in possession', the contingent remainder was to go to sons John, Cornwallis and Edmund, and to his daughter Frances Dove's little daughter, her mother being dead. So likewise with the rectory of Rolvenden, 'if it be not sold by my wife to pay debts; and for Braxted, all my wife's rights reserved in it at her pleasure'. Notes of his sermons were left to his clerical son John: 'they are jewels, if he will use them right'.

[1] The Lord Keeper's presentation was revoked. *Cal. S.P. Dom.*, *1603–10*, 143, 180.
[2] *Salisbury Mss.*, XIX. 42–3.
[3] C2/James 1, H24/43.
[4] P.C.C., Wood 97.

'My books to be sold or given as my wife will. I make Alice, my wife, my sole executor for gathering in my debts and answering all mine: which is not much, knowing her wisdom and fidelity.'

Knowing her as we do – thanks to Simon – we have less confidence in her wisdom and fidelity: without the poor Dean to take the consequences of her silliness, she proceeded to get herself into a horrible mess. We can follow what happened to her from a couple of cases in Chancery that survive, though it is often difficult to arrive at the rights and wrongs on either side, from the way Elizabethans would swear and forswear without regard for truth. About a twelve-month after the Dean's death Alice married again. The essence of the trouble that ensued was the ignorance of each partner as to how much the other was worth: each was engaged in putting something over on the other – a familiar enough proceeding in matrimony – and both were taken in. There followed a state of disenchantment, and worse; we will try and extract the sense of the matter from the complicated transactions.

It was to be expected that Mrs Blague would be anxious to dispose of her charms again; the fortunate – or, rather, unfortunate – fellow upon whom they lighted was Walter Meysey, merely keeper of one part of the Gatehouse prison at Westminster. But he represented to the all-too-willing lady – we know how credulous she was – that he had the reversion of the Lieutenancy of the Tower of London, was worth £500 a year and would soon be knighted. 'He had sent into Flanders to Captain Herle for four mares for a carotch' – a coach: that must have fetched her; 'with other wooing brags, which so flowed out of his fluent tongue as thereby he [persuaded] the poor gentlewoman and brought your poor orators [her sons] into a fool's paradise'.[1] We are not surprised to hear that the lady 'believed him and was greatly affected to him'. She had a great deception.

But so also had Walter Meysey on his side. The estate the Dean had left was so encumbered with mortgages and debts that there was hardly anything left of it. We well understand why. Among the debts was one that had been owing to a London tailor

[1] C2 James I, B15/20.

for years, some £60 – multiply by perhaps a hundred for comparable valuation – 'for apparel by him made for the said Alice in the lifetime of Dr Blague'. As for the properties the poor man had acquired to provide for his family, they had either been purchased on a mortgage or been eaten up by mortgages subsequently. The Dean's eldest son, John, a cleric, had purchased the reversion of 'The White Hart' in St Giles in the Fields, 'for his advancement in marriage' – as jointure for a wife; but the Dean had entered into bonds for £100 a year to raise the money. The rectory of Rolvenden had been mortgaged to Francis Butler, 'the ally of the said Alice'; there were other complicated transactions concerning Braxted. Meysey found that there was nothing for him, and hardly anything for him and his treasure to live on.

Hereupon Meysey pushed Alice's sons out of her 'mansion-house', where they had all been brought together under a misapprehension; the sons were 'compelled to take a chamber in an obscure place for fear of being arrested' for what were now the joint debts of their mother and her husband. Shortly after Meysey left her house and abjured her company. But this did not save him from arrest for the good Dean's debts which he had shouldered by entering into marriage with the widow. He pleaded three years later that he had been imprisoned in King's Bench for the Dean's debts of £400.[1] The sons rejoined that Meysey had not married their mother in expectation of any wealth so much as the prestige and credit he might acquire by her 'great friends' sake'. Likely enough, the Dean had had that in mind too in marrying such a lady. The sons deposed that Meysey treated her so badly that if they 'had not a care of her ever since, she might have begged'.

This is the end of her; we do not know what became of her; her foolery had caught up with her at last.

We know a little more about other members of the family. The eldest son John matriculated at Oriel, but moved to Cambridge, where he was a Fellow of Jesus, 1600–6. He did not enter the Church until the year after his father's death, evidently for a

[1] C2 James I, M7/68.

living; for he was ordained only upon presentation to All Saints, Cambridge, where he was vicar, 1612–17.[1] Younger brother, Edmund, was also a Jesus man. Simon has more to tell us about the poor young sister, who had been provided for by marrying her to a not very nice cleric years older than herself. Frances had been born at Lambeth in 1586. 'This was a very untoward thing in her youth. When she was born she was all hairy, and much long hair on her shoulders.'[2] She was only fourteen when she was married off to Dr John Dove, 'a very Judas and cursed villainous and treacherous unkind priest. She had but one child, and died 1604', when she was only eighteen. Simon hardly ever speaks so unkindly as he does of this cleric: he cannot have been a nice man.

Dr Dove was in his fortieth year when he married little Frances Blague. A Westminster scholar at Christ Church, he was presented to a Wiltshire living by Egerton, his patron. If it had not been for this he had 'resolved to die within the precincts of the college, like a monk shut up in his cell, or an hermit mured up within the compass of a wall – without hope of ever being called to any ecclesiastical preferment in this corrupt and simoniacal age'.[3] Now he was in a position to let his light shine before men. In the blithe spring of 1597 he departed abroad as preceptor, or bear-leader, to the sons of Sir Thomas Gorges, with four servants and £100 – the Elizabethan equivalent of the Continental tour.[4] From the fact that Egerton was his patron, that he accompanied Dean Blague in the dealings with the Lord Keeper which got the Dean into trouble with him, we may infer that Simon's description of him as treacherous relates to this.

In November 1600, the year of his marriage, Dr Dove consults Forman medically: he has 'a hoarseness and stuffing in his lungs that he cannot speak when he preacheth'.[5] In March and April he wants astrological advice how best to proceed with Mr Fish for Burghfield in Berkshire – evidently a benefice, which he did not

[1] Venn, loc. cit.
[2] 206.
[3] q. *D.N.B.*, under John Dove.
[4] *Cal. S.P. Dom., 1595–7*, 398.
[5] 236.

get.[1] Perhaps the disappointment made him ill, for in April he has pains in the head, great heat in the lungs and a rheum – he is ordered to purge. Dr Dove wrote several books, mostly devoted to attacks on Catholics and unbelievers, which merit Simon's description of him also as unkind. I have given some account of his intellectual position elsewhere:[2] he had no objection to the tortures of the Spanish Inquisition being applied to atheists, i.e. such men of genius as Christopher Marlowe and Thomas Hariot. However, he advanced no further in the Church; his last work was therefore 'a direction to holiness of life'.

Forman's dealings with another Cambridge cleric were in marked contrast: they were purely business dealings, over money. This being so they erupted into a series of charges and counter-charges, mutual arrests, threats and law-suits. They are rather empty of personal information and not easy to make out: all we have are the snail-tracks in slime of the references in the Case-Books. Not that this cleric, Peter Sefton, came to consult Forman medically or astrologically; it was Forman who consulted the planets as to how to deal with his opponent, and to learn what next to expect of him.

Peter Sefton matriculated as a sizar from St John's at Easter 1574.[3] He took his M.A. in 1582, having been ordained deacon at Ely on Easter Day two years before. He does not seem to have proceeded any further, and was therefore unbeneficed. Forman describes him as 'preacher'; which means that he was one of those ministers supported by puritanically inclined merchants in the City to vex the Establishment. But Sefton had no objection to trafficking in benefices – after all, a deacon must live; he seems to have been a troublesome operator.

The Seftons were neighbours of Forman in the Stone House in Billingsgate. The first thing we hear, in July 1596, is some Billingsgate language when the Seftons and their ally Atkins fell out with Simon.[4] Mrs Sefton addressed lewd speeches to him,

---

[1] 411.
[2] cf. *The Elizabethan Renaissance: The Cultural Achievement*, 329–30.
[3] Venn, op. cit., IV. 41.
[4] v. later, Autobiography, p. 294–5.

Mr Sefton filed a bill of covenants against him – they were entangled financially. In this heroic year 1596, when Essex and Ralegh were hammering at the gates of Cadiz, Simon had a peck of troubles. He was in and out of Clink and Counter; his troubles with the Doctors were at their height. Being in and out of prison was nothing exceptional in Elizabethan London. In September Forman brought a suit against Sefton in the Court of Common Pleas, in regard to a debt owing to him – we have only Simon's note of expenses, for attorney's fees, for arresting Sefton, and for three times going to the Attorney-General by water, i.e. up the river to Westminster.[1] On 14 September he was

arrested to the peace [i.e. by warrant to keep the peace] the next morning at 7 a.m. And, going to Alderman Martin's to get a *supersedeas* [a writ to stay proceedings], was taken by the Doctors of Physic and Sheriffs, and carried before my Lord Mayor. Who committed me to the Counter, where I lay till 23 September; then was bailed by the Doctors, yet could not be delivered till 24th, 9 a.m. At 11.20 I came out of prison home.[2]

At the end of the month he was in prison again, at the suit of the Doctors, for twelve days. 'I agreed with them and am bound in £40 not to meddle in London after Mayday next.'

The next thing we hear is that one Jarvis, evidently Simon's ally, 'stabbed Atkins in my chamber'. This gave Sefton the opportunity to sue out a warrant against Forman. What with one thing and another, he thought it best to decamp for a bit. But, buoyant as a cork, he was back again at the end of November, when 'my man and I fell at square and he went from me of his own accord'. No wonder he considered whether it were 'best to go into India [i.e. West Indies] with Watts' ships'; and also cast to know where his man was: 'he was not in prison but about my business'.

On 10 December 'I was before the Queen's Attorney [i.e. Sir Edward Coke] and discharged the 13th. I was there again by Sefton's procurement and discharged again.' Now Forman took

1 226.
2 234.

the offensive, after casting on 13 January 1597 whether to go to the Attorney-General. 'I went not that night,' for it was best not to go when the aspect of the moon was unfavourable. Next day he was successful; he had Sefton arrested: 'he made agreement with me forthwith, and I had a silver bowl for my money'. This was a pledge for the remainder of the money Sefton owed him; upon which the Attorney-General 'entreated me to stay the matter'. In December Forman had arrested Atkins: we only know from a note of the charges, of interest to those who wish to learn how this kind of thing was carried out. For entering the action, 6d; 'for myself' 6d; to two sergeants, 2s; 'for my host, 6d; for my action and my host's, 2s; for execution, and other fees, 8s 3d. To Lightborne the serjeant for arresting him, 10s.' It is curious that the odd name Marlowe took for the murderer of Edward II in his play should have been that of a minion of the law about in London at the time.

Few Elizabethan law-suits seem to come to a precise end – no wonder the lawyers prospered, and so many county families were founded on a legal fortune. At the end of February, after a dream of Forman's betokening trouble, 'that day Sefton came before arbitrators and said that I occupied a wench upon a stool, with many other false villainies for the which I could have killed him with a good will'.[1] Simon, who thought of himself as a respectable citizen, much resented this aspersion upon his moral character. In March he casts several times to know whether Sefton would renew the matter, and whether it were best to bring him before a J.P. to swear the peace. On 9 March 'Sefton arrested me and I arrested him for £1000 [a nominal sum]. I put in sureties. Sefton sent that he would bail me if I would bail him. But I would not do it.' On 20 April, in Bow Church, Cheapside, Sefton acknowledged by his bond that he owed Forman £200; he refused to pay Simon's claim of £40 for damages, but handed over £10 by way of amends, and on this agreement was reached. This seemed a happy consummation, but at once Simon cast the horoscope to know whether they would continue friends or who would break first; would the end be 'death or hurt to any of us?'

[1] 226.

Clearly Forman was in a position to lend money to Sefton for his activities. What these were we learn when, in September 1598, the preacher 'moved the matter to buy the benefice of my Lord of Northumberland'.[1] Perfectly proper, of course: benefices were property. During the peace that endured for more than a year between these two we learn something about a neighbour in this delectable quarter. Before noon on 31 August, 'Mrs Bestow came to the two Spaniards that lay in the warehouse [evidently prisoners or detainees], and she came alone. Mrs Sefton watched her, and she stole out when they were at dinner about 1 o'clock. Bess went home to her house and inquired for her; she was not at home.' An interesting sidelight on fraternising during the long war with Spain.

In May 1599 war broke out with Sefton again, and in his methodical way Forman gives us the occasion, noting down the words that 'Peter Sefton of the Stone House, clerk' uttered on the evening of 9 May – that Simon 'had six, seven, eight, nine whores and had killed two children. That I suffered Sir William Monson twice to occupy Mrs Bestow in my chamber; also that Mr Wheatley and myself did carry her to the Spaniards in the warehouse and there they did occupy her also.'[2] Simon marshalled his five witnesses to this shocking defamation, which gave him an advantage over his clerical neighbour. After consulting the stars, which were propitious, Simon had him arrested a couple of days later, by Rudgley the serjeant in Gracechurch Street, 'for which I paid him 3*s*'. Sefton was put in prison, Simon going bail for him. 'And within one hour after the setting of this figure we agreed. He delivered me up a bond of £200, and I released him on condition that after this he should abuse me no more in word nor deed, but keep himself honest and in quiet. On this condition . . . I caused the action to be withdrawn and discharged him.'[3]

Was this the end? No: in October Sefton was muttering about a premunire – a vague threat which was not the less ominous for the very effective use Henry VIII had made of it against the bishops.

[1] 195.
[2] 219.
[3] 354.

This, and the covey of clerics descending upon him to know whether they would become bishops, inclined Simon to wonder whether he mightn't become a bishop too – 'as Rainwell told me. – It seems rather that I shall die or escape hard before that time. He said I should go into the field with a multitude of men first, or [ere] four years be out I should be bishop, and give [as arms] four saints in squares in a green field and a square cap on the crest.'[1]

Sefton evidently owed Forman £200, but now he would not pay his creditor the 20*s* he owed him, expenses of the suit. In April 1600 Forman consulted his attorney, Robert Delahay of Furnivall's Inn, touching the forfeiture of Sefton's bond and whether to put it in suit in the Court of Common Pleas. Forman had made Delahay's acquaintance a couple of years before when two lusty fellows had robbed him of bed-clothes and apparel.[2] Simon paid his lawyer 20*s* for doing so, though he did not omit to consult his horoscope as to the result. The bond was produced in court by Sefton's attorney, lawyer Sparrow, but the hearing put off in the usual manner.[3]

In July there were further threats from Sefton; Simon was anxious to know what Sefton intended and could do against him. The comforting answer came: 'he himself will run into great trouble by his own folly'.[4] In January 1601 Simon is still anxious to know, and that is the last that we hear of their dealings.[5] Everything shows how litigious Elizabethans were, and how much they needed to be when the law was so imprecise, uncertain and dilatory. Though these proceedings are rather empty of personal content, they indicate a relevant pattern: by sheer tenacity Forman comes through his troubles and comes out on top.

It is a relief to turn from these scuffles with a shadow to a real person: Mr Broughton, celebrated as scholar and divine in his own day and admired even in the Victorian age. Hugh Broughton

[1] 219.
[2] 226.
[3] C.P. 40/1651.
[4] 236.
[5] 411.

was a Shropshire man of old family and estate; armigerous, he bore on his coat-of-arms owls, which might be thought to refer to his subject but in fact relate to his native place, Owlbury. He was as a lad taken up by the 'Apostle of the North', Bernard Gilpin, whose living – Houghton-le-Spring – he is said to have aspired to, for it was very valuable. There supervened a coolness between these ardent Protestants, for in his will Gilpin enjoined the return of the books Broughton had borrowed, and 'I trust he will withhold none of them'.[1]

At Cambridge Broughton was a Fellow of the puritanical college of Christ's from 1572–8; from this he advanced to a prebend at Durham, and from that to the fat rectory of Washington, 1580–3.[2] But he desired the prospects London offered; transferring himself there he could not – with his Celtic blood (he called himself a Cambrian) and his aggressive temperament – resist the delights of theological controversy. Though he was a better scholar than most, and rather more sensible, this impeded his preferment. It was all right, in that age, to hold the view that the text of Holy Writ was totally uncorrupt and immaculate even to the Hebrew points, for was it not written by the finger of God? But when he put forward the kindly point of view that Hades never meant a place of torment but merely of departed souls, this was held to undermine religion – to be what we should describe as Modernist. The view was anathema to a more strict Puritan, Dr Reynolds of Oxford, who – we remember – abhorred stage-plays.[3] A good deal of ill-feeling was aroused on this excruciating point – the more so because, since it was a nonsense issue, there was no settling it. The theological fires burned brightly.

Somewhat discountenanced but not discouraged Broughton passed over to Germany, where he was more highly regarded and did not hesitate to dispute the Hebrew text with the most eminent rabbinical scholars. He tilted against Beza in the fiercest Greek; the nasty Scaliger, who didn't think highly of anyone except himself, called him 'furiosus et maledicus'. The Romans were

---

[1] q. *D.N.B.* under Broughton.

[2] Venn, Part I, I. 231.

[3] cf. *The Elizabethan Renaissance: The Cultural Achievement,* 10.

oddly more tolerant; perhaps they hoped to catch him, but he returned before so improbable a step.[1] Arrived home he required, perhaps he needed, preferment. Though puritanical in theology, he considered episcopacy to be Apostolic, which was as well in one who aspired to it. For in May 1595 we find him petitioning Burghley for the archbishopric of Tuam, asking that he might discuss the points in dispute with Dr Reynolds before the Lord Treasurer.[2] That in itself was enough to put that wise old owl off: *Quieta non movere* was the motto for that sated power.

Frustrated of his hopes Broughton consults the astrologer. In July 1596 he comes to know what his fortune will be. The answer was, 'he shall have preferment after a while by his lordship' – perhaps become a dean.[3] In September his query concerns money – on which he was held to be keen – and he wants to know whether Dr Dodd will be bishop of Chester or no. The answer: 'he shall have the bishopric hardly, but it shall be impaired and some stipend given out of it yearly, or it will cost money.' We see what these people were really interested in: bishoprics, deaneries, rectories and vicarages were all property. From the point of view of astrological faith, we may point out that Dr Dodd never did become bishop of Chester. But Mr Broughton was willing to settle for the chancellorship – after all, so near home. In October he is with Forman again to know whether he will get it. In November Simon himself wants to know whether Dr Dodd, whose name was much bandied about, would become bishop of London. He did not: the admirable Bancroft did. Amusing to relate, the Crown made Bancroft resign one of his London livings to our friend, Dean Wood.[4] After all, he, like Dean Blague, was a chaplain to the Queen. (Later on, at the time of Essex's rising in February the deleterious Dean Wood was held in custody for a while – the Woods being followers of his.)[5]

In the new year 1597 Broughton's anxiety, and his addiction,

[1] This corrects the *D.N.B.* account: he did not remain abroad till the death of Queen Elizabeth.

[2] *Cat. Lansdowne Mss.*, 150.

[3] 234.

[4] *Cal. S.P. Dom., 1595–7*, 404.

[5] *Cal. S.P. Dom., 1598–1601*, 590.

are at their height. In January he wants to know to whom it is best to deliver the letter, petitioning for preferment; in February whether it is propitious to deliver it yet.[1] Next, he has the question put, on behalf of the man, whether there will be a marriage between Richard Wilbraham and Mary Egerton – naturally those old Cheshire families would be of neighbourly interest to him. In March is it best for him to go into the country and return again, or no? A few days later he inquires for Dr Dodd, whether the Earl of Essex will move the question. The planets answered oddly, 'it seems the preferment shall be given to a woman. Neither doth it seem Dodd shall absolutely have it; if he doth it will be for money. Whoever has it shall be in peril of death shortly after.' On 18 March Broughton put the question 'upon the answer the Earl of Essex gave him touching Dr Dodd – what would follow?' Broughton came again that afternoon to know, lowering his sights, 'whether ever he shall be Dean of Chester or no'.

On 18 April Mr Broughton came to learn whether any bishopric shall be given between this and Whitsun – it 'seems he shall be bishop of Chester'. Four days later when he came to know whether he should be a D.D., get Chester or go home, the stars gave a contrary answer. It 'seems he shall not be bishop, best to go home. He that shall be bishop either will not keep it long or else he will die.' This might be taken to be consoling in its way. The cleric went on to inquire, if he delivered the letter at Court, whether he should prevail on behalf of Dr Dodd; also what would be the end touching his parsonage and tithes and Sir Randall Brereton – evidently a tithe-dispute with a Cheshire neighbour. I do not know that Broughton ever became a D.D.; it is characteristic of Forman's correctness that he always refers to him as Mr Broughton.

This same day Hugh Broughton put in his petition for preferment to Burghley.[2] Two days later he wrote to the great man explaining his stand in his controversy with the famous Lancelot Andrewes on the meanings of the words Sheol and Hades.

[1] 226.
[2] *Cat. Lansdowne Mss.*, 163.

However right he may have been, it was a mistake: politicians do not relish donnish controversies. Perhaps the Archbishop at Lambeth was against him, as was said, as being too independent a personality and scholar. On 20 April Mr Broughton put the question whether Lady Wolley – a lady-in-waiting – would move the Queen for Dr Dodd for the bishopric and whether he shall speed. (The Wolleys were a Lincolnshire family, where Dr Dodd had a good benefice; one sees how local affiliations operated at Court.) A few days later Broughton is asking 'whether Dr Vaughan shall go down to Chester and be bishop there'. In fact he was translated there from Bangor and made an effective bishop in his difficult diocese, holding up his head against both Puritans and Catholics, which was what the government wanted and the diocese needed.[1] Though Dr Vaughan was modern-minded about the sacred healing of the King's Evil by the royal touch, he held marriage with a deceased wife's sister to be 'impious, scandalous, not to be endured'.

Who was Dr Dodd whom Dr Broughton fancied his rival for preferment? There are a number of Dodds, and dodderers, among these clerics; but Simon's marginal notes are, as usual, invaluable for purposes of identification. He was vicar of Epping. So he was Roger Dodd, a Cambridge man, who was archdeacon of Salop (Shropshire) as well as vicar of Epping.[2] He did eventually make the Apostolic Succession, being promoted to the bishopric of the Isle of Man in 1604,[3] from which he may have made the leap to Meath next year.

This was the end of Broughton's consultations with Forman, but not of his hopes. In 1602 he wrote a rude letter to Archbishop Whitgift, accusing him of preventing her Majesty's intentions of preferring Broughton to St David's, Christ Church, or London.[4] For good measure he sent Whitgift two treatises exposing his errors and Bishop Bilson's, which he had prepared for the Scottish King. Unfortunately for him, when James succeeded to the

---

[1] White, 352–6.
[2] Venn, Pt. I, II. 50.
[3] *Cal. S.P. Dom., 1598–1601*, 360.
[4] *Salisbury Mss.*, XII. 306.

English throne Whitgift was still Archbishop. Queen Elizabeth said, 'Anger makes dull men witty, but it keeps them poor.' Broughton was not a dull man, simply too disputatious. He had been the chief advocate of a new translation of the Bible; yet when King James succeeded, the scheme put forward by Reynolds for an Authorised Version was accepted. Though a better scholar, Broughton was excluded from the translators. Naturally he criticised the new translation unsparingly, and it seems that his corrections were largely right. He was himself held up to ridicule by Ben Jonson in *Volpone*, and again in *The Alchemist*.

He was treated unjustly; he was properly arrogant, for he knew he was a better scholar than the rest. His real fault was that he did not belong to a party: 'had he stood with a party, his language would have seemed temperate enough according to the fashion of his day'.[1] His pupils adored him; good-looking and gracious, he was of 'a sweet, affable and loving carriage' among friends. But he was sharp with his pen, and had no opinion of the run of the mill; however, since he was an individual of marked gifts, he was remembered when they were forgotten. The great Victorian scholar, Bishop Lightfoot, could still say that his writings 'do carry in them a kind of holy and happy fascination'.

In Richard Napier, rector of Great Linford in Buckinghamshire, Forman had a pupil and colleague in the arts, or sciences, of astrology and medicine. Since they were true believers we find them consulting each other over their difficult cases and helping each other, the one being in town the other in the country. Richard Napier, his brother Sir Robert and nephew Sir Richard, are quite well known: all three have their place in the *Dictionary of National Biography*. Sir Robert was a highly successful Turkey merchant, who lived in Bishopsgate Street, and so was able to purchase the estate of Luton Hoo in Bedfordshire. His son, Sir Richard, the favourite and pupil of his uncle, went up to Wadham and became a Fellow of All Souls. He continued his uncle's practice in medicine and astrology; it was not until the Royal Society got going that astrology was dropped from academic

[1] *D.N.B.*, under Broughton.

teaching – though it now has its professors again in progressive India. The good rector left his nephew all his property, including the voluminous manuscripts Forman had bequeathed to his colleague and friend. Sir Richard's son handed them over to Elias Ashmole, as much addicted to astrology as to science – he would not have made a distinction.[1] Thus it is that Forman's invaluable papers have fetched up with Napier's and Ashmole's in the Bodleian Library at Oxford.

The Napiers were Scots by origin, of the family of the famous inventor of logarithms. But Richard Napier's father was alternatively known as Sandy; this is the name by which Forman always refers to him – we had better stick to that. Born at Exeter in 1559, he matriculated from Exeter College, Oxford, in 1577; presented to the rectory of Great Linford in 1590 he remained there for the rest of his life, forty-four years. He had a large income from his dual practice; for the rest he was as abstemious and charitable as he was pious. It was probably his prosperity that enabled him to enlarge his rectory house by adding on the gabled wings to the medieval hall we see today.[2] He also built a good tithe-barn to house the corn he garnered from his rectory.

Great Linford is now practically in the suburbs of squalid, demotic Wolverton. The advowson had been bought by Christopher Troughton. In neighbouring Newport Pagnell church there is a brass of 1611 to John Uvedale and his wife, he in ruff and long cloak, she in a farthingale. These also are names that appear in Forman's papers

Richard Sandy first approached Forman, 20 January 1597, for help – astrological of course – concerning some things stolen.[3] Four days later he has great heat in the back and reins and is troubled with gravel. His humour was melancholic, full of red choler – he was to prepare and purge. His age is given as thirty-seven, which is correct. In May Forman is sending to Mr Sandy by Foster, 'the carrier of Newport, who lodgeth at "The Castle" at Smithfield Bars'. In August Forman prepares to follow; he

[1] *Elias Ashmole*, ed. C. H. Josten, I. 210.
[2] *V.C.H., Bucks.*, IV. 391.
[3] 226.

notes the way – 'Barnet, St Albans, Dunstable, Hockley in the Hole, Brickhill, Stony Stratford, Linford,' along Watling Street all the way until the last turn-off. However in September he 'rode to Cambridge to meet Mr Sandy – spent much', but his journey was in vain. In January 1598 he notes, in Latin, that the rector conferred on him the ecclesiastical power of blessing and cursing according to the order of the Church. Henceforth they were brothers, and Simon sometimes writes 'Brother Sandy'. In May 1599 when he was to pay a visit to Linford, he did not omit to put the question, 'how I shall speed on my journey to Parson Sandy's'.[1] All went well there and so 'to Mr Marsh's to Waresley in Huntingdon, who used me kindly and came to London with me'.[2]

On 19 September 1599 Simon writes to 'Brother Sandy' reporting that the book he had told him of is half done.[3] 'Therefore I pray forget not your promise for the answering of all invectives against our profession.' There was a great deal of discussion of it at just this time.[4] 'I do wish that you had Bruceldoro, my gelding, to keep this winter.' If so, send word by the carrier next week: 'if you come to London on him you shall be welcome. This winter I mean to study hard. I thank you for my cheeses.' Later, we find Forman providing Sandy not only with advice for his cases but drugs and medicines for his practice.

Bruceldoro is the name of Orlando's horse in Ariosto's *Orlando Furioso*. Sir John Harington, in his translation, anglicised Brigliadoro (bridle of gold) as Brilliadoro. In his letter Simon goes on to pun about gold. He had evidently read Harington's Ariosto – both kindred spirits. This reminds us that, unfortunately, we know nothing about his reading, otherwise than what he regarded as professional, books of astrology, alchemy, magic. We know that he was fond of plays – did he read those of Mrs Mountjoy's lodger? How much we should like to know!

An undated letter is evidently an example of bantering Eliza-

[1] 219.
[2] 354.
[3] 240.
[4] cf. *The Elizabethan Renaissance: The Life of the Society*, c. IX.

bethan humour, which goes to confirm the information of the astrologer Lilly that Forman had regarded Sandy as a 'dunce', a word he was apt to use of others.

> Scholar, I received your letter by the carrier . . . and withal a pasty of some turkey, as I suppose, fast closed in boards like a wooden dagger on a leaden sheath – a worse I saw not this seven years. I gave the fellow 2*s* for his pains: for the messenger was worthy of his hire.

We perceive that this is Elizabethan humour.

> And also I know that your good will was better, or else my deserts and good will hath been in vain; for I have done that for thee, scholar, that I have done for no man the like . . . Men say a man should not look a gift horse in the mouth. No more did I this, but I looked in his belly, and there I thought to have found gold . . . Alack, alack, poor genny [i.e. jennet, little horse] metaphorsised! . . .
> Other demands also I find in your letter, namely to know in which side of a man or woman the disease lieth. I have oftentimes told you this question before.

Forman explains the astrological formulas, and those for other questions Parson Sandy had put, whether best to sell land or no, and concerning parties troubled in mind.

> My business is such now that I had much ado to have time to write this letter. And so with a thousand commendations I commit you to Christ Jesus and the holy Trinity, my schoolmaster and teacher, to whom be bliss. And to yourself thanks for ever, etc.

Forman meant that Christ and the Trinity, so as to include the Spirit, constituted his schoolmaster and teacher. Sandy, though capable of passing on spiritual power as an ordained priest, was Forman's pupil in medicine and astrology. His letters bring out another side of his personality, his intellectual arrogance; his experience of life brought home to him the idiocy of average humanity, the inferiority-complex of earlier days had given way to confidence in himself and a sense of superiority over others.

Another letter shows Forman helping Sandy with drugs and medicines from London.[1]

> Sandy, I have bought and sent you such parcels of drugs as are

[1] 1488.

specified in the note herein enclosed. But we have no hypocon water, nor can get none. Endive water is to be had, but we know not how to send it for spilling. In the meantime make your infusions with white wine; for every dram of rhubarb put ½ pint of white wine or Rhenish wine. I have sent you but ½ lb of hameck, because it is somewhat old.

You write unto me also to let you know how and when a maid's virginity is loosed.

In this matter the celibate rector was very much Forman's pupil.

I answer you, when the velme [membrane] or string of her virginity is broken. If you will know otherwise then it must be upon a question and by sight of the party. [He gives astrological directions.] And when you will open a vein to bring down the course of a woman, do it in the middle of the foot under the ankle, and sometimes the vein lieth above the ankle in the inside of the foot; and that upon the ankle on the outside of the foot is to stop the course . . . You will find it in the little written book I gave you. Your brother paid me 20*s* for the drugs, but they came to 26*s* 9*d*. My boy delivered the things to Warren the carrier packed in a candle-basket.

These exchanges went to and fro between Linford and Lambeth: in May 1607 'Warren brought a pie from Mr Sandy' – that would be a very large one.[1]

Forman did not achieve security from being troubled. On 16 March 1603 he writes to Sandy: 'I know, dear friend, since my last being with you, you long much to hear of me and of my estate.' There follows a characteristic passage about the storms and tempests buffeting him. 'No, not any humble entreaty of my friends, no offers of peace, no gifts, nor rewards, no conditions, no submission' could stop the Doctors from persecuting him. Forman looked up to the heavens while they said, Crucify him, Crucify him.

I caused both my honourable Lord of Hertford and my Lady also [Frances Howard, a regular client] to write most effectually to my Lord's grace [i.e. the Archbishop] in my behalf to give me his licence, but it will not be. He gives me fair words and so drives me off with delays, saying the Doctors have written unto him desiring him most instantly not to take part with nor to get me any licence; for if he should

[1] 802.

it would be much prejudice to them, to their privilege and also to their proceedings – which makes his Grace cold in that he absolutely of his own clemency promised me at first.

Again I caused my Lady to write in my behalf to my Lord Chief Justice and to Sir Francis Popham, his son, that his lordship should not take part with the Doctors against me. He answered that he knew me not nor had granted any warrant against me, but only set his hand to a general warrant of the Doctors, and 'henceforth he would be better advised'.

The Doctors had sent their attorney to Forman at Lambeth; he felt strong enough to answer them to be better advised than they had been and that no one should enter his house as they had done. He asks for Sandy's prayers, with a million commendations to Mrs Grimes, to Sandy's sister, to Joan, William and the rest of the household, with which he was familiar. Also to Mr Uvedale and Mr Blundell and their wives, 'and the rest of our friends'. He adds that 'tronco [his pet name for his wife] commends her to you', and asks Sandy to send by a trusty friend 'the parchment book you gave me of astrology, send it to Mr Leate's: he will send it to me. Bind it safe in something that it takes not wet'.

Mr Leate was a leading merchant in the City and, as we shall see, a regular client. The letters show what a circle of friends Forman had, besides his devoted following of clients from the first people in the land downwards. Besides being very gregarious he clearly had a gift for friendship.

His sister Jane lived with the family at Lambeth and helped him with the work that kept the household busy. In 1611, the last year of his life, she wrote to ask parson Sandy for his advice about a suitor, 'your countryman, an Exeter man, student at Exeter College, Oxford: a grave gentleman'. This was Mr Thomas, a councillor at law, who had been well acquainted with Sandy at the university; he had a house in Chancery Lane, another at Ham in Essex, and Jane would like 'your absolute opinion of him . . . I have now ended my business in the spiritual court to some charge – my unnatural kinsman, Mr Lanne, hath done me despite.' He had caused her brother to lie one night in Newgate and to be bound over to answer before the Lord Mayor and Aldermen –

'knowing I had no one else to defend me to be sent to. I find the want of my dear and beloved husband.' She had received the box with the heavy glass; the urine tested was not streaked with gold. Urinology was a regular and popular part of contemporary medicine; though Forman did not set much store by it, he practised it like other medical men.

Forman's last letter to Parson Sandy, 23 July 1611, shows the two men helping each other with perfect confidence in their science.

Your loving and kind letters came unto me by Rutland the carrier, who brought withal two cheeses and a little book of Merlin's as tokens of your kind goodwill and powerful courtesy. Touching those brazen moulds for carats of the plan Aretis [i.e. the constellation Aries, the Ram, in the zodiac], if you have them – if you can tell how to use them, you have a good thing for curing diseases, as for other purposes to cast therein.

Now Forman asks his clerical colleague's help over a question of robbery. Ralph Glaste, the cheesemonger, was robbed of plate and money worth £300 while at church. Would Sandy please search thoroughly who did it and what has become of the money and plate, how we may know them, etc. 'Send me word by this carrier next week – I will do as much for you.' Perfect belief, we observe. Forman now had a son and heir: 'son Clement salutes you'.

A couple of months later Simon was dead.

Meanwhile, what had happened to Forman's old Wiltshire patron, John Thornborough, in whose service he had first come to Oxford? Thornborough had climbed up and up the episcopal ladder, really as a government servant. As such he achieved a place in the *Dictionary of National Biography*, though a smaller one than his former servitor – we may suppose that this would be more of a surprise to the Bishop than to Simon.

With the patronage of the Herberts, Thornborough acquired several valuable livings in Wiltshire and Dorset. Simon had had a poor opinion of Thornborough's idle life at Oxford, and there seems to have been no further contact – certainly Simon got no help in his early troubles from this well-beneficed cleric. We learn, however, that the girl for whom Thornborough jilted Dr Lawrence's daughter at Cowley was the daughter of the furious Dr Bowles, schoolmaster at Salisbury – no advance in station. In 1590 Thornborough was made Dean of York, and as such a member of the Council of the North; what the government expected of him was that he would chase up the Recusants in that refractory Province, and in this he did not disappoint them. In order to meet the expenses of his installation we find him raising a loan of £900 on his fat vicarage of Chilmark, worth £140 a year.[1] In this case Robert Pinckney makes his last appearance, going surety for his friend.

Thornborough considered that his services merited reward; in June 1592 he petitioned Burghley for the bishopric of Limerick, in August he offered to resign the Mastership of the Savoy if he got Limerick.[2] He got it, and next year offered that, 'if he could be employed about the state with the Deputy and Council in Ireland, he would give immediate intelligence of everything concerning the Queen's service there'.[3] He asked Burghley 'to wrap up my proffered service and duty in silence, not oblivion'. We perceive that this was a bid for an Irish archbishopric, such as Broughton had hoped for.

He did not get it. The Archbishop of York was unfriendly, in spite of the Queen's direction 'for the well-using of my lord of Limerick'.[4] We learn from him that

the common cause of religion has received some disgrace by his unfortunate marriages, especially by the last, which is flat contrary to her Majesty's ecclesiastical laws of the land, and much misliked by most of the clergy of this realm. Yet I think that *pars innocens* by the law of God may marry. Albeit the presumptions are pregnant that the woman was with child by him at the time of his divorce, yet hath he now protested to me that he was no offender with her or any other at the

[1] C2 Eliz., T1/34.
[2] *Cat. Lansdowne Mss.*, 137.
[3] *Lansdowne Mss.*, 76/91.
[4] *Cal. S.P. Dom., 1598–1601*, 178.

time of his divorce. If it be true, then in my judgement this marriage is lawful.

So Thornborough's second wife may have been the guilty party, the Bishop an innocent one, in a divorce-suit. The Bishop's valuable services against the Recusants were retained at York; he had to send his chancellor to look after the diocese – or, rather, the revenues – of Limerick.[1] Anyhow in 1603 he was promoted to the see of Bristol. He remained at York, a thorn in the side of obdurate Catholics, who abounded there. He reported his activities faithfully to Cecil, now Lord Salisbury, with mingled complacency, sycophancy and hope.[2] A Northern peer who was sympathetic to his Catholic neighbours, Lord Sheffield, protested against the bishop's officiousness. 'It was his course in the Queen's time, and has been in the King's, to insinuate himself into favour by seeking to disgrace other men's services. Consider how scandalous it is to our Church that one of our bishops should leave the charge of his bishopric to follow such base courses, only for his own gain.'[3] Whether this was true or no, Thornborough received his reward, being promoted in 1617 to the desirable see of Worcester, with delectable Hartlebury Castle to live in.

Meanwhile he had encountered some *contretemps* in his family life. We learn from John Chamberlain that the bishop's eldest son, of nineteen or twenty had 'killed himself with a knife to avoid the disgrace of breeching, which his mother-in-law [i.e. stepmother] would needs have put him to for losing his money at tennis'.[4] The stepmother was a Suffolk woman, like Mrs Blague, and evidently as silly. She was a sycophantic friend of the young Countess of Essex, Forman's client, the poisoner of Sir Thomas Overbury. For her notorious wedding to Robert Carr dressed as a virgin-bride, Mrs Thornborough had been among those who won

[1] *Cal. Carew Mss., 1601–3*, 34.

[2] *Salisbury Mss.*, XVIII. 138; XIX. 145.

[3] *Salisbury Mss.*, XIX. 274.

[4] *The Letters of John Chamberlain*, ed. N. E. McClure, I. 335. Chamberlain had found the bishop's sermon at Paul's Cross on the Queen's last Accession Day, 1602, 'dull'. Ibid., I. 172. I do not suppose he was much of a preacher.

notice by their presents – the silly Stuart king gave £10,000 worth of jewels. Mrs Thornborough gave the bridal-cake, a curious and elaborate affair which cost £5.[1] (Multiply!)

When the circumstances of Overbury's murder came to light the Bishop's wife was delated as 'a suspicious person in the affair. She is intimate with the Countess of Somerset and her mother [Countess of Suffolk], and given to chemistry.'[2] She was also an intimate of Lady Walsingham – Sir Thomas and his lady were Keepers of the Wardrobe to Queen Anne, and the lady a great performer in the masques the Queen favoured, especially Ben Jonson's Masques of Blackness and of Beauty.[3] Now Mrs Thornborough went to prison, whence she was summoned before the Overbury Commissioners to give an account of herself.

This untoward association did not prevent her husband's nomination to Worcester next year. Here, too, the Bishop's family involved him in a scandal. One of his sons abducted an under-age heiress and took her to his father's residence; the Bishop was impelled to marry them, for fear of worse.[4] Then the bride's fortune disappeared, was consumed; the Bishop, forced to provide for her, was not generous. However, in the growing conflict between Charles 1 and Parliament, Thornborough took the popular side.[5] He was thought to be currying favour with the people; but it may have been at least as much because the upright rule of Archbishop Laud vetoed the appointment of Thornborough's son-in-law and chaplain to the two best benefices in the diocese.

It is amusing to find that the bishop of the diocese was one of the patients of Shakespeare's son-in-law, Dr John Hall. When over eighty Thornborough had been 'long tormented with a scorbutic wandering gout', and suffered from terrors in his sleep because of a sudden slaughter in his household, which afflicted him with

[1] ibid., 1. 498.
[2] *Cal. S.P. Dom., 1611–18*, 336, 345.
[3] E.A.Webb, G.W.Miller and J.Beckwith, *The History of Chislehurst*, 141.
[4] W.Moore Ede, *The Cathedral Church of Worcester*, 132 foll.
[5] cf. H.R.Trevor-Roper, *Archbishop Laud*, 178, where he is, however, described with characteristic inaccuracy as having been bishop of Waterford; it should read, of course, Limerick.

melancholy. Hall treated him with his special scorbutic beer, with which he had cured his wife of scurvy – beer boiled with scurvy grass, water-cress, fumitory, fennel, and juniper berries.[1]

What is interesting from our point of view is that all his life Thornborough was an addict to, and student of, alchemy; in 1621 he published a book on it and on Pythagorean philosophy, the mystique of numbers. At the age of seventy-seven he put up his large, columbed four-poster of a tomb in the cathedral, himself lying in effigy in scarlet robes within. In addition to crests and coats-of-arms the monument is plastered with inscriptions, alchemical and astrological signs. On one side, 'Denarius Philosophorum, Dum Spiro, Spero'; on the other, 'In Uno 20, 30, 4 or 10 Spirans Sperabo.' Such Pythagorean symbolism is all very odd for a bishop, but it somehow draws him nearer to his former servitor, whom he outlived by thirty years.

John Thornborough, the gay young dog of Magdalen, must have been tough; he was over ninety when he died in 1641, the Civil War already on its way, which made such havoc in his cathedral. For all his cultivating the popular cause, it took no thought for his tomb: this bears the marks of the damage it received in those popular entertainments.

[1] Mark Eccles, *Shakespeare in Warwickshire*, 114–15.

Chapter VIII

Sir William Monson and Mr Leate; Merchants and Seamen

It is not surprising that Forman had a following among merchants, particularly those trading overseas, with their liability to losses, still more among seamen and their wives wanting to know where their husbands were and whether they would return home. All this gives us a precious insight into simple folks' minds, their fears and hopes. But it so happens that two of the most constant clients were leaders in these classes. Nicholas Leate was a leading merchant in the City, Ironmonger, and a member of the Levant Company, heavily involved in the export trade. Sir William Monson was perhaps the best known seaman of the last years of Elizabeth, after the deaths of the great generation of Hawkins, Drake and Frobisher. He is all the better known to posterity for being the one naval commander of the time to give us a personal account of maritime affairs in the last phase of the war with Spain and his voluminous Naval Tracts.[1]

Actually Sir John Hawkins's wife sent for Forman in March 1595, on the eve of the last fatal voyage to the West Indies on which both Hawkins and Drake died.[2] That was in the last stage of the fitting out of the ships, before their assembling at Plymouth. We have already noticed the interest these inhabitants of Billingsgate took in the goings-on in the river, the visits of Mrs Allen and her friends to the Earl of Cumberland's fine new ship, their trips down the Thames. Forman was very conveniently placed for the resort of seamen anxious to know what their luck would be on a voyage, or whether to set out; and again for their

[1] *The Naval Tracts of Sir William Monson*, ed. M. Oppenheim in 5 vols., *Navy Records Society*.

[2] v. below, Autobiography, p. 290.

wives in the absence of their menfolk – notably from Ratcliffe, Limehouse and Wapping.

The Monsons were of an old Lincolnshire family several members of which came to Forman at various times; but the sea-captain was a regular, who hardly ever put to sea without consulting his astrologer. William was a younger son of the family, born in 1569 and sent up to Balliol. From this fate he absconded and fled to sea, without leave of father or mother, and took to privateering. This was in 1585, when he was sixteen. Two years later, already Captain Monson, he came to Forman to know how he should speed in his voyage for Sir George Carey;[1] this was Hunsdon's son, Governor of the Isle of Wight, who was much engaged in privateering. 'He came home about the 26 May 1588, and brought nothing, sped very evil; but met with such a rich ship as I told him three days before Easter, at that very hour as I told him. But took her not through his own negligence – let her pass by him till it was too late, and she got under a castle in the coast of Spain. And he rescued the ship' – i.e. his own.[2] No wonder the sea-captain of eighteen was Forman's man from that time forth.

Next year he served as a volunteer in the Queen's pinnace, *Charles*, against the Armada. In March 1591 Monson then in Sussex sent a messenger to Forman to know how he should speed going to sea. Simon noted that this man had been taken prisoner in Spain, going on land for water. Monson was serving under the Earl of Cumberland as Captain of the *Garland*; put in charge of a Dutch ship which was taken by the Spaniards, he was captured and spent the next two years on the prison-galleys in Lisbon harbour or in the Castle. In 1592 Simon is anxious to know for himself what has happened at the famous fight of the *Revenge* at Flores in the Azores: 'whether the Queen's ship in which Sir Richard Grenville be lost?' He added later: 'this ship was lost,

---

[1] Forman always spells him Carew; but Carew, Carey and Cary were all pronounced Cary and spelt interchangeably. It is desirable for scholars to distinguish them by different spellings: Carey for the Hunsdon family, Carew for the main West Country and Irish stocks, Cary for those of Cockington.

[2] 802.

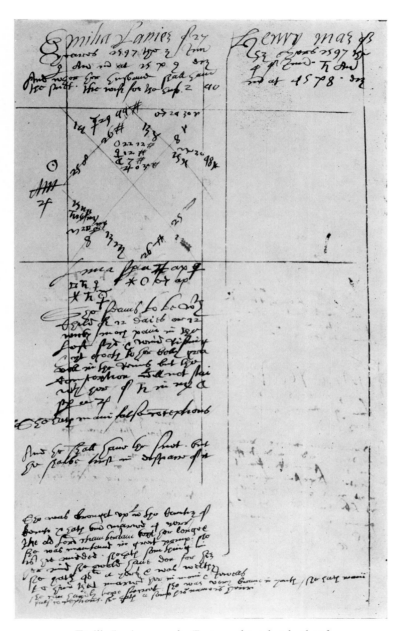

Emilia Lanier consults Forman about her husband

left   Lord Chamberlain
Hunsdon's tomb in Westminster
Abbey

above   Nicholas Leate, Levant
merchant

right   Monument to Richard
Staper, Levant merchant

following page   Frances Howard as
Countess of Hertford

first taken by the Spaniards and, being much rent and torn, sunk with all that were in her, before this question was made'.[1]

In 1593 Monson's father died; the elder brother Thomas succeeded to the family estates, but the sea-captain was left some property, which enabled him to purchase his freedom – for the rest he had to make his own way. He continued to serve on Cumberland's privateering expeditions, on which the Earl spent a fortune. In January and February 1593 Captain Monson – spelled out in Greek letters, in case anyone looked into Simon's books – wants to know his prospects in the voyage he intends.[2] The Captain had a dangerous time of it; when the Earl left him to examine the Spanish ships they had captured, Monson was almost overpowered, had to jump overboard into his boat, suffering a leg injury which he felt the rest of his life. Next year, sick, he spent on land, using the opportunity to take a (useless) M.A. at Oxford.

In 1595 he married Dorothy, daughter of Richard Wallop and a widow – so he must have got something with her. In May he put the question three separate times how he should speed 'if he went to sea a-roaming in the *Alcidor*, Mr Watts's ship.' He had no luck. Simon tells us, 'he went out about 20 June to the South Cape, where his main-mast brake and so was glad to come home; his victuals stank, because not well salted, and so left the voyage and was like to be killed himself; came in at Plymouth, 29 July'. This is corroborated by Monson's own account; out of Plymouth, the temperamental Earl had turned back, putting another captain in command of the *Scourge of Malice*, 'which did so much disconcert me that I abandoned the company of his ship at sea, and betook myself to my own adventure. This bred an after-quarrel between my lord and me, and it was a long time before we were reconciled.'[3]

We may append as a note to this unfortunate year the anxiety of a poor sailor's wife, Rose Davis, who came four times that winter to know what had become of her husband, who had gone

[1] 354.
[2] 205.
[3] Monson V. 183.

with Drake and Hawkins to the West Indies. Forman notes that both commanders died; but Davis 'came home again well. Within a year after he was killed in fight at his own door.'[1] One sees the daily dangers of Elizabethan life, quite apart from war and going to sea.

Would 1596 bring better luck?

In April a seaman's wife, Ellen Flower, came to inquire for her husband gone to Stade, the river port for Bremen.[2] Next came Captain Fleming, of forty-five; he 'has disordered himself and fretteth much – full of melancholy'. Monson has a rather crabbing mention of him, but he will always be of interest to us as the seaman who brought the first news of the Armada off the Lizard. He had a series of commands of Queen's ships all through the 1590s. In December 1597 he was back again consulting Forman about his aches and pains. On 13 April Captain Monson came to know whether he would return or no from Cadiz, which was to be the last great blow against Spain of the whole war. 'He shall be in some danger – yet return.' Three days later Monson put the question again, and in the middle of May he wrote for a further forecast. He was given command of the *Rainbow*, a Queen's ship, in the powerful fleet that was gathering for a shattering blow. Just before putting to sea he inquired once more as to his prospects in the ship: 'Let him: they shall prosper well and take good purchase.' Before sailing he put the question for his wife; she had pains in head and back, with fever and a cough, but 'she will not die'. Nor did she.

Monson served as Essex's flag-captain, and landed with him at Cadiz, fighting his way to the market-place and having one or two narrow escapes. He was among the large number knighted by Essex – so many that it cheapened the order and provided a common joke against a 'knight of Cales', i.e. Cadiz. But Monson brought back some loot: he had taken a small fly-boat with seventy-nine bags of specie, worth some £2000.[3] This went to the government, of course.

[1] 802.

[2] 234.

[3] *Cal. S.P. Dom., 1595–1597*, 275.

Meanwhile another member of the Monson family had been consulting Forman: 'Mr Monson the elder'. What will come of his fortune? Then, in Latin for privacy, whether he is in love with any other, and whether there is any man living by whom he may reap benefit, i.e. probably by a legacy.

It seems he loves one base-born that belongs to some lady; he hath loved another which now he loveth not; he loveth not his wife. There is none by whom he shall have any benefit of living by, and the prince shall do him little favour. He shall begin to fall before he rise and after his fall he shall rise again to greater wealth. His wife, it seemeth, he married against his will, by whom he hath three daughters and no son. She is a tall brown woman, somewhat long visage, very gentle and courteous, but hard-favoured; it seemeth he loveth her little. He hath spent much, consumed much, and is much in debt: wavering-minded and incredulous.

I.e. inconstant and sceptical. Poor lady, to be married to such a man! The more one looks into these people's lives the more one is saddened at the human condition.

This summer, as we have seen, Simon was at the height of his troubles with the Doctors, and worried about Avis Allen. In September he lost his book of medicine. In October he questions when the *Richard* of Hampton, i.e. Southampton, would return and with what result – evidently a little privateering vessel. On 26 November he inquires whether it is best for himself to go into India, i.e. the West Indies, with Watts's ships – this is Alderman Watts, the great City merchant, who was heavily invested in privateering, which grew mightily in this last phase of the long war. Mrs Webb's son, Thomas, was bound to sea in Mr Watts's *Centaur*; both he and his mother sought to know through Forman how he would speed. Then there was *The Lion's Whelp* in the same enterprise; Edward Davis wanted to know how he would speed in her: 'it seems he shall get wealth by the death of one or some dead body' – this is the kind of thing the stars could tell one. One of the Allens, Thomas, Master of the *Recovery* of London, is now in the Yssell in Holland and stays for want of an eastern wind. That same day Forman reminds himself to write to Henry Brooke, Lord Cobham's son and heir – who later played such a contemptible part in the conspiracy that ruined himself and Ralegh. Forman twice reminds himself to write to Sir George Carey, Sir William Monson, 'and to Sir John North and to Lord North. Comptroller to her Majesty.' The popular astrologer certainly made his existence felt, his desires known.

More Monsons in 1597: on 10 January Sir Thomas comes, suffering from weakness and pain in his reins; he is of a dry humour and full of scabs. This was Sir William's elder brother, who was in town for the meeting of Parliament this year, for which he was returned as knight of the shire for Lincoln. He had been up at Magdalen as a youth of fifteen, five or six years after Simon, but left without taking a degree; we shall hear more of him. In March came 'Madam Monson', probably Sir William's wife: 'with child, likely to be delivered before her time'. It was no sinecure being the sea-captain's wife: she had a large family by him. She wanted to know 'whether there will be any going to sea, and whether Sir William will go'; is it best for her to go into the country or stay here? In April came an unknown sailor's wife, to know whether her husband was alive or dead, 'which went to Bordeaux; all the rest came home, and he was not heard of'.

Essex and Ralegh, the younger generation all in favour of carrying on the war, were bent on following up their triumph at Cadiz with a *coup* against the homeward-coming treasure-fleet off the Azores. The Queen and Burghley were reluctant, but the young men got their way. Thus took shape the Islands Voyage of 1597. On 21 May Sir William came to know how he should speed – he was to be in command of the *Rainbow* again in Essex's squadron – and whether it would be a lucky voyage. Answer: 'it seems the General of the fleet shall die, or be in great peril. They shall get wealth.'[1] On 30 May Monson sent again by letter to set the horoscope. Forman also inquired for himself whether to go with him. The answer was discouraging: 'there will be great sickness, scarcity and death; they will have shipwreck, great winds and loss'. On 9 June Sir William inquired again, this time for his folk, i.e. his seamen. Towards the end of the month Mr John Aske

[1] 226.

came 'to know how he shall speed in the voyage with my lord Essex, life or death, riches or honour. – He shall be hurt in the head, neither shall he enjoy anything he gets.' I do not know whether this discouraged the young man from going; next year we find him inquiring whether to go and serve in Ireland, and if he would win a knighthood by so doing. Men's motives are as completely exposed in Simon's books as their fears, desires and hopes. Mr Aske, presumably of the well-known Yorkshire family of the leader of the Pilgrimage of Grace, became a regular client: he lived in Cold Harbour.

Early in October Sir Thomas Monson's wife sent for Forman; in accordance with his usual practice he cast the figure to know whether it was best to go – 'Go not: there is treachery at hand.' He also set a geomantical figure to know 'why Madam Monson sent for me, to what end, good or ill' – 'you shall be in danger of imprisonment'. He added, 'he is not sick but out of quiet, with a fever of two fits, full of melancholy passions'. A week later Sir William's lady came. We learn that she was thirty, 'much subject to melancholy and full of fancies . . . She cannot sleep; she hath many ill thoughts and cogitations. She hath not her course and the menstrual blood runneth to her head . . . And she thinks the devil doth tempt her to do evil to herself; she doubteth whether there is a God, with many such evil thoughts.' – 'Give her the water of hecarick: minister at 10.'

This is extremely interesting; for, for obvious reasons, in the sixteenth century people hardly ever dared to express disbelief in God. It is no less obvious that there must have been unbelievers of whom we hear nothing: here is a case.

Meanwhile Ellen Flower is inquiring for her absent husband, and also for one Stope going to Bordeaux, whether he would return. (She was no better than she should be with Simon.) Philip Sammon went to sea in the little *Greyhound* of Aldborough on St Stephen's day last, 1596, for the West Indies. His wife wants to know what has become of him. A later note: 'he was taken prisoner to Spain and died there about Michaelmas'. Mrs Porter of Ratcliffe inquires after Robert Porter who went to the Straits a year ago, i.e. into the Mediterranean. The fever to go a-roving,

privateering or plain piracy, possessed people – though the chances
of making a profit on an investment were nine to one against.
Most investors lost heavily; but for ordinary seamen, it was
employment, a way of life – or death. Simon himself wondered
again whether to go. His half-brother, Stephen Michell did,
leaving 'with me one cloak, green, a hat, a pair of breeches, etc.,
till he return. If he return not, Sybil to have cloak, his brother
John the rest.' He did return, but the day was not far off when,
serving under Monson, he was killed.

Stephen was twenty years younger than Simon and had served
in the household of Alderman Watts for some five years.[1] In 1591
he was captain of the *Pegasus*, one of Watts's five little ships roving
in the Caribbean. Stephen had known Sir George Carey since
Armada year.

In the year 1598 Monson was unemployed; he had quarrelled
again with Cumberland over missing the treasure-fleet in the
Azores and sent him a challenge. It seems that Monson had
advised Essex correctly to take station on the course by which
the *flota* was approaching. Essex, himself no seaman, followed the
advice of his landsmen and so missed it. Monson went in pursuit,
in company with Southampton's *Garland*; but Southampton
turned aside to capture a frigate, and the *flota* with its treasure –
Spain's sinews of war – escaped within the shelter of the guns of
Terceira. Recriminations, quarrels raged throughout Essex's
fleet: he had achieved a fiasco, and no large fleet was sent to sea
again. Privateering became the order of the day.

The celebrated Shirley brothers – of beautiful Wiston under the
Sussex Downs – thought they saw a chance of making a fortune,
as Drake had done when the going was good. Sir Anthony Shirley
had already made two unsuccessful voyages, and lost everything
by them; after which he set out on the travels that made him an
extraordinary career in Turkey and Persia. Forman has a succinct
note: 'Anthony Shirley, son of Sir Thomas of Wiston, born 20
August 1565. This man, being disgraced by Queen Elizabeth,
forsook his country and went into Persia about the thirty-second

[1] K. R. Andrews, *English Privateering Voyages, 1588–1595 (Hakluyt Society)*, 97, 132,
170.

year of his age. And was there in great credit for a time with the Turks and Soldan of Persia, as it was reported.'[1]

In spite of Anthony's failure, his elder brother Sir Thomas now proposed to follow his example and go to sea. Mr Shaw the elder, merchant, came to know whether it was best to deal with Shirley 'for ware in his intended voyage or no'.[2] The answer was very much conditioned astrologically, the upshot: 'Do it not,' for the moon's aspect was unfavourable. Elizabeth Negro came for her son Ambrose 'which was gone beyond sea two years ago'. A later note yields: 'her son came home the week afore Midsummer following. He had been taken prisoner in Sicily, had been at Venice, Rome, and over all Italy. He had been sick, but not long – came home in Alderman Hammon's ship.' On 20 April Mrs Webb, curious as ever, wanted to know how Sir Thomas would speed in his voyage. The father of the Shirleys had bankrupted himself to set forth Sir Anthony; his brother, confessing that his 'poverty did wrap me in many inconveniences', was forced to part with the ownership of the *Golden Dragon* and the *Primrose* to John Skinner.[3] Putting to sea, he rounded up four Lübeckers which were not lawful prize and had to be returned. Another Shirley fiasco.

However, the spirited were not discouraged: to them privateering had the compelling appeal of gambling. In October the little *Mayflower* and the *Swan* were going on a venture to the Caribbean. Stephen Michell made the question whether to go or no. 'It seemeth . . . they shall come in some league of friendship with the people of the country where they go and afterwards they shall conspire some treason against them.' Next day Simon inquired for himself 'whether I should speed well if I should now make a voyage to India [i.e. West Indies] and be captain myself'. But – 'take heed of stabbing twelve days hence, or twelve weeks, or twelve months.' On 18 October, 'questo, if I go presently [i.e. immediately] to Sir William Monson whether he will let me have a ship or no. I went to him forthwith, but he had no ship left: he had sold them. But he used me kindly; I found him lame

[1] 206.
[2] 195.
[3] q. D. W. Davies, *Elizabethans Errant*, 62.

on his bed.' Evidently from the leg-hurt Monson tells us he had received in 1593; we see how Forman's compulsive exactitude is corroborated in the smallest detail. Astrological prediction was another matter. In May the Peace of Vervins had been concluded between France and Spain. That same 18 October Forman consulted whether a peace would be concluded between England and Spain by the end of February. 'There will be a peace speedily, it seems within seven weeks or seven months.' There was not – not until 1604.

Now William Bagley of Ratcliffe came to know how he should speed in his voyage to the West Indies. 'This ship never made any voyage before; they loosed from anchor 29 October.' We learn from a later note that this ship was the *Refusal* of Sir John Gilbert, Ralegh's half-brother.[1] All this group, Robert Cecil too, invested in privateering, though he kept it secret: 'that which were another man's paternoster would be accounted in me a charm'.[2] What a way of putting it the clever Secretary of State had! The seamen came home safe and had 20s a share each of the proceeds; this besides wages and keep – 40s a share was accounted a good voyage. On 4 November Stephen inquired whether it was best to go to the Caribbean in the *Neptune*. Forman is corroborated by the documents that have survived: the Master of the *Neptune* was a Ratcliffe man, John Paul, who made two voyages in her that year.[3] Stephen got the answer, 'he may go, but he shall get little'. Actually 'he went forth and made a reasonable good voyage'.[4] Sanguine Simon, methodical as ever and as hopeful, has notes on how to victual a ship. These give us useful historical information; easy as it is to find out the public facts of history, the dates of battles, the deaths of monarchs, here is the kind of information that is hard to come by. 'In a ship they go five to a mess and every mess is allowed 7 lb of flesh; flesh days three a week, four days fish. If you victual a ship for one month, wherein are forty men, you must have 84 lb for every five men, that

[1] 802.

[2] q. K. R. Andrews, 'Sir Robert Cecil and Mediterranean Plunder', *E.H.R.*, 1972, 513.

[3] Andrews, *English Privateering Voyages*, 185.

[4] 802.

is 14 stone (10 stone is 80 lb beef): for five men a month at 16*d* a stone; for fifty men 840 lb.'[1] There follows a list of other things necessary; pease, oatmeal, cheese, pork, stockfish, vinegar, and so on. That summer, in July and August, Simon had been unwell: he notes various symptoms, heat in the reins; then taken in the neck, a darkness in the right eye, cramp in the shoulder and could not sleep. He was forty-five; it turned out to be nothing much; he must have been tough, but he never went a-roving.

In November Stephen consults whether to go in the *Rebecca* to The West Indies and Barbary, or later to take service 'in the brewers' flyboat'.[2] Early in 1599 there was a scare of a new Armada; the Armada of 1588, it is not generally realised, had been followed by two more Armadas, in 1596 and 1597, both dispersed by storms before reaching the Channel, and with great losses. In early 1599 ships and galleys were gathering at Corunna, and this coincided with the most dangerous crisis of the war in Ireland, after the disaster at the Yellow Ford in 1598. Essex was to leave in March with the largest army yet sent, to crush the resistance in Ulster. Forman gives us an account of his send-off from the City. A fleet was collected in the Channel, an army around London, in case of another attempted invasion. Monson was given command of the *Defiance* in the Channel fleet.

In February before leaving he put the question whether he should overcome his adversary for the land he had in suit.[3] He was followed by the Flowers of Ratcliffe. 'Goodman Flower' was to go in the *Rose Lion* to Stade, but she had been long delayed. A big ship like this would be set forth by a syndicate of City merchants. Again he inquired how the voyage would go and whether they would be free from enemies. This ship was a powerful armed merchantman that had already made several privateering expeditions; she was also engaged in the Levant trade, for which merchant ships needed to be heavily armed, to run the gauntlet of the Straits and the coasts of Spain and Barbary. In the conditions of the sea-war it was not easy to draw lines of distinction between

[1] 195.
[2] 802.
[3] 219.

war and trade, legitimate or illegitimate, trading with the enemy –
as the Dutch did all through their war – and sometimes between
licenced privateering and plain piracy. So it is superfluous to be
primly ethical and censorious on the subject: men are what they
are, and men must live. And seamen's wives too. On 22 March
Ellen Flower wants to know – this is partly in Latin – when her
husband will be back and whether they are at their way's end.
'It seems they came to their way's end four days ago and will not
come till forty-four days hence.' Anxious, she next wants to know
whether she is pregnant; she was twenty-six, and 'should be with
child of a false conception of six weeks'. In July she inquires for
Nicholas Robinson, a butcher of forty-five, who has run away.
Answer: 'he is gone south-west and by south; a black [i.e. dark]
fellow, lean and long face, of reasonable stature. About thirteen
days hence they shall hear of him.' Did they? I wonder.

In the emergency Sir Thomas Shirley was given command of an
old ship of 300 tons, the *Foresight*. What would become of him?
In March 'it seems he will go, but come short of the place he
intendeth. He will die in that voyage or scape exceeding hard.
Most of his soldiers will die.' Nothing of the sort happened;
never mind, *ça n'empêche pas*. Mrs Webb wanted advice whether
her son should go with Shirley. 'Let him not go, for he will be
very sick or die.' A fortnight before we had his note, 'halek Martha
Webb . . . *plene et volenter*'. All this along with crowded daily
business, the leading merchant, Mr Leate, for his ships, quarrels
with Sefton, wondering whether to lend him money, Ellen
Bagley again for her husband, Mrs Blague and her nonsense
agonising about Dean Wood, and so on.

Then there are the Monsons. In May Forman puts the question,
in Latin, whether to go and see Monson's sister, Anne Lee,
whether she loves him and might marry him. A few days later
Lady Monson comes, with 'a stopping of the heart through much
grief and fearfulness' (i.e. anxiety and apprehension). In July
between questioning whether to keep and marry Anne Baker and
dreaming of two white swans and two young ones, Forman
consults whether best to adventure with Mr Lock and others into
the East Indies.

In August Mary Alcock of St Katherine's inquired after 'her servant, Daniel Fleshman, that went forth with Mr Harry White in the *Little John* Tuesday before Michaelmas day to the Indians', i.e. the West Indies. Would he have been taken or no? 'She shall hear of him seven days or thirty-two days hence. He seems to be well and not in prison.' She came again shortly after, to inquire for her husband and her man. Actually her man had been in prison in the Havana, but came home on Mayday next year; her husband, however, was slain at sea.[1] In September Goodman Bagley, who had come home safe, consulted whether to go in the *Margaret and John* to the Cape. This dandy ship belonged to Alderman Watts and had already made two or three privateering voyages. But, this time, 'let him not go in her – in danger of death'.[2] Very well, what about the *Pilgrim*? This little vessel of 90 tons had been owned by the privateering Earl of Cumberland and she had already been on two expeditions to the Spanish preserve of the Caribbean, from which they meant to exclude all others, if they could. The answer to Bagley's question was 'No – in peril of life'; then what about another ship, he queried. Meanwhile, having put ashore, Monson wanted to know what would come of the business about the money of which he had been robbed about six years ago, £150; he 'hath now heard who did it and sent for him by a poursuivant'.

In March 1600 Mary Alcock came to inquire for her Francis Nelson, imprisoned in Dunkirk two months ago.[3] It would seem that this woman traded on her own, possibly the widow of a merchant carrying on the business. In April Anne Lock of nineteen came twice for her husband. He had gone out in the *Marigold* at Michaelmas 1599; they had captured a prize, which was driven ashore at Lisbon. The *Marigold* came home, but he was not heard of. He had been taken prisoner and was held for seven months; two months before he came home he went in a Fleming eastwards – into the Mediterranean presumably: perhaps that is how he got away, for 'he came home well, 14 May'.

[1] 802.
[2] 219.
[3] 236.

Forman inquired for himself 'whether to buy the part of the ship that Whitfield goeth in and how he shall speed in the voyage'. For some years now he had been prospering and had surplus money to invest.

The apprehension of invasion the year before was completely mistaken. As Monson wrote, 'never was greater expectation of war with less performance'. The fact was that Spain was unable to mount another armada at sea; the war was sputtering to its conclusion in commerce-raiding and hits upon the Spanish coast. Monson put the question whether to take command of the Queen's ship, *Warspite*. Next, how he should speed in serving with the fleet in the Channel. Stephen wants to know whether to go in the pinnace with John Becket of Limehouse, captain; or in the *Green Dragon*, captain Pepperell, to the South Cape. He went with this man, from Gravesend, 2 July. 'On 25 July they met thirty sail of the Spanish Indian fleet [the treasure-fleet] bound homeward.'[1] Three days later they met three Spanish ships coming from the West Indies; they kept company with them for a week, but after a running fight during three days failed to take any of them. So they lay in wait about the Cape for a month till in September they went into the Straits and took a ship of Marseilles, 'not lawful prize, for which they had trouble.' One sees that there was a law of the sea, which was honoured not only in the breach – as one might suppose from recent writers obsessed with the idea of 'plunder', though they know very well that to lose was far more frequent than to gain.

Bagley and his wife must have been persons of some little substance to be referred to as 'Goodman' and 'Goodwife'. In July she and Elizabeth Smith came to know what had happened to their husbands who had gone to the West Indies at Michaelmas last in the *Desire*. Simon learned later that the ship was lost and the men taken prisoner through their own folly by running the boat [i.e. ship's boat] ashore. Half the company were lost or taken prisoner; the other half came home in a prize they took after the ship was lost – presumably their ship was lost in the fight in which they took the prize. 'At Midsummer they were at

[1] 802.

the Islands homewards', i.e. the Azores. Goodman Bagley must have been among those lost: he never appears again.

Now the Shirleys descend upon Forman for consultations upon their complicated affairs. Early in 1600 Sir Thomas had put to sea with the *Golden Dragon* and the *George*.[1] Shirley was desperately short of money and supplies; he begged Cecil for another £100 loan – so that even the Secretary's investment in a venture was not always of his own volition and might be throwing good money after bad. Shirley brought in two prizes, one of them laden with part-enemy, part-neutral goods. His creditors were after him for that part of the goods that might be adjudged to him, but how much of it was lawful prize? The case came before the Court of Admiralty. In July Shirley consulted Forman by letter as to the most propitious time for his examination, the best time to go to the Lord Admiral – Howard of Effingham, created Earl of Nottingham (to Essex's disgust) in 1597. Forman's answer was, 'Let him go to the Lord Admiral on 12 July between seven till eight.'[2]

The day that Simon had Shirley's letter he had a visit from Frances Vavasour. She was now twenty-nine, and she wanted to know whom she should marry. Who was she?

She was the sister of the celebrated Anne Vavasour, the mistress of Sir Henry Lee, Queen Elizabeth's champion, creator of the famous Accession Day tilts, Master of the Armoury at the Tower. These two Yorkshire girls both started their careers as maids-of-honour to the Queen. As early as 1590 a courtier was writing, 'our new maid, Mistress Vavasour, flourisheth like the lily and the rose'.[3] That was nine years ago, and still no marriage had been found for the young woman. The truth was that that maiden lady, the Queen, did not much like her maids-of-honour marrying; she preferred to keep them in her service, ageing virgins like Blanche Parry and herself, till they dropped. Frances Vavasour was said to have been contracted to Leicester's handsome, if illegitimate, son Sir Robert Dudley; but the Queen refused her

[1] Davies, 66 foll.
[2] 236.
[3] q. E. K. Chambers, *Sir Henry Lee*, 161.

consent. He, like his father, was irresistible to women, and she became his mistress. Then he married – which didn't prevent him having other mistresses, with one of whom, dressed as a page, he ultimately absconded from the country; becoming a Catholic in Italy, he was able to invalidate his marriage on the ground of a pre-contract. Frances Vavasour was left high and dry, on the strand, and twenty-nine – an advanced age for an Elizabethan maiden to acquire a husband.

The next inquiry is to know whether Lord Cobham has gone. Yes – he went to Flanders. And what is the significance of that? We shall see.

On 22 August Shirley put the question whether to go to sea. Answer: 'it seems about sixteen days hence; he will be taken prisoner or scape hard, for he will run ship on shore and want victuals'. The same day Sir Thomas's father put 'the same question as the young man. I was first with the young man 3 July.' He did not put to sea; he had other hazards to run nearer home.

Young Sir Thomas had engaged himself to a promising widow; it was always a good thing for an Elizabethan to marry a widow, for she had her 'widow's thirds', one-third of her previous husband's estate. The more often she was widowed the better the bargain. Thus some celebrated ladies, like Lettice Knollys – detested by the Queen, her cousin, for catching Leicester – and Frances Walsingham, were able to marry four times over. But young Sir Thomas's widow was the sister-in-law of Sir Robert Cecil – now we know why the canny Robert was induced to throw good money after bad.[1] The lady was the sister of Lord Cobham; now we know why Lord Cobham was wanted out of the way: Sir Thomas was backing out of his bargain.

Some time that year Sir Thomas secretly married Frances Vavasour, while continuing to assure his father, Lord Cobham and the young widow herself of his continuing affection. When found out, he explained that he took this course 'for fear of offending my father with my double dealing; neither durst I in outward show to him to seem to leave my first desires till I had found some good means to win him to like the second'. Well,

[1] Davies, 32.

women have the privilege of changing their minds, why not men? Cecil, however, was furious at having been made a fool of, though – politic as ever, even in private relations – he explained that he would not resent the wrong to himself but the injury to Shirley's father. The Queen also was angered by this behaviour, as she often had reason to be at secret marriages to maids-of-honour under her nose. 'Graciously she hath always furthered,' she said, *'in good sort* any honest and honourable purposes of marriage or preferment to any of hers, when without scandal and infamy they have been orderly broken unto her'.[1]

Sir Thomas was sent to the Marshalsea to cool his heels. Instead of a widow's portion he got nothing with his wife, three years older than himself. They did, however, produce the dramatist, Henry Shirley, whose promising career was cut short in his twenties, by being run through with a sword by a Member of Parliament – an event which caused odious Prynne, who hated the stage, to crow.

Sir Thomas Shirley did not appear in Forman's books again. His sister Margaret did, of whom nothing is known, though her brothers were so celebrated. Born in 1569, she had been married off at fifteen to one Pepsall. 'It seems she was enchanted to marry him. It seems she will be married to him twenty-four years before free.' In 1608 she was not free; but 'she shall be free at forty and do well' – evidently as a widow. Forman annotates, 'overcome by enchantment'.[2]

It is extraordinary to think that these brief entries in his case-books are the traces of such human stories, with their passions and their sufferings. There must be, there are, many more.

His involvement with Sir William Monson continues, as also the frequent consultations with all kinds. Here we are concerned only with mariners and merchants. Twice Joan Ede of Ratcliffe came to know about her husband that went to the Caribbean four years ago, was captured and sent prisoner to Seville. Did he ever come home? A seaman of Ratcliffe who was going to the Azores in the

[1] q. Chambers, 161.
[2] 206.

Godspeed, and the wife of another, wanted to know how they should do – the stars spoke variously.[1] She struck bad luck off the Cornish coast: 'she went to sea a-roving, but the company were taken about Penzance by the Dunkirkers and lost all. They were stripped of their clothes and came home naked. The Master was taken prisoner to Dunkirk.' The fact was that the Channel and western approaches were alive with privateers, and, within the Straits, were not only the Spaniards but the Barbary pirates.

We are intrigued by 'the gentlewoman of Deptford that was so behanged with jewels, that left the grasshopper with me'.[2] Her husband had gone into Ireland, but returned at length. In December Mrs Webb wished to learn whether her son Richard should go with the fleet to the Indies.[3] This could mean the East Indies, or rather India. A spirit of rivalry arose in the City at the spectacular success of the Dutch East India Company. On the last day of the year the rival English company got its charter – one-third of the members coming from the Levant Company. A fleet was gathering: James Lancaster's flagship was our old friend, *The Scourge of Malice* – the Queen's sententious name for her – now renamed *The Red Dragon*.[4] She was accompanied by the *Hector*, of 300 tons, the *Ascension* and the *Susan*. They left Woolwich on the historic voyage – from which flowed so much, ultimately an empire – on 13 February, but were delayed six weeks by contrary winds in the Channel.

Channel trade and shipping suffered. In January two merchants come to inquire for the *Diamond* of Fowey – which Elizabethans sensibly spelt Foy – laden from thence for London ten days before and not heard of since.[5] In June Stephen Michell wanted to know how he would speed in the *Desire* of Fowey; answer, 'best to go down to Fowey'. But 'he went not'. Instead he went to Stade in July, in the *Elizabeth*, and came back in November. Mrs Flower continued to come when her husband was at sea. Lucy

[1] 802.
[2] 354.
[3] 236.
[4] Sir William Foster, *England's Quest of Eastern Trade*, 154–5.
[5] 411.

Ashmore inquired for her husband in Russia – English ships went by the Archangel route; he came home in October.

In 1602 a squadron was put to sea for a last effort in the Queen's reign to intercept the treasure-fleet. The commander was Sir Richard Leveson – whose bronze figure we see in Wolverhampton church; for the rest, he kept Mary Fitton, after her disgrace at the hands, if that is the word, of the young Earl of Pembroke. Sir William Monson was to go as Vice-Admiral. There are full accounts of the events that ensued at sea, but Forman's notes give us new information. The Vice-Admiral came for his horoscope on 26 February; 'he went away from me at Lambeth 3 March'.[1] Ordered to await a Dutch contingent, Monson was too late to reinforce Leveson and make him strong enough to attack the armed guard of the treasure-ships. Forman tells us that 'he took a Hamburger and a Brazilman, and sent them into Plymouth at the end of May'. Baulked of his main objective, Monson made a determined onslaught on a richly laden East Indian carrack right under the guns of the castle of Cezimbra, captured her and her guard of eleven galleys, one of which was that on which he had been imprisoned years before. Forman says that the carrack was 'worth £300,000 at least; her worst commodity was callico and pepper. He got great credit thereby, came to London 4 July and went to Court.'

The government was expecting Spanish intervention in Ireland, and sent Monson to sea again that stormy summer to keep watch on the ships at Corunna. Simon fills in for us with the information that Monson sent his servant with a letter, 2 July, for advice 'whether best to go to sea again with those eight Queen's ships of the fleet'. The answer was discouraging: there was 'danger of being betrayed by one that goes with him'. The figure showed 'first, favour of the prince and, after, treachery wrought against him'. This was likely enough in contemporary circumstances; and it may be because of this that Forman went down to Plymouth to aid and protect Monson by his arts.

We have a fascinating account of the episode in a letter from William Stalling, Queen's Victualler and an official in the Customs

[1] 802.

at Plymouth, to Cecil. Monson took a chamber for Forman in the house of a goldsmith there, William Bentley. There took place the conjurations which the suspicious official took to be 'a mass or the like exercises . . . by one Simon Forman, whose dwelling, as he says, is at Lambeth by London'.[1] So, on Sunday 8 August, the house was searched, where a 'portmantey' was opened,

'wherein were found certain wicked books of conjuration, and some calculations what shall become of her Majesty's ships in this service . . . The mayor has bound Forman to appear before the judges at Exeter; but what information will be given against him I know not, for Sir William much favours him. The matter here by many is thought very dangerous, and I can hardly have a good conceit thereof, and yet dare not condemn any.

There were some half-a-dozen persons in the room at the proceedings, and the official enclosed the oath such persons took never to divulge them and to 'be true and trusty to thee [the astrologer] for evermore, to do for thee the uttermost in my power'; the rest in cipher. Here is another explanation of the hold that Forman had over his clients.

Monson wrote a long disingenuous account to Cecil, to clear himself, making light of the matter. He put it down to a mad boy in his service who thought he had lighted on a mass being said and ran to the mayor. There had been found 'two books and a piece of paper full of figures touching diseases, and one about the success of one of the Queen's ships with the name of one Stephen unto it, sailor, that was to go in the same ship'. All the fuss that had been made was owing to the folly of the mayor; mass would never have been said at that time of day, and as for Monson 'I was abroad that day from one o'clock until eight at night.' Forman had as much as £50 in his chest; 'what the books imported I know not, but it is like no great matter, for of the £50 he kept but £20 for the answering it. My countenancing him was to clear myself, who, through the mayor's indiscretion, might have been brought to utter discredit.'[2]

---

[1] *Salisbury Mss.*, XII. 290.
[2] ibid., 551–3.

Now we know what the disclaimers of Elizabethans may cover, and how disingenuous people can be – one would think that Monson had hardly heard of Simon! As for poor Stephen, it was his last voyage: Simon tells us that he was slain at sea under Monson.

One of Stephen's services had been to bring home tobacco for Forman's use, as we learn. 'I dreamt of Stephen that he was come from sea and brought more tobacco . . . They had sailed in the dark long, and could get nothing.' At last they got something; when they came home Captain Watts sent to the ship for tobacco. 'We walked in a green church – lay by a wall and found two great cherries.' Stephen 'said they did ill to let them lie there till they did stink'. Next Simon dreamed that Dr Blague had lent him many books of magic. The same morning Mrs Blague sent to borrow £12, which Simon would not lend without a pawn.[1]

We do not know the upshot of the affair at Plymouth, but it had its consequences. While Forman was away he naturally did not keep up his regular Case-Books. He did not resume them; he continued his practice, but his notes of cases are disparate, separate jottings. We have no information of him until next year, 1603, when he took steps to defend himself by getting a licence to practise medicine from Cambridge. Nor is there any further entry relating to Monson, though the Monsons turn up again, mentioned along with Forman posthumously, in the proceedings after the murder of Sir Thomas Overbury in the Tower.

Among City merchants Forman came to have also a leading figure as his most regular client, Nicholas Leate. He did not become so until 1599; after that he came to consult frequently about the ships on which his goods were laden. He was a regular Levant merchant, with no interests in privateering; but these ships had to run the gauntlet of the Straits in these exciting years. From the Stonehouse in Billingsgate and with his friendship with the Allens, Forman had a number of earlier contacts with merchants. We cannot identify them all; since most of them were involved in

[1] 236.

shipping, they are closely involved with the seamen. The coal trade with Newcastle was growing fast, and had frequent losses along the coast in winter. A Limehouse woman inquires twice for her husband in December 1596. 'He went nine weeks ago in a carvell [a small light ship] to Newcastle and since they have not heard of him. – This man was drowned, the ship also and was never heard of.'

In the course of the war with Spain, English ships were beginning to penetrate into the Mediterranean. Sir Edward Osborne and Richard Staper had been the driving forces in developing trade with the Levant; in 1592 a new charter established the Levant Company on a firmer foundation.[1] In that year Forman notes that Thomas Allen made a voyage into the Straits, was nearly cast away on his way out, but did accomplish his voyage and return home.[2] This was probably his acquaintance, Mr Allen of Thames Street, whose ship, sent to Flanders in September 1594 was overdue, and 'like to have been cast away by mighty winds'. Next September we hear of Avis Allen and her husband, and 'Mrs Allen of the ship' supping with Simon.[3] There are other such entertainments with Osbornes and Challoners, names that appear among the fishmongers and haberdashers; Avis's cuckolded husband was a cheesemonger. In June, Staper, on behalf of the Levant Company, presented Sir Robert Cecil with two Turkey carpets for the favour of his obtaining the Queen's letters to the Sultan.[4]

In July Master Lumley, of the Three Kings in Watling Street, came several times about a robbery – 'the thief came again at night'.[5] This was Martin Lumley, draper, who was to become an important figure in the City, sheriff, alderman, Lord Mayor. Elaborate calculations indicated 'someone that worketh in the house'; whereupon Mr Lumley came again twice to know 'whether his man be the thief'. His man found a length of the cloth in the

---

[1] A.C.Wood, *A History of the Levant Company*, 20.
[2] 802.
[3] v. later, Autobiography, pp. 292, 293.
[4] *Salisbury Mss.*, VI. 215.
[5] 226.

inner shop, 'the stealth thereof in the full of the moon the same morning'.

A more regular client is Henry Wood of Swan Alley in Coleman Street. 'This is a fair and large street, on both sides builded with divers fair houses besides alleys, with small tenements in great number.'[1] In December 1596 two hoys went from London to Amsterdam – Dutch boats with Dutch masters, carrying his goods. 'They shall arrive safe, but to take heed,' etc. In January 1598 he puts the question whether best to buy bay-salt or no: this was the name it still had in the little grocer's shop of my boyhood in Cornwall, i.e. salt from the Bay of Biscay. We find Mr Wood consulting Forman several times this year: he has various troubles on his mind. We have already learned that he was in love with Mrs Mountjoy, Shakespeare's landlady – Coleman Street was not far from Silver Street where her husband kept shop. All Mr Wood had to do was walk up Coleman Street, along the City Wall and down to little Silver Street.

Mr Wood was worried. In April, was there ill towards him?[2] In May, in Latin, was there trouble threatened against him? In August, again in Latin, what would happen to him after this? The answer is safely in English: 'it seemeth that his goods shall be attached, some great enemy shall proffer him fair friendship, but treachery will follow'. In December he inquires whether he shall have good sale for his holland cloth in France. He himself goes over with his goods to Flanders or Amsterdam, for his wife puts the question whether 'taken by the Dunkirkers. – He was passed over and not taken, but well.'[3] That month a question is put for Mr Hawes, Sir George Carey and Sir Thomas Gorges whether they will 'obtain stock for a case of things of certain merchandise'.[4] Answer, 'he shall be in great possibility thereof; and, for money, it may be had, but the prince will be angry before it is granted and repent for doing it.' Evidently 'stock' meant a joint stock; the great increase in London's trade and prosperity

[1] Stow, I. 284.
[2] 195.
[3] 354.
[4] 195.

brought with it the development of the joint-stock company, such as the Levant and East India companies. The joining together of a number of merchants to lade a vessel for trade (or privateering) were analogous steps in the development.

Next day, was it best for Mr Hawes to proceed to obtain a commission of coals? – He may, but the process will be long delayed by someone's death. Who were these people? We know Sir George Carey. Sir Thomas Gorges – of the West Country family that produced Sir Ferdinando, founder of the province of Maine – was the builder of triangular Longford Castle near Salisbury, and husband of the Swedish Marchioness of Northampton, a favourite lady with the Queen.[1] We find her writing to Burghley this year urging that John Hawes may succeed to his father's post in the Customs-house.[2] The Hawes were a leading merchant family that had produced a Lord Mayor, a Clothworker, in the previous generation: Alderman Watts, also a Clothworker, had married his daughter Margaret.[3]

At New Year 1599 Mr Leate comes for the first time; he becomes the most regular of clients, understandably, because his ships are engaged in the long and dangerous voyages through the Straits to the Levant. He is inquiring for the *John Francis*, a ship that had made good takings at Cadiz.[4] She went from the English coast in September 1598: is she now at Algiers, or has she left there for Alexandria? The answer was that she was safe on her way homeward with much goods of price, but that there had been sickness among her people.[5] In February, March and even as late as August, he inquires yet again for her. 'She came back well, his man [i.e. factor] not with her.'[6] Mr Leate, trading on a large scale, lades goods in a number of ships. Five times in February and March he puts the question for the *Angel*: 'what is become of her that she comes not? . . . She should come from Alexandretta in the bottom of the Strait' – evidently the Elizabethans used the

[1] cf. C. A. Bradford, *Helena, Marchioness of Northampton*.

[2] *Cal. S.P. Dom., 1598–1601*, 42.

[3] *Remembrancia, 1579–1664*, 287.

[4] R. Hakluyt, *Principal Navigations*, MacLehose edn., V. 243.

[5] 802.

[6] 219.

term for the whole Mediterranean. The horoscope indicated: 'this ship seems to have had some great mishap but now she is set out homeward again'. The ship had been Captain Amias Preston's, raiding in the West Indies four years before.[1] Parson Sandy's brother Robert, the merchant in Bishopsgate Street – a couple of years before, Shakespeare had moved thence to Southwark – is inquiring whether the *Darling*, which went to Leghorn and had been stayed by the Duke, should come. 'She came home well about 14 April.'[2] She also had been in Preston's raid into the Caribbean.

In March Mr Leate inquires for 'the *Hector* of London that went with the present to the Turk, how she shall speed and what state she is in now, whether taken by the Spaniards or no'. She was a powerful armed merchantman, newly built, of 300 tons, and could give a good account of herself with her armament of twenty-seven guns. (At the beginning of the Queen's reign England had been dependent on foreigners for guns, at the end she was exporting them, even to Spain.) She was carrying a remarkable present to the Turk, which made news: a mechanical organ made by the organ-builder, Thomas Dallam, to mollify the Sultan with concord of sweet sounds into granting trading concessions.[3] At the beginning of the Queen's reign over a hundred organs had been dismantled in the churches, in deference to philistine Protestant prejudice; not until the end of the reign were the English building them again. A demonstration of the instrument had been made before that musical connoisseur, the Queen, before leaving. Thomas Dallam went in the *Hector* to set it up in the Seraglio in Constantinople, but got into some trouble for taking too much interest in the ladies in the harem. At the end of March the indication is that 'they be past the enemy and well, but have had a hard skrudge [? journey]; they are at the mouth of the Straits'.

In April Mr Leate was inquiring for the *Charity* 'that came from the Straits: when she will come or where she is'. This vessel had

[1] Hakluyt, X. 213.

[2] 802.

[3] cf. S. Mayes, *An Organ for the Sultan.*

been employed by the Turkey merchants before; she had evidently been reported to be out of the Straits. In May he wanted to know whether the *George* of London was safe. In September little John Leate, aged two, was ill with smallpox: give him manna and rose-water. At New Year, 2 January 1600, Mr Leate paid Forman a courtesy call; on 25 January at 11 a.m. 'Mr Henry Billingsley came to be acquainted with me'.[1] Haberdasher, alderman and briefly Lord Mayor, he is better known as the first translator of Euclid into English, inspired thereto by Dr Dee, who was now too much taken up with mystagoguery and Hermetic nonsense to do it himself. The geographical interests of the circle were more worthy of respect. In February 1602 Mr Leate put the question 'to know whether there be any North-West Passage to Cathay and whether the ships now intended to send shall find it; whether best to adventure his goods in them or no.'[2] Nothing came of this, however. A couple of years later we find Forman meeting the celebrated and mysterious Doctor himself.

In February 1600 Mr Hawes put the question for his letters patents, and whether they would be profitable or no. In March a further question elicits that they concern a property that has passed through so many hands that 'it will be hard to effect it to his mind'.[3] On 28 May would he get his letter from the Council this day? Answer – either this day at night or nine days hence. In August 1601 Mr Hawes wants to know what has become of his servant Richard Adams. Meanwhile Mr Leate was putting regular inquiries and Forman later collected the information he acquired as to what happened to the various ships. At the time of Mr Leate's last question (April 1599) as to the *Angel*, about which he was so anxious, she was 'about Dover, coming home well, rich and safe'.[4] The *Charity* returned safe, and was at Woolwich on Mayday 1600. In February 1599 the fast-sailing little *Lanneret* (which means female-hawk) had gone out with the *Hector* for protection, as far as the Adriatic. She was bound for Venice, thence to Aleppo.

[1] 236.
[2] 802.
[3] 236.
[4] 802.

Leate had his man in her, who was left behind sick at Scanderoon, (Alexandretta), where he died. In October the ship was at Zante, off the south-west coast of Greece, the centre of the currant trade; currants were the staple imports from the Levant and the trade increased mightily with an improving standard of living. Zante belonged then to Venice and remained an exquisite jewel with its sixteenth-century architecture unimpaired, until 1953, when – in addition to the general devastation wrought by man in our time – Nature destroyed it by an earthquake.

Forman's notes tell us about the homeward journey of the good ship *Hector*, which was to inaugurate the direct trade with India via the Cape of Good Hope. Leaving Constantinople in mid-September they made for Zante, where they picked up five ships of London and two of Bristol. Coming from the Straits they sank a big Biscayan with 500 men, and spoiled another Spaniard. The *Hector* arrived on the English coast, with a dozen ships, 'came home very rich'. This is what it was to have entered the Mediterranean at last in force.

In December 1601 and January 1602 Mr Leate is anxious about the *Mermaid*, which should come from Petrossa, i.e. Patras. She had been owned by Sir Anthony Shirley and taken over by Essex for the Cadiz expedition.[1] She had left Patras on 26 October and hovered off the island of Formentera in the Balearics, where she had taken a prize and 1000 dollars more.[2] Off the coast of Spain they had contrary winds and, though they saw three ships coming for England, could not come near them. On 23 January 1602 they entered the Sound at Scilly in extreme foul weather, with a great fog all next day. They came up to London on 3 or 4 February. Then there was the *Swallow*, which had gone a-roving for Sir George Carey in the West Indies in 1591.[3] Her horoscope was unfavourable, when Mr Leate put the question: 'she would be burnt or suffer loss'.[4] In fact she was 'taken by the Spaniards at the Straits, and another also'.

[1] Hakluyt, X. 266.
[2] 802.
[3] Hakluyt, X. 179.
[4] 802.

In June 1602 both Mr Leate and Mr Richard Staper came to inquire for the *Maryan* coming from Leghorn; she had in fact been taken by the Spaniards, and Mr Staper had the question put whether the King of Spain would re-deliver the goods in her. Mr Staper was one of the oldest Levant merchants, having been in Turkey as early as 1578.[1] We can still see him, long-bearded and kneeling, facing his wife with their children behind them, on his monument in St Helen's, Bishopsgate. In January 1604 Mr Leate inquired about the *Centurion*, to come from the Straits. This armed merchantman had had a gallant fight with five Spanish galleys in 1581, recorded by Hakluyt. 'The *Centurion* was fired five several times, with wild fire and other provision, which the Spaniards threw in for that purpose . . . In every of the galleys there were about two hundred soldiers, who, together with the shot, spoiled, rent and battered the *Centurion* very sore.'[2] Though grappled and boarded, the crew fought them off, forced them to ungrapple and got away. In April 1605, after peace had been made, Mr Leate is putting the question for the *Triumph* to come from Tripoli. In June his wife comes to consult Forman medically, to know the cause of her sleepish heaviness; evidently she was unable to defy lethargy.[3] She had been to consult him medically a couple of years before, for herself and her child.[4]

Forman's later notes are mere jottings, no longer the meticulous and full Case-Books up to 1601. In October 1603 rich Sheriff Swynnerton sent his man for help with regard to £200 lost out of a chest; 'the chest was broke up.'[5] We have a tantalising note of the meeting at last of the two mystagogues, Dr Dee and Dr Forman, 'at dinner at Mr Staper's house, 26 July 1604, 12.40'.[6] We can imagine the direction of their conversation from their mutual interests. The respectable Dee was now ageing and discouraged, a little crazy with paranoia; Forman was not without paranoia either, but he had emerged from a disreputable back-

[1] M. Epstein, *The Early History of the Levant Company*, 54.
[2] Hakluyt, VII. 37.
[3] 204.
[4] 236.
[5] 205.
[6] 1488.

ground, and far worse troubles, into a respectable social life, with substantial friends and eminent patrons, into prosperity. They talked magic and alchemy. Both depended on books: to them books were power. 'Dr Dee entreated for Raymond Lully' – evidently a manuscript Forman possessed of the medieval Spanish alchemist, who fascinated Montaigne. 'He showed me a little book of one Hooger, of transmutation of metals wrought by a noble Scot.' This would seem to be a fairly recent book on alchemy, by Hoghelande, published at Cologne in 1594 – it would be so like Dee to be keeping up with the subject. Credulous as ever – each was as bemused as the other.

On 5 June 1607, 4 p.m. there came a supremely practical man, Sir James Lancaster, the able commander who had carried through the first voyage of the Company to India with success.[1] Forman calls him 'Mr' Lancaster, but it was quite common to refer to knights in that age as 'Mr' – as with Sir Francis Bacon, or the Countess of Southampton's second husband, Sir Thomas Heneage, whom she always refers to as 'Mr' Heneage, and, similarly, 'Mr W.H.', her third husband, Sir William Harvey – the publisher's dedicatee of Shakespeare's Sonnets (*not* the poet's).

In 1608 came Margaret Stevens for her husband that went to Russia in the *White Lion* of Hamburg. 'They heard he was cast away, because all men came home but him. He had returned and was at that time not far from home; but kept himself close that he might see how his wife regarded him and how she behaved herself.'[2] A very Forman theme to close with. This entry reminds us that the Elizabethans were the first to open up the sea-route to Russia: all part of the lively, throbbing expansion at sea which was a grand theme of the age, and which we observe in all its human aspects – gains and losses, privateering and merchanting, triumph and overthrow, life, suffering and death – in this chapter.

It is hardly surprising that the dramatist who expressed the whole life of the age (except its religious squabbles) should have expressed this aspect of it too, at just this time, in *The Merchant of Venice*, written shortly after Cadiz.

[1] 802.
[2] 205.

Antonio's friends, Solanio and Salerio, think that his sadness is owing to anxiety over his ships and ventures overseas. Solanio thinks he understands:

> Believe me, sir, had I such venture forth,
> The better part of my affections would
> Be with my hopes abroad. I should be still
> Plucking the grass to know where sits the wind,
> Peering in maps for ports, and piers and roads . . .

As Mr Leate constantly consulted Forman. Salerio felt,

> My wind, cooling my broth,
> Would blow me to an ague when I thought
> What harm a wind too great might do at sea.
> I should not see the sandy hour-glass run
> But I should think of shallows and of flats.
> And see my wealthy Andrew docked in sand
> Vailing her high top lower than her ribs
> To kiss her burial . . .

The big *St Andrew*, one of the Spanish flagships, vice-admiral of the fleet, had been captured at Cadiz. Antonio reassures his friends:

> My ventures are not in one bottom trusted,
> Nor to one place; nor is my whole estate
> Upon the fortune of this present year.

Nevertheless, luck turned against the merchant of Venice as it did against the merchant of London, Mr Leate; for a while around 1613 he was in difficulties and had to ask forbearance from his creditors.[1] The Council asked the Lord Mayor to mediate with them, 'and if any of them were so void of compassion that they could not be prevailed upon to assent thereto' – like Shylock – they were to be summoned before the lords of the Council.

Like Antonio, Mr Leate recovered his prosperity. He went on to become three times Master of the Ironmongers' Company. There one sees what he looked like from a fine convincing portrait

---

[1] *Remembrancia*, 496.

on the staircase: a handsome man with dark brown hair, dark eyes and well-shaped eyebrows; a small shapely nose, flowing beard just beginning to turn grey. Evidently a man of about forty, with benevolent kindly expression, like his disposition. For he did a number of good works, including that of draining the land about the Barbican, where the Hall of his Company now stands.

He was a benefactor to his country in other ways. Devoted to gardening, he introduced many rare plants into the up-and-coming country. John Gerard, the botanist, paid tribute to him at just this time, in that he 'doth carefully send into Syria, having a servant there at Aleppo, and in many other countries, for the which myself and likewise the whole land are much bound unto'.[1] We should remember him for bringing from Constantinople to this country the first double yellow rose.

[1] q. *D.N.B.*, under Leate.

Chapter IX

All Sorts and Conditions of Men

We have already seen what a variety of persons came to consult Forman as astrologer and medical practitioner; we must now widen the spectrum to show what a representative cross-section of society his Case-Books present. In addition to the seamen, merchants, clerics and their wives, we shall find almost all classes represented: great Court-ladies, gentry from town and country, officials, ordinary middle-class townspeople, theatre-folk, credulous women and valetudinarian men, all kinds of women with menstrual troubles, sailors and their wives, servants and prostitutes. To these classes there are three significant exceptions: politicians and lawyers, themselves experts in human credulity, and doctors, who are hostile.

There are a few even of these, but they are exceptional. It is impossible henceforth to go into detail into the hundreds of cases that came to him, sometimes five or six a day – we must broaden the palette or, rather, select. In any case it would be impossible to identify the large majority of the names: enough to identify a minority – even that takes a considerable knowledge of the people of the time to locate who is who. Often we are given no clue, if the first name does not appear. On the other hand, we are often given a clue with the age of a person or the address and occupation. One could spend the rest of one's life tracking them down; but there is a law of diminishing returns: enough is enough.

Let us begin with the gentry – the most significant class in English society, from the Middle Ages to the social revolution of our time: they provided the vertebrate structure of the nation. (One of the deepest troubles of our time is that we are now without one: a lower middle-class bureaucracy does not provide a satisfactory framework.) Two of the distinguished Kentish

clan of Wotton are clients. In February 1599 Mr Wotton suffers
from chilliness in his limbs, sweat in his face, much water and
much wind: he is to be let blood and in spring to be given a diet.[1]
In March he appears again: he is John Wotton aged thirty-one.
In April he undergoes his diet for twenty-two days, at 2*s* a day.
Early next year he appears with the same complaint. He makes
half-a-dozen appearances in the books. In August 1599 we have
Mr Henry Wotton, with a great heat in his blood: he is to diet
three days and to purge. It is disappointing that this was not the
famous Sir Henry Wotton, the ambassador and writer, who was
at this moment serving as secretary to Essex in Ireland. Sir
Henry's father had five sons by his first marriage, among them a
John.

John Wotton had been with Essex on the Normandy expedition
of 1591 – which had helped to give Shakespeare's *Henry VI* plays,
with so much of Normandy in them, their popularity. Southampton, at seventeen, had followed his adored leader across the
Channel. Essex had carried out a piece of foolhardy *bravura*, a dash
with a small body of horsemen to meet Henri IV across enemy
country, in which he lost his brother, 'the half-arch of my house'.
John Wotton had risked his life to rescue the body.[2]

There is no difficulty with a name like Sir Barrington Molyns,
or Mullings, or Mullins; moreover, he comes at a critical turn in
his affairs, so we learn something about him. In June 1597 he
appears for medical treatment: 'he is infected with the melancholy
and salt phlegm – breeds worms in his nose of stinking sweet and
venomous humour'.[3] What appalling things Elizabethans suffered
from we shall learn more and more; I have heard of this idiosyncratic complaint in our time only in Germany, under the name
of *Stink-Nasel*. Sir Barrington was to diet twenty days to scour the
blood; '*aqua salsa* and wormwood to wash his face with fumitory'.
In spite of his unsavoury person, Sir Barrington is very anxious
to marry; he comes again and again, questing for Mary Hampden,
then Madam Southwell, the sister of Sir Robert Southwell.

[1] 219.
[2] W. B. Devereux, *Lives and Letters of the Devereux Earls of Essex*, I. 231.
[3] 226.

Perhaps no one was very anxious to couple with Sir Barrington. Who was he?

He was one of Essex's cheap Cadiz knights, the son of Sir Michael Molyns of Mackney, now Court Farm, outside Wallingford.[1] He had been sent to Oxford at thirteen as Dr Case's scholar, not to a college, which means that he was probably a Catholic. In August 1597 he inquired concerning Mary Hampden and touching going into France. This is corroborated, for he was present at the capture of Amiens from the Spaniards in September. On 22 March 1598 – when Forman dealt with nine cases – Sir Barrington wanted to know whether Elizabeth Southwell's engagement to him would hold; in April whether he would obtain Mary Hampden, if he gave over the other match.[2] Meanwhile, in Latin, would he be taken to prison, would there be trouble for him? In June he comes several times to know what shall be the end between him and Mistress Southwell, and then 'whether it will come on again after this breach'. He had obtained a licence to marry Miss Southwell, and the engagement had evidently been broken. The horoscope said, 'it will never be a match, as it seems. In the last of August his state will mend.' In September, what will happen to himself and his friends? In December Mullins's gentlewoman, one Bridget or Frances – of twenty-three 'hath the green sickness and hath taken thought and grief, very faint at the heart and her mind much troubled'.

In February 1599 Mullins's maid – they lived in Chelsea – has much putrefaction in the womb, her blood is corrupted; she is to purge, be let blood, sweat and diet.[3] July: would Sir Barrington obtain the money from Mr Bromley according to his promise? Answer: 'he is in possibility'. In September he wants to know again whether his estate will mend. His anxiety relates to his prospects of marriage. We learn in January 1600 that Madam Southwell has three suitors; 'she hath the second's answer already, but yet he will not be so answered, and she will not have the

---

[1] W. A. Shaw, *The Knights of England*, II. 94; *The Visitations of Berkshire*, ed. W. H. Rylands (*Harleian Soc.*), I. 112.

[2] 192.

[3] 219.

third'. Elsewhere we learn that she was thirty: no time to lose – she did marry Mullins and an only son was born in 1602. (Her niece, another Elizabeth Southwell, was fancied by another client, Sir Clement Heigham, but later eloped with Robert Dudley.) His affair settled, Mullins returned no more; anyway the forecast was wrong, the match came off. Among the gossips to christen Robert Sidney's daughter Barbara in December 1599, grandees like the Earl of Worcester, Lady Nottingham and Lady Buckhurst, came 'my Lady Moleyns, she that was Mistress Southwell, the maid-of-honour, with my Lady Effingham'.[1] Sir Barrington had made it.

Sir Barrington was respectable, or at least heterosexual. Humphrey Stafford – of that ancient family of the dukes of Buckingham – was not; and Forman's information about him corrects an entry in the *Dictionary of National Biography*.[2] Stafford belonged to the Blatherwick branch in Northamptonshire and had married Elizabeth, daughter of Sir John Cutts of Childerley in Cambridgeshire, when she was twenty. Her husband was 'a lewd consumptive fellow, his father disinherited him of his possessions for his lewd life and for buggery. She had two daughters and he forsook her; she lived in much care and sorrow to her father, who did much for her.'[3] The situation is corroborated by the Visitation of Cambridgeshire, which gives the poor lady only one daughter; another may have died.[4] The county histories of Northamptonshire are suspiciously silent at this point in the Stafford pedigree.

Sylvanus Scory, who came to consult Forman in April 1598, had had a gay and dissolute life; himself charming and attractive, his tastes were otherwise than Stafford's. He was then forty-seven, son of the bishop of Hereford. Aubrey tells us, 'he was a very handsome gentleman, and had an excellent wit [i.e. intelligence]; his father gave him the best education, both at home

---

[1] A. Collins, *Sidney Papers*, II. 152.

[2] cf. *D.N.B.*, under Anthony Stafford; this devotional writer was not the son of Elizabeth Cutts, nor of her husband.

[3] 206.

[4] *Visitation of Cambridge*, ed. J. W. Clay (*Harleian Soc.*), 31.

and beyond the seas, that that age would afford. And loved him so dearly that he fleeced the church of Hereford to leave him a good estate,' i.e. by letting too long or too favourable leases for large fines, which he could pocket himself. Aubrey heard that Scory had been left an estate of £1500 a year, 'which he reduced to nothing – allowing himself the liberty to enjoy all the pleasures of this world – and left his son so poor that, when he came among gentlemen, they would fancy a crown or ten shillings for him'.[1]

Scory was a favourite with the Duke of Anjou, Queen Elizabeth's 'Frog', who gave him a warm recommendation to her favour, which Sylvanus neglected to make use of. He became, too, a friend and patron of Ben Jonson; altogether a 'most accomplished gentleman'. This is what he had come to now, viewed by Forman: 'the humour abounding is that of melancholy, which breeds a stone . . . He hath had it long and can never be cured thereof . . . weakness in his genitals *quod non potest coire* [so that he cannot copulate] and grieveth much', i.e. suffers from anxiety.[2] 'It comes through much lechery. He is unfortunate by accident and will not be ruled.' He may have been an accomplished and witty gentleman; he was evidently also a waster and a fool. His son went up to Balliol, but left without taking a degree, to travel like his father in France.[3] The father, 'giving way to fate in the parish of St Peter near St Paul's Wharf, London, in September or October 1617, was buried in the chancel of St Leonard's church by Shoreditch, near to the grave of his mother Elizabeth'.[4]

Of well-known country gentry we recognise a number of names. Here is John Tregonwell – Forman does not always get the name right – the great-grandson of the eminent Cornish lawyer who, from his services to Henry VIII, acquired beautiful Milton abbey in Dorset. The young man was unwell; a friend brought his urine unknown to him: Simon diagnosed, 'full of wind, colic, imposthume [ulcer], will die or escape hard within

---

[1] J. Aubrey, *Brief Lives*, ed. A.Clark, II. 216 foll.
[2] 195.
[3] J.Foster, *Alumni Oxon.*, 1324.
[4] A.Wood, *Athenae Oxon.*, II. 770.

three days'.[1] He did not die. We next hear of him through his mother, Mrs Waller – married again and living near Winchester – who puts the question whether they will overcome John Rives in his suit for Lyscombe farm, near Milton. Three questions on this yield the following piece of wisdom – 'very hard to be brought to agreement'.[2]

It is fascinating to find the grandson of St Thomas More coming to consult the astrologer – for his health, not his soul. This is Cressacre More, aged twenty-nine in 1601 – correct, for he was born in 1572: he has pain in his stomach, much wind, and is anxious.[3] He lived to a good old age, to be seventy-seven and see Charles I's execution in 1649. More lived on his grandfather's estate at North Mimms, which had been restored to the family by Queen Mary, a kindly woman – except where her faith was concerned. It does not seem that Thomas More of Newington was a member of the martyr's family; he was eighty-five in 1598, 'his legs do swell . . . he will die eighteen days hence'. But he survived until May, when he came with a stuffing in the stomach: to purge two days, but 'will swell shortly'.[4]

Nor is it possible to identify Mr Digby, who dances attendance day after day in 1601.[5] We should say that he was suffering from paranoia: is there any evil towards him by John Woodbury and the rest? Does John Woodbury go about to betray him? Is he himself in peril, and what will follow? Has Ursula Savile another lover, namely William? Sometimes Mr Digby has both astrological and geomantical figures cast; often Forman merely notes his name – he must have thought him a fool. He kept him on a string by feeding his fancies, regularly telling Digby to 'take heed', 'a plot is laid', etc. He was a gentleman; but the Digbys were an odd lot, producing Gunpowder plotters a few years later, and a practitioner of occult arts in the next generation in Sir Kenelm Digby.

What one notices in this section of the *clientèle* is that quite a

[1] 234.
[2] 195.
[3] 411.
[4] 195.
[5] 411.

number of these gentry – More, Mullins, Cornwallis, Digby, Fortescue, Arundell – are Catholic in their sympathies: more credulous, or more in need of reassurance.

Officials, government servants, were a less numerous class then, but they are well represented. In May 1596 an important Customs official, Richard Carmarden, was suffering from anxiety and melancholy, self-induced – as well might be the case, from the circumstances of his post. He sent his urine for diagnosis; in August 'he mended and was well again'.[1] It was as well, for his was a very teasing and responsible office, Surveyor of the subsidies of tonnage and poundage in London.[2] He had come up as a follower of Lord Burghley, but was now in some disfavour with the great man who was getting querulous as he grew old and feeble. Next year Carmarden was answering him back as few dared to do: 'But truly, my lord, I will rather crave pardon of her Majesty from any employment to your lordship than endure such open checks and taunts from you, as this day and before I have done, for doing her Majesty's commandment.'[3] Carmarden, a good watchdog of the Queen's interests, was secure in her confidence and was of much Burghley's seniority: he died in 1604.

More regular clients were Mr Auditor Conyers, of the Exchequer, and his family; we hear of another Exchequer official, John Pond, who pines and consumes away. Not so old John Conyers, a *protégé* of Burghley from Nottingham, who at sixty-four in 1596 suffers from stone and strangury, has a cough in his lungs and vomits oft.[4] In May 1597 the Auditor seeks advice whether to go to Lord Buckhurst and deliver his bill.[5] About All Hallow-tide his wife died, but the Auditor is still attending Forman over the years till 1601. Son Thomas and wife are clients too. Cuthbert Stillingfleet was the elderly Messenger of her Majesty's Chamber, entrusted with confidential messages of

[1] 234.

[2] J. U. Nef, 'Richard Carmarden's "A Caveat for the Queen", 1570', *Journal of Pol. Economy*, XLI. 33 foll.

[3] *Cal. S.P. Dom., 1595–7*, 412.

[4] 234.

[5] 226.

importance, as to Essex in Ireland. In 1601 he was fifty-three, suffering from a melancholy humour in blood and stomach – this was the usual 'humours' doctrine of the medicine of the time – and, more to the point for a messenger, from sciatica.[1] However, he drank Forman's strong water and 'it cured him'. No wonder that his wife became a regular, always something wrong with her. She wants also to be advised whether it is best for her daughter to marry Thomas Baillie; a couple of days later the daughter wants to know too. The Stillingfleets naturally lived at Westminster; in 1600 brother Anthony turns up thence to consult about his health.[2]

In May 1599 Mr Hanson wanted to know whether Mr Suckling would obtain the Lord Treasurer's hand for him for his office.[3] The poet Sir John Suckling's father became a Treasury official, the poet spent the cash.

Grimstons appear: Edith and Dorothy who live in the Crutched Friars.[4] In April 1601 comes Edward Grimston, forty-seven, from Great St Bartholomew's, a fashionable quarter: pains in his leg, the figure says he is in danger of strangury in the foot.[5] This may be the voluminous translator; but there are two brothers, each named Edward, at the time.[6] This reminds us that writers form another class that did not patronise Forman. It is not likely that the Mr Chapman who appears in 1598 was the poet and dramatist, George Chapman, odd as he was. This man wished to learn 'whether he be bewitched or forspoken. – He is in the hands of his enemies – many pains and stitches in the right side.'[7]

I do not know whether 'Mr Milward of the Tower,' who is always described as such, was an official there.[8] He comes in May 1596 – 'himself knows of it'; what does this mean? That he knows the cause of his disease? He has pain in lungs, stomach,

[1] 411.
[2] 236.
[3] 219.
[4] 195.
[5] 411.
[6] cf. G. N. Clark, 'Edward Grimeston, the Translator', *E.H.R.*, 1928, 585 foll.
[7] 195.
[8] 234.

head. Then Mrs Milward of the Tower – they must surely belong there; she has bitterness rising in the stomach, gall like to vomit. In May 1597 comes Nathaniel, 'at Mrs Milward's at the Tower, twenty-four: he is much bruised in the stomach and body with treading on at Paul's, 8 May, at the sermon, upon the uproar'.[1] Evidently a demonstration of mass-foolery at some sermon. (A clever woman like the Queen had to put up with them, but always found them unutterably boring; or, rather, she occasionally burst out and uttered what she thought.)

Among lawyers we have seen Robert Delahay consulting Forman professionally, as Forman consulted him. In 1597 he was only twenty-three; Jane Briscote a widow of forty-six is interested in him: Forman describes her as daughter of the late wife of Sebastian Brusket, which suggests a relationship to Ludovic Brysket (Bruschetti), Italian immigrant friend of Sir Philip Sidney. In spite of the attraction of a widow to a rising young man, Delahay did not marry the woman twice his age. 'About Christmas after he married another, a young gentlewoman of twenty-eight years in Surrey.'[2]

Thomas Watkins of Lincoln's Inn comes for medical treatment, suffering from sprouting of blood, pimples on hands, heat of blood; he is fearful and faint-hearted. In Lincoln's Inn is one Roper, a recognisable figure: 'it seems he will be fantastical by reason of much drieth of the brains, wine, and a former of two teeth', apparently wisdom-teeth.[3] Forman conveniently distinguishes Mrs Phillips of King's Bench for us, evidently the wife of a lawyer or legal official. In January, aged thirty-eight, she thinks herself with child: 'I think not, much wind and water.'[4] She comes several times; in March her name is given in Greek letters, for she thinks she has been poisoned: 'hot and burning, like to be light-headed, some impostumation', i.e. ulceration.

In April 1597 Mrs Phillips of Southwark wants to know – in Latin – whether she is pregnant. In March 1592 there was a

[1] 226.
[2] 354.
[3] 195.
[4] 226.

question whether Austin Phillips would ever marry Eleanor
Auger – 'he married her not, but married another man's wife'.[1]
Six days later, alongside this, a certain person put the question 'if
he went awooing to Mr Notting's daughter, whether he would
obtain her in matrimony' – 'He married her not, yet he had her
good will and her friends'; 'she received an angel of him in token
thereof'. This may well have been Augustine Phillips, the actor,
who joined the Chamberlain's Company on its formation in
1594.

For this leads us to a number of people whose names connect
them with the theatre, Henslowes and Burbages, even if we cannot
identify them individually. In August 1596 a Mr Henslowe
inquires concerning stolen goods: 'the goods are near the house,
buried in the earth in a neighbour's house'.[2] No clue as to who he
was. In February 1597 Mr Philip Henslowe has pain in the reins,
side, head and water in the stomach: he is to purge.[3] In July
Bridget Henslowe sent earnestly to know whether she would live
or die – 'she will die on Friday next – light in the head'. She was
forty and had a miscarriage. But she did not die; we learn in
January next year that she had had a long sickness and lived at
St Mary Hill, close to Forman in Billingsgate.

In 1598 a Mr Hemming turns up – apparently he is Roger, not
John, the actor. In January 1600 Forman is questing whether to
take 'the house by the stone carvers in Southwark' – this would
be the workshop of the Janssens or Johnsons, whence so many
monuments went forth to ornament the churches and carved
chimney-pieces for great houses.[4] Among Forman's regular
Southwark clients were Mr and Mrs Cure; these would appear
to be not the foreign artists but the family of Thomas Cure,
Saddler to Edward vi, Mary and Elizabeth, who has a monument
in Southwark cathedral and founded almshouses in Park Street.[5]
Mr Cure comes often with trouble in chest and lungs; he is sixty-

[1] 354.
[2] 234.
[3] 226.
[4] 411.
[5] W. Taylor, *Annals of St Mary Overy*, 96.

two in 1597, 'an enemy to himself, surfeits in drinking wine, which is ill'.[1] In May 1601 Mr Cure is prescribed a diet of fifteen days, at 6*s* a glass, when Mrs Blague is paying 8*s* a glass for twenty-one days. Mr Ferdinando Clutterbuck pays 2*s* for a purge, 8*s* for a glass. With so individual a name he is easily identifiable: he lived in the parish of St Martin Oteswich by Bishopsgate Street and was very well off, rated at £70 for the Subsidy.[2]

In May 1601 Elizabeth Burbage, aged thirty-two, is having trouble with her pregnancy. In October Humphry Burbage, of twenty-five, has a purge prescribed. There is still no corroboration whether these people belonged to the well-known theatrical families. But in February 1601 there is a note that is indubitable: Forman's brother George was 'robbed by one Towne, a player; he at last confessed and made recompense, though not the goods'.[3] This was Thomas Towne of the Admiral's Company, who therefore played in Marlowe's plays. When the Lord Chamberlain's became the King's Men, the Admiral's became Prince Henry's. Towne died, not old, in 1612, leaving £3 to his Fellows 'to make them a supper when it shall please them to call for it'.[4]

Forman, for his part, kept up a sniping warfare against the Doctors who persecuted him; he notes down his confrontations with them and cases where he considers they have killed their patients. And indeed it is probable that they were more lethal than he was. In October 1597 'Dr Paddy and I met in Lombard Street' – so they evidently knew each other.[5] Paddy was a distinguished figure in the medical world, at this moment Censor of the College of Physicians, on his way to becoming President, attending Southampton in the Tower and King James in his last illness. There follows something difficult to make out: Simon seems to wonder what would happen concerning some fault

[1] 226, 411.
[2] *The Visitation of London,* ed. cit., 151.
[3] 354.
[4] q. E. K. Chambers, *The Elizabethan Stage,* II. 347.
[5] 226.

committed. In 1598, of Dr Poe (?) 'it is reported that he gave a
purge to one that wrought in the Queen's slaughter-house at
Greenwich at 7, and the party was dead by 9 the same day. He
gave a vintner's wife beyond St Nicholas Shambles a purge also,
and she died with it.'[1] Forman was imprisoned first by Dr
Barnsdale in November 1595. We can locate this man: he lived
in St Sepulchre's parish and was rated for Subsidy at only £10
in fees – evidently not very successful and therefore jealous.[2]
When he came out of prison after a fortnight, Forman fell out
over the treatment of a sick person in Chancery Lane with 'Dr
Wilkins': this is Dr Wilkinson, who lived in St Bartholomew the
Less.[3] He was no more successful a physician than Barnsdale;
Forman was put in prison again for a few days.

In January 1598 Forman took the offensive. 'Dr Barnsdale was
served with a *subpoena* [writ] to put in an answer to my bill in
Chancery . . . and my matter was removed out of the lewd court
of Wood Street to the Chancery by a *certiorari*,' i.e. a writ to bring
the matter to a higher court.[4]

In March Dr Daniel is in question: a woman in Cornhill 'hath
taken physic of Dr Daniel, two purges, and is not the better for
it'.[5] We note the implication that a cure is expected, and on one
occasion Forman was given ill words by a woman because he
would not undertake to cure her. In August 1599 Forman was
sent to the Counter for six hours for calling Dr Adrian a dunce.[6]
All these are rather unsuccessful doctors who have left little traces
of themselves. Simon picked up a piece of information – whether
against Dr Barnsdale or Dr Friar, he was not sure – about a lady
in Lothbury who had been let blood 'and the same night her
course came down, and she died'.[7] We learn how Simon got his
information: 'the mistress that makes head-tires [wigs] in Tower
Street told me this, when she came to ask counsel'. Forman

[1] 195.
[2] *The Visitation of London*, ed. cit., 160.
[3] ibid.
[4] 226.
[5] 195.
[6] 219.
[7] 236.

himself prescribed blood-letting very sparingly. In January 1601 he considers whether 'best to enterprise to obtain Dr James's place, physician to the Queen'.[1] James was a highly qualified man, medically as well as linguistically; the first graduate of the university of Leyden, he had been her doctor only since 1595 and died in January 1601.[2] Forman had no 'qualifications' or university degree; but he considered himself as good a doctor as those who had – and probably was.

Printers and publishers formed a small profession, and few turn up; but those who do, excite our interest. On 30 August 1596 Richard Field comes: he has 'swallowed a portugue', i.e. a valuable Portuguese gold coin: 'it lies in the pit of the mouth of the stomach'.[3] His age is given as thirty-seven, which tallies well enough with that of Shakespeare's Stratford school-fellow, baptised in 1561.[4] The fact that the coin was a portugue makes it more likely, for Field specialised in printing foreign books, Spanish as well as French and Italian. This year he printed Spenser's *Faerie Queene*, as three years before he had printed Shakespeare's *Venus and Adonis*.

In April 1598 the two Jaggard brothers appear, the age of both is given as thirty-two: William is in danger of yellow jaundice, John has a fever.[5] These brothers were sons of a barber-surgeon of Aldersgate.[6] Having set up shop in the churchyard of St Dunstan in the West, their first publication was a sermon by our friend Dr Dove in 1594, dedicated to one of his charges, the boy Francis Gorges. Their second publication was a selection from the secrets – herbal, mineral, alchemical – of Albertus Magnus: interests dear to Forman's heart. What won William Jaggard notoriety was his publication in 1599 – the year after coming to Forman – of a selection of poems by various people, including Shakespeare, and then putting the popular actor-dramatist's name on the title-page to sell it. It was this last that gave offence,

---

[1] 411.
[2] C. H. and T. Cooper, *Athenae Cantab.*, II. 178.
[3] 234.
[4] M. Eccles, *Shakespeare in Warwickshire*, 59.
[5] 195.
[6] E. E. Willoughby, *A Printer of Shakespeare*, 39 foll.

for the poems themselves were fair game, the practice with regard to copyright being different then. Thomas Heywood tells us, 'so the author, I know, much offended with Master Jaggard that, altogether unknown to him, presumed to make so bold with his name'.[1]

How much we wish we could identify William Larkin, forty-seven in 1601, whose 'disease is plague in the groin – he is very whole: strong water cured him'.[2] From his age he could be the distinguished painter of the time whose late Elizabethan and Jacobean portraits are now highly regarded. No birth-date appears to be known for him; Forman's client would have been born *c.* 1556. An odd clergyman turns up – Parson Randall of St Andrew Hubbert's, three times in April 1600: he 'has much shogged his body, having ridden a great journey'.[3] Dr Cradock of Oxford consults Forman about his son – this is a New College civilian from Hampshire, probably a Wykehamist.[4] Young William Bradish, twenty, wants to know 'whether he shall obtain the place or Fellowship in Cambridge he sueth for now or no'. He did – he became a Fellow of Emmanuel, and then got a Dorset vicarage.[5]

Servants offer a rather small class – naturally, for they have not much money; but their employers cast horoscopes for them when in trouble, or to know whether best to employ them; often enough female servants are pregnant by their masters – Forman was not an exceptional offender in this respect. Joan, Mr Borace's servant, of Ratcliffe, it seems, 'is pregnant by her master; he hath given her some ill medicine and gone to somebody to bewitch her that she should die'.[6] Her illness comes from 'putrefaction of some dead conception in her womb'. William Price, my Lady Borace's (? Borlase) man, was an epileptic: 'the falling evil taketh him at certain times; he falleth not, but sometimes vomiteth'. A servant to a merchant in Gracechurch Street, aged nineteen,

[1] q. E. K. Chambers, *William Shakespeare*, II. 218.
[2] 411.
[3] 236.
[4] 219; Foster, I. 344.
[5] 236; Venn, I, 1. 200.
[6] 195.

inquires whether his fellow, aged eighteen, is true or false, for 'he misseth money often in his accounts'.[1]

Eustace, Forman's man, queried whether his leg could be cured 'without peril of his life and leg. – Either he will lose his leg, or be lame for ever. The humour abounding is phlegm and melancholy with the blood. First break it – so soon as it is broke purge him strongly. Then, the corruption out, heal him with *deum medendi doloribus*, or bate [abate, diminish] him or send him to the bath.' Forman treats 'my Lady Leighton's maid' as well as the lady. What trade is it best for Robert Frank of the Turk's Head in Fleet Street to follow for his living? 'He is very unfortunate in the end of his actions, for the end of all his doing is naught. His wife is more fortunate than he: let her deal for him, yet somewhat negligent. Let him stay where he is – if he goes into the country, he will not stay there long.'[2] Forman regularly cast to know whether his servants would be faithful or no. In his case it was particularly important that they should be trustworthy; for, in addition to the maid-servants, there were the men who helped him in his operations. Sometimes one of them would set the figure, having been taught how to do it. On 8 August 1597 'we began to make our glass and to pray; John fasted the Monday before and the same day. We bought the glass 8 August and drew the circle in Virgam presently,' i.e. immediately.[3] I do not know what they were up to, crystal-gazing (like Dr Dee) or what not.

When Simon loses his scissors he casts a figure to find them; they were 'taken by the maid, found in her chamber by the mistress of the house'. Is it best to take Alice Cousins to service or no? – the figure is irrevocably cast. Or he casts for his brother-in-law Sandys to find out whether Dorcas was false or no, 'doubting of her truth, he put her away this day'.[4] Or 'whether my sister shall have Elizabeth Hill to be her servant'. This girl was expecting an offer of marriage, which did not eventuate; so 'she came to my sister, but would not stay with her'. Even Elizabethan servants

[1] 411.
[2] 219.
[3] 226.
[4] 335.

had their freedom to choose, or a measure of choice. Mrs Lucas comes to learn 'whether Bess, her maid be with child'. Several times he casts for Thomas Janssen, Sandy's workman, or for the sickness of his own man. In all the cases there is only one reference to toothache; evidently people took it in their stride and had the tooth out with no fuss – Forman himself was above tooth-drawing, which would be done by a mere mechanic. Again, ordinary people's diet was simpler and better for the teeth – the Queen was liable to toothache from her addiction to sweetmeats.

Since we cannot deal individually with the hundreds of cases that occur in the books, we may note a few of the names. Without following the example of the insolent young Canning who – when a deputation of working men waited upon him – was found making rhymes out of their uncouth names, we may observe that Elizabethans, like modern Americans, were more enterprising in the names they fancied. There is Appelina Proudlove, about whom Forman has a note, in Latin, whether she will be secret. Living in Bishopsgate Street, she has been married only two years: 'her husband is now beyond sea in the East. He will come about a week after midsummer. She hath a wart under her right cheek.'[1] She was twenty-three. Then there was Appelina Fairfax, or Actaeon Dove – it sounds like a name out of the *Faerie Queene* – or Peter Dearlove. We have Aquila Gould and Temperance Slaughter, Cognata Stocker and Cassandra Potter; even when the surnames are ordinary enough the imagination of the time declares itself in the Christian names, Ferdinando and Orlando – Shakespeare is not remote from the time; Sylvanus Scory – Spenser had a son called Sylvanus; Peregrine Willoughby's name is cited, along with Counsel Clark, Eusebius Andrews, Ethelred James. This in addition to the regulars appearing over the years, Mrs Lydiard of Woolwich, Mrs Davies of Fleet Street, Dorothy Madison, Mrs Blague and all the family of Spidells.

One more exception – few foreign immigrants appear, whatever the reason. In June 1600 the mother-in-law of Samuel de Glans alias Druet inquires, without his or his wife's consent, 'whether

1 236.

he hath the pox or no. – He is deaf and hath the pox dry inward.'
Then the poor young wife of nineteen comes – 'he hath been
sweated for it eighteen times'. But this was an astrological answer.
Hortense the Italian at the Black Boy in Grub Street, just outside
Cripplegate, was suffering from fever, a throat full of phlegm:
'he hath the sensonic or pox and will die or scape hard: he is to
prepare [i.e. diet], purge, let blood and gargle'.[1] In 1601 Jochanan
Vauxpena – one can *hear* her pronouncing her name Juana in the
Spanish way to Simon: 'I received £6 and must have £6 more
when she is well. If she be not well at all, I must give her £5
again.'[2] Here again is the implication that if a cure is not effected,
one expects one's money back, or part of it.

Forman's practice was dominantly medical, secondly for the
purpose of forecasting the future; people also came to him to
find things lost, as they did to Dr Dee. Sometimes children or
young people are lost or stolen, as today. Edward Price of seventeen years went from his parents on 17 December 1598 at 6 a.m.
and 'was never heard of since'.[3] He was the son of a cooper at the
Blue Lion in St Clement Danes. A month later his mother,
Swythin Price, put the question for him, whether he was killed or
no. Answer – he is gone westward, would be heard of within
fifty-eight days. Next Mrs Cure is inquiring for the youth. 'He
seemeth now to be in prison with some kinsman.' In fact, it
transpired that 'his uncle had stole him away to marry him to one
in Wales'.[4] In mid-February he came back, but to a neighbour's
house; his kinsman had intended to marry his daughter to him.[5]

In October 1597 'a certain gentlewoman, going abroad to see
the going of her Majesty to Parliament, left at home her daughter
of twenty'. When she returned, her daughter was not there; she
did not know whether stolen, or had run away, or killed herself.
The lady putting the question was a neighbour and client at
Lambeth, Mrs Pole. 'The maid was not heard of for a sennight

[1] 219.
[2] 411.
[3] 195.
[4] 354.
[5] For the practice of forcibly marrying children or under-age persons v. *The
Elizabethan Renaissance: The Life of the Society*, 210–12.

[week], at this time she was at Westminster also,' evidently to see the show; and afterwards went to Newington Butts – where there was a playhouse – and there stayed, with obvious danger to her virtue. Mr and Mrs Clark were friends of Simon, Mrs Clark something more; one June morning 1599 she lost her boy. What had become of him? 'She could not find nor hear of him by any means till 7 p.m. One took him up in Cheapside and carried him to a garden in Shoreditch, a friend.' We have seen that going to a garden was a regular amusement, like going into the park in subsequent centuries.

People attached more importance, oddly enough, to their dogs than to their cats. John and Ann Fletcher of St Dunstan's Hill lost their dog one Sunday in the Crutched Friars: 'a little bitch with six silver beads about her neck, and a greenish and blueish velvet collar; a white bitch, on each side a red foot, red cheeks and ears, a white star in the forehead and all the hinder part white'.[1] Ann came back a few days later to know whether 'to inquire for her little dog where the parrot was to sell'. A dog of more consequence was a greyhound of the Earl of Cumberland's, that broke loose from a house in Water Lane where it was kept. 'The dog ran straight to Charterhouse [where the Earl was living], thence to Gray's Inn Fields, where it was taken up by a leather-dresser, who sold it to a tapster for 5s. The tapster used to take the dog daily into Gray's Inn Fields, where the dog was spied by one that knew him.'[2]

Then there was the danger of being bewitched or enchanted – Mrs Blague and her husband thought she must be enchanted by Dean Wood, when it was merely sex. We have a charm 'to help those that be bewitched:

> The water is not thirsty,
> The bread is not hungry:
> In the name of the Father, the Son and the Holy Ghost,
> Come forth, fair Angel, and help thy brother.

For those that be troubled in their mind and planet-struck, hang

[1] 226.
[2] 240; G. C. Williamson, *George, Third Earl of Cumberland*, 132.

a horse-shoe over their bed and wear valerian.'[1] We may not hang horse-shoes over our beds, but many people still do over their doors – that is the only difference. As for valerian, there is something about its smell that attracts cats – hence, perhaps, the association with witchery.

A parent came to know whether his year-old child 'be forspoken or bewitched or a changeling'. Obviously there was something wrong with it, probably an idiot. The figure showed that 'it is forspoken – some ill sprite doth vex and consume the child'. Substantial Mr Brewer came for his daughter to know 'whether she be enchanted or no'.[2] Shortly after 'Margery Skelton, that dwells in the little lane that goes into the fields beyond Holborn bridge, is haunted at night with a ghost or spirits continually that she hears often. Her husband's sister causes her to be bewitched by an old woman – Jane Taylor, a witch of Hammersmith, that bewitched Elizabeth Fisher.' What was at work would seem to be the familiar jealousies between in-laws.

Mrs Condwell was a regular client, who came to Forman in a despairing state of health; from this she graduated to more intimate relations, and her health improved. Her husband also became a friend and told Simon of 'a poulterer that transformed himself to a bear and met one in Bishopsgate Street; when he wrestled with him he turned to a man'. Again, 'one of my Lord Walsingham's men was haunted with one like a devil in divers shapes; at length he struck at him with a sword, and it was a man.' With such tales were supper-parties at the Condwells' regaled; one sees how the imaginations of dramatists were fed in such a society, where all things were possible. And we may add that the scene-ending in *The Winter's Tale*, to which critics have taken such objection – 'Exit, pursued by a bear' – had nothing improbable in it for an Elizabethan audience, so accustomed to bear-baitings, performing bears, or an occasional bear breaking loose in the streets.

With the credulity of the age everybody believed in buried treasure – a state of mind I have come across in our time with a

[1] 219.
[2] 236.

convent of Carmelite nuns in Cornwall, who believed there was treasure buried in their garden. The Elizabethans had the excuse that people often did bury their treasure. We have already noticed Forman digging hopefully, but in vain. When he got his house in Lambeth, he cast to know, in Latin for security's sake, whether there was treasure concealed in the middle of his bedroom.[1] Then he inquires 'whether the treasure has been taken away in St Katherine's right against the conduit where Sir Francis Drake dwelt.'[2] This feature was at the crossing of Dowgate with Chequer Lane by Skinners' Hall. Drake inhabited the large mansion known as the Erber – tribute both to the wealth he had won and the ostentation he enjoyed.

In May 1597 'Mr Howard, Carey and others' are searching for treasure at Crowborough. 'At Eridge in Sussex, Lord Burgavenny's house now in the tenure of Mr Edward Neville, Sir Henry Neville hid £5000 in a cellar before he died' – this was some twenty-five years ago.[3] The question was made by someone of no kin, but had been 'sent by the kinsman that hid it'. Stephen Ballard of Ramsbury in Wiltshire sent his son Robert to know whether there was treasure in the chapel-close now in his tenure. The figure showed that 'there was something hid in the south-east part of the ground, but of no great value. There should be £2200 in a green chest, a common way near the place.'[4]

All kinds of odd inquiries came Forman's way. Should a lady sell her dowry? Should a couple sell up and go to live in Ireland? Was it best for Margaret, wife of George Gray, to stay in London and keep her trade or to go and dwell in the country; would her boarder, John Ferne, continue a good friend to her? The answer was – 'best to go, but not into Lincolnshire'. A cattleman, or possibly a butcher, of East Cheap holds some ground at Blackwall, where 'in a certain marsh his cattle do die always in the springtime in that one close; and that which they make most reckoning of doth always die'. What is the cause?

[1] 236.
[2] 354; Stow, I. 231.
[3] 226.
[4] 236.

Or Mr Lambrey comes *pro suo phallo*, in Greek letters: the woman held responsible for his state, 'a youngish wench of mean stature, a pleasant face, round, of an amiable brown countenance, black brows, blackish hair'.[1] Information as to other people's illicit loves is noted down – one never knows when it may come in handy. 'Sparrow, the clerk's man at the Counter in Wood Street [Simon had a grudge against this place where he had been several times confined] loves an unknown person, lodges in a bedroom at the house of a stationer.' 'Mark Frost in Mart Lane' – servant to Mr Snelling, a brewer, the other side of the water – he 'loveth one Thomson's wife in Walnut Tree Lane against St Tooley's church-door'.

This introduces us to the idiosyncrasies, the oddities, the enormities of people's lives, the 'facts of life' in depth. Robert Goodridge, after he married, was 'troubled with a perverse humour of gadding: he would go out of door from his wife and friends without any cause and say he would go walk. Many times they should not see him again in a month or two after. Often. A surgeon by trade.'[2]

Susan Cuckston of Westminster at forty fell into a melancholy despair and

was possessed by a sprite which would often provoke her to kill or drown herself and bid her cut her own throat when she had a knife in her hand. If she came by a well or any water he would bid her drown herself. Twice she hanged herself and was cut down; once she was drowned and brought back. The sprite that was in her said he was a sprite of the water but had his being in the air. She could not abide any pins about her but she must thrust them in her flesh. She was a little short woman, poor, somewhat discoloured and lean, looked like one feared [afraid] and sometimes she saw the sprite. Her husband was a tailor, a tall black fellow, long black beard and hair; he did falter in his tongue.

William Atkins, of Rutham in Norfolk, was given to art, astronomy and physic; he had 'a natural gift of seeing angels,

[1] 226.
[2] 206.

and was subject to much trouble by his kindred'. Another who could see spirits was a seafaring man, Edward Gaul:

this man hath power to see spirits and divers shapes and things in the air that others could not see. George Coomey was tall and slender, whitely face, thin brown beard, somewhat purblind and would talk very thick; angry and furious. Given to astronomy and to cast nativities, and to speculations with which he was once frented [i.e. frenzied] almost out of his wits and in despair. He was fearful and timorous in magical arts and durst not attempt any more. A gentleman born, but spent his stock and patrimony lewdly on lewd women, and kept two several men's wives long time. By one he had a child for the death of which he was like to have been endangered. Much given to the flesh, and had for and about women much trouble and imprisonment 1598, 1599, 1600 and 1601. He married a kinswoman in October 1602.

Simon could have got this from Mrs Coomey, who was a client.

Love – or sex – had its complications and led people, in the contemporary state of knowledge, to incorrect conclusions in physiology. Jane Hills 'married at twenty-three and had two boys at a burden: they had two several men to their fathers, for she loved another beside her husband – whom she had loved before marriage'. Thomas Colford was

a bastard: his mother confessed that Philip and Leonard Holmes did both keep her; one of them was the father of it, but she knew not which. They were two brothers – it seems to be the son of Leonard. When it was but fifteen weeks old, it was most grievously pinched with the fairies with black spots on his breasts, sides, belly, back, arms, thighs and legs, on the buttocks and throat; and scratched as if with pins.

Here for a change is a good fellow, a virtuous Walloon.

This Conrad Himmlet was an honest, painful [i.e. painstaking], studious, true and trusty, kind fellow. He had the high German tongue, the Walloon tongue, the French, Latin, English and part of the Welsh tongue. He was given much to travel for knowledge, loved well astronomy and all arts, was very studious therein, quick of conceit and of deep judgment, apt to anything. But he had a dimness of his eyes, a black man of good stature, not proud but stout.

Not all immigrants were as virtuous. Dorothy Powell, a girl from Blandford, had been kept by a Frenchman, who gave her two or three children but did not marry her. 'He forsook her and went into France. She was fair and tall, of good colour, soft white flesh.'

Forman had a vivid gift of describing not only a personality, with conciseness like a contemporary miniature, but a whole life. Here is the story of a woman's life. Clemence Scarborough at fifteen by chance came into a house when a fellow came a-wooing to a widow. 'He left off the widow, and fell in with an old woman and persuaded her to marry him.' He sold all she had and next married Clemence, left her to try for herself and was five years away. Meantime she married another man with a yellow beard. The first came back, sued for a divorce, sold all she had and left her again. She came to misery at twenty-five, with four children, and 'then was meretrix [a whore], glad to shift for herself. She was a little black woman. He used the sea much as a soldier and captain, and would consume all.' One sees him as a kind of Parolles.

We are given glimpses into the adventures of women with the soldiers and sailors of the time: they bring home to us how close a transcript from life are the goings-on of Falstaff and Doll Tearsheet at the Boar's Head in East Cheap. 'The same night that Mary Best was married she came to John Cole's bedside and told him she should be married the morning following. He took her into the bed and did halek. Now at Shrovetide last, when he went to sea, he and one Laurence and company went to a tavern in Bishopsgate Street and were there all day. And Mary sent Cole a bracelet of her hair with her name therein.'[1] It is like Doll's parting words to Falstaff: 'Come, I'll be friends with thee, Jack. Thou art going to the wars, and whether I shall ever see thee again or no, there is nobody cares.'

Here are one or two actual Doll Tearsheets in the flesh.

Alice Materday, wife of Edward Elliot, was straight, slender and tall, somewhat long visage, ruddy and brown of complexion, could talk

[1] 236.

well, and very liberal if she had it [i.e. money]. When she was twenty-five years old she began to grow into great misery and want; continued for three or four years and made many hard shifts. She had well to live, but consumed it . . . She turned whore and was at last a very harlot, and thereby lived.[1]

These poor creatures come alive under Simon's pen, with his gift for veracious miniature. Moralistic as he was, he was no better than they. 'Susan Lovett, born in Gloucester, had great living left her by her friends, but by marriage and adultery spoiled all. She had two or three husbands, and two or three bastards, and consumed all vainly . . . She was a woman thick-set, of reasonable stature, fat and very black hair; and she of a brown complexion, compacted of lechery.'

Young Christian Hobson, of 'the upper ground at Holy Ghost stairs', had more success in this line. 'This maiden at fourteen years old was a proper, fair, well-made maiden, good face and speckled, or tadipoled. A white fair flaxen head, good eyes, a long hand and small fingers; witty and apt to learn anything; gentle, somewhat a big voice and . . . She had a hurt in the forehead and in the neck, a red natural spot and a cut in the throat with an inkle string.' Inkle means tape: we recall Costard in *Love's Labour's Lost*.

What's the price of this inkle? – One penny.

Or Autolycus's wares, in *The Winter's Tale*: 'inkles, caddises, cambrics, lawns'. Christian was 'somewhat dry of nature', able to look after herself. At seventeen she became 'the concubine of a knight of fifty-six years, which had a wife, he kept her, maintained her, and gave her £40 per annum'.

This was the figure, we remember, with which Lord Chamberlain Hunsdon provided for his mistress, Emilia Bassano, the Dark Lady of Shakespeare's Sonnets.

[1] 206.

Chapter X

Public Persons and Events; Frances, Countess of Hertford

With so very full and active a life Forman had no call to be particularly interested in public affairs. He was, as we have seen, professionally and personally interested in the seafaring life of the time, the voyages and privateering, and through his numerous clients involved in them. And we shall see that his curiosity was aroused by Virginia in 1609, when the second charter for establishing the colony produced a wave of public excitement and nearly six hundred persons became 'venturers'. This was like him: Forman reacted like any other London citizen. Nothing exceptional: in this respect his notes on public events have the historical interest of being those of any average, alert middle-class person of the time.

We have observed that he was struck, in 1592, by the loss of the *Revenge* in Sir Richard Grenville's last sea-fight in the Azores. In November that year he has a note, in Latin, questioning what would happen to the King of Spain in the future, whether he would send another Armada against England, or peace be concluded in 1593.[1] He later added: 'there was no peace concluded, neither did he send any army against England this year. But our merchants and thievish ships did rob and spoil many of his ships, took great prizes from him and a great carrack this year.' This was the rich East Indiaman, the *Madre de Dios*, the cargo of which opened envious eyes to the returns on Oriental trade. A further note enters up, 'he [Philip II] died 1598 in September'.

We saw Mrs Pole of Lambeth among the crowd that gathered to see the Queen at Westminster go by in procession to open Parliament; indeed Forman himself was there, and picked up a

[1] 354.

woman, Joan Harington. On 28 October 1597 he put the question to know 'what should be done in the Parliament and what would come thereof in the end – quietness or strife'. This has its interest as an indication of the ordinary person's attitude to Parliament. He annotated: 'many statutes concluded on and it ended in peace. Statutes for the relieving of the poor and for soldiers, etc.; and four 15ths and two subsidies granted; and for punishment of beggars and that everyone should go where he or she was born'. Here is what interested the average person in the legislation of that Parliament. He adds: 'this figure was also set by another for the same purpose at the same time.'

We have a few jottings as to the influence of the planets on prices – for those that are interested in such things. 'These things are cheaper than they were' – an entry that strikes a note disagreeably unfamiliar to us: 'currants, 28*s* a cwt; grains, 12*d* a lb; ginger, 12*d* a lb; woollen cloth etc., 23*s* a wt; castell [Castille] soap was dear; black soap, 23*s* a cwt; hops, 40*s* a cwt; pease, 8 groats [farthings]; butter, 4*d* a lb'.[1]

He recalls for us the apprehensive atmosphere of early 1587, the near-panic, with the unprecedented Armada in its final stage of preparation against the small country, the state of mind in which the Catholic candidate for the throne – in case the invasion was successful – was brought to book. 'Many lies, false tales and strange news running, like to make an uproar, which made many folks at their wits' end to hear thereof. For the most part all false. The Queen of Scots beheaded, noise of wars, and our ships stayed in France.'

All this book is an exposure of the Elizabethan mentality, its mercurial character, credulity and sense of illimitable possibilities – hence the stimulus to the imagination for its poetry and drama: life itself had the tone of drama. But here again is some evidence of the difficulties in interpreting these authentic relics of the age. The name Eure appears in three different forms: Eure, Evers, Every. The most common is Evers, and that was fairly certainly how it was pronounced. We can now identify Forman's client, William Evers, as the brother of Ralph, Lord Eure, Warden of

[1] 384.

the Middle Marches. They belonged to an ancient Border Family, and the brothers were much attached to each other. William Evers came to consult Forman, 13 May 1597, when he was twenty-seven; he was suffering from some poisoned air and bad medicines; 'he hath a slimy flux – matter in bowels and reins'. Next day he 'took first, 3*s*, of my strong water'.[1]

Mr Evers told Simon something that fascinated him, of the boy with the Golden Tooth at Prague, and 'whether he shall prove a prophet or no: this boy is at Prague with a nobleman. He is between eleven and twelve years old: he is prophetical and wonderful in many things. He saith there shall come one with an iron tooth, and then it shall be known what he is. He saith all his teeth shall be gold.' Simon gives us information, otherwise unknown, that Lord Eure's brother was born 19 January 1569. This Border fighting tough believed this kind of thing just as much as Simon. Even that wise old owl, the great Lord Burghley, had believed that Dr Dee coined dross into gold when he was in Prague in 1588, and besought him at the crisis of the Armada to come home for the benefit of his country and coin gold to pay for its defence.[2] The point is that most people believed nonsense, as always – it is only the character of the nonsense that varies with the time.

In June Mr Evers came to inquire how he should 'speed in this voyage'.[3] This is the Islands Voyage. It seems he will alter his estate in this voyage three times: from worse to better, then from better to worse, and shall be lord of substance, but not have the use for his own profit. He shall be dignified by the general. He was: a note adds, 'he was knighted'. It does not appear to be known otherwise how and when he acquired his knighthood – evidently from Essex, and this is the grouping to which we find subsequently he belonged. Mr John Aske, who lived in the aristocratic enclave of Cold Harbour on the Thames next Billingsgate, was a regular client: he too wanted to know how he should speed in this voyage. I do not know whether he went.

[1] 226.
[2] cf. *The Elizabethan Renaissance: the Life of the Society*, 251.
[3] 226.

On 14 May Forman casts to know whether Sir William Evers be slain or no.[1] Next day he went to dress him for his wound. This is interpreted for us by John Chamberlain, writing to Carleton: Lord Eure and Sir William, walking in the street with one page, had been attacked by five Widdringtons 'about a country quarrel' – a Border feud.[2] They had both been hurt, Sir William seriously, but likely to recover. In December 1599 Sir William's young nephew, called after him, son and heir of Lord Eure, has a licence to travel abroad for three years.[3] Meanwhile, in May 1598, Forman had noted the conclusion of peace between France and Spain: the Peace of Vervins.

The winter of 1598–9 in London was filled with preparations for equipping and dispatching the largest army that had ever been sent into Ireland, to conquer the resistance of Ulster. Essex was to be in command; he took his leading follower with him, young Southampton, as his General of Horse. The play that Southampton's former poet was writing that year, *Henry V*, is topically full of the preparations:

> Now all the youth of England are on fire,
> And silken dalliance in the wardrobe lies;
> Now thrive the armourers, and honour's thought
> Reigns solely in the breast of every man.

The play was written and performed before Essex's disgraceful return in September, after the fiasco he perpetrated in Ireland; for Shakespeare writes in the last Chorus of the play:

> Were now the General of our gracious Empress –
> As in good time he may – from Ireland coming,
> Bringing rebellion broached on his sword,
> How many would the peaceful city quit
> To welcome him!

Always popular (in spite of, or, more probably because of, his

[1] 195.
[2] *The Letters of John Chamberlain*, ed. N. E. McClure, I. 37.
[3] *Cal. S.P. Dom., 1598–1601*, 355.

defects), he had been given a grand send-off from the City in March:

> But now behold
> In the quick forge and working-house of thought,
> How London doth pour out her citizens!

Like everyone else Forman was greatly excited. On 19 March he put the question to know how the Earl of Essex would speed and whether he would prevail or no. The calculations from the horoscope follow.

There seems to be in the end of his voyage negligence, treason, hunger, sickness and death. He shall not do much good to bring it to effect. At his return much treachery shall be wrought against him; the end will be evil to himself, for he shall be imprisoned or have great trouble. He shall find many enemies in his return and have great loss of goods and honour; much villainy and treason shall be wrought against him to the hazard of his life, because the moon goeth to Jupiter. Yet he shall escape it with much ado after long time, much infamy and trouble.[1]

This follows the regular style of Forman's forecasts, yet it comes oddly close to what ensued. Other people may have had similar apprehensions, but with Forman there seems to have been an element of the psychic.

On 27 March Forman put the question as to how Essex would speed, at 2.15 p.m. It seems that Simon was among the citizens who saw him leave.

He took horse at the Tower about 1 o'clock, up the Crutched Friars and up Cheapside with some hundred horse. About 2 o'clock it began to rain, and at 3 till 4 there fell such a hail-shower that was very great. Then it thundered withal and the wind turned to the north; after the shower was past it turned to the south-east again. And there were many and mighty clouds up. But all the day, before 1 o'clock, was a very fair day, and four or five days before bright and clear, and very hot like summer.

The moon's aspect was unfavourable.

Others, too, noted the sudden and ominous turn in the weather.

[1] 219.

Camden tells us, Essex was 'accompanied out of London with a gallant train of the flower of the nobility and followed by the people with joyful acclamations. But it happened to thunder in the clear day, and a violent shower followed soon after.'[1] Forman was not the only one to take it for 'an ominous prodigy'.[2] The event was in keeping with the forecast.

As usual Essex exceeded his commission by creating an enormous number of knights, nearly sixty, and Forman notes them down. Essex was engaged in building up a personal following within the state, to have the decisive word and jockey himself into arbitrary control at the Queen's death. For this purpose he made the traitorous truce with Tyrone, and was in touch with the King of Scots, anxious to advance the happy day of his march south into the promised land.

Sir William Evers was one of his emissaries, for early in 1601 – while Essex was planning his *coup* in the City – Evers was in Scotland, having secret conference with James at dead of night. This was reported by Sir Robert Carey to Cecil; when Evers returned to London he was confined to his house and made to explain himself to the Queen.[3] His forwardness, however, won him high favour with James when he at length succeeded. Meanwhile it had kept him out of harm's way during Essex's fatal outbreak into the City.

At once upon the outbreak, on 8 February, Forman casts to know, in Latin, what would come to Essex, whether he would be taken and imprisoned, whether guilty and what his enemies would do against him.[4] A note adds, 'he was taken in his house the night following and carried to the Tower'. Next day, Forman cast 'whether Lord Essex will be executed, life or death'. On 18 February Frances Bevill and Frances Howard put their first question, 'whether Essex and Southampton will die'. Two days later Forman casts to know whether Southampton dies; another couple of days, whether Essex will live or die. The answer came: 'they

---

[1] W. Camden, *The History . . . of Elizabeth*, ed. 1675, 569.
[2] q. J. E. Neale, *Queen Elizabeth*, 355.
[3] *Salisbury Mss.*, XI. 90, 567.
[4] 411.

shall not die, but live in prison'. This was wrong, for on 25 February, 'Essex was beheaded this day about 7.30 a.m.' Next day, the question was whether Southampton would be beheaded. He was not, but remained in the Tower – with the occasional attendance of Dr Paddy for his health – until he emerged into the light of day, and royal favour, with James's accession.

On 7 September 1599 Dorothy Killigrew came from fashionable Canon Row to consult Forman about her health. She was thirty-five; her symptoms were much colour and phlegm in the blood and in the lungs; in Latin, she is pregnant at this time.[1] This poor lady was having a bad time of it, with her husband, John Killigrew of Arwennack, the manor-house that still remains in part upon Falmouth harbour, close by Pendennis Castle. His father and grandfather had been governors of it; his uncle was Sir Henry Killigrew, the strait-laced diplomat and brother-in-law of Burghley; his cousin, William, in intimate attendance upon the Queen as Groom of the Privy Chamber.

Nothing of this could save John Killigrew from the consequences of his depredations upon shipping in and about Falmouth, being hand-in-glove with pirates, receiving stolen goods, etc., and the general extravagance and disorder of his conduct. His wife was the daughter of Sir Thomas Monk, of the family of General Monk who brought about the Restoration.[2] The poor lady had replied to her husband's request for money, 'sorry I am, but help you I cannot. Pawns I have not. I have sent to your tenants according to your directions, but none will come near me, neither do know by what means to get you money. I have passed all that ever I have or can make shift for.'[3]

Her husband was writing to cousin Robert Cecil:

All the good that ever we received, saving by my father, came only from your Honour's father . . . The Lord knows my innocency, only I have confessed that I have bought and sold with men of war that were

---

[1] 219.

[2] J. L. Vivian, *The Visitations of Cornwall*, 269.

[3] *Salisbury Mss.*, VIII. 155.

allowed in the service of her Majesty, set out and maintained at sea by great persons. I have been close prisoner this three months, not knowing certainly my offence, my living taken from me, my woods, and my necessary places about my house utterly ruinated. These be my comforts, this is my reward for thirty years' service in the Court. Happy had my wife been and her children if, when the Spaniards were at my house, they had the spoil of it. Then had their miserable days been ended.

This was mere rhetoric: the family continued and flourished in the next two generations. It seems that this member of it had made a great fool of himself. We cannot go into his story here, but, for all his grand connections at Court, he did not get out of prison. He was still in prison in 1604, and seems to have died there: he must have been much to blame.

A more unfortunate prisoner was James Fitzgerald, known as the Tower Earl or the Queen's Earl of Desmond, who had been held in the Tower for sixteen years after the Munster rebellion of his father. Upon the outbreak of rebellion in Ulster the politic Tyrone put forward the lad's cousin as rightful Earl. To break the unity of the factions Sir George Carew, governing Munster, suggested sending the imprisoned Fitzgerald over with the title restored. The English government was doubtful of success, but eventually agreed to try it. On 23 September 1600 Forman cast to know 'how James Fitzgerald, Earl of Desmond, shall speed in Ireland when he comes there. – He went away to Ireland some eight days after.'[1]

He sped quite well and was well received by his people – until a Sunday came, when, instead of going to Mass as they expected, he went to the Protestant church. This finished him with his expectant people, and he returned in despair to England. He was a sickly fellow, who had constantly needed medical attention in the Tower. On his return to Westminster in October he came to consult Forman who diagnosed 'a cold palsy', a kind of stroke; he was forty-one. A mysterious message sent on his behalf inquires whether it was best to marry; but a note adds, 'he died 11 November following, and some did suppose that some of his

[1] 236.

countrymen had given him some dram to rid him out of the way'.[1]
This was the rumour at the time, which subsequent Irish writers
have transposed into the suggestion that the English poisoned
him! They had every reason not to do so: he was their man; nor
is there any reason to suppose that the Irish poisoned him either,
though they had more of a motive for doing so. Enough to know
that sickly as he was, he just died.

Another Court figure who appears in April 1601 is Gilbert
Talbot, who 'himself sent', presumably his urine. The diagnosis is
'cold phlegm, melancholy in the stomach, full of cold humours'.
His age is given as forty-eight, which was that of Gilbert Talbot,
the rich but valetudinarian seventh Earl of Shrewsbury, who
married Bess of Hardwick's daughter. A Catholic convert, she
inherited her mother's formidable gift for intrigue, and tried to
spirit her niece, Arabella Stuart, out of the country as a candidate
for James's throne. It is quite likely that the Earl preferred to
drop his title for purposes of consultation.

This seems to have been the case, too, with a lady who consulted Forman at 4.15 p.m., 22 March 1598, 'against the Chequer
in the Strand'.[2] This sounds like a place of appointment; great
ladies could come to one in secrecy or disguise. The lady came as
Bridget Kingsmill –

alias the Lady Norris, of twenty-four years. She hath not been well long
time. She took it in child-bed by some ointment or other thing that she
did put into her quent, which did infect and envenom her blood. She
hath a truckling in her flesh, like the stinging of nettles, and a rising of
blood into her lungs, periplomania, much gravel in the reins, catarrh,
fearfulness and trembling . . . strangury and pain in the poll and hinder
part of her head. She is an enemy to herself and will not be ruled; not
well in her matrix . . . a venomous humour so that she is often in great
pain.

Who was this young lady, who seems to have given an alias
and had such a plethora of ill symptoms, that one would have
thought she had not long to live? She was the great Robert
Cecil's niece, daughter of the gifted but neurotically unstable

[1] 411.
[2] 195.

Earl of Oxford, who wasted the whole of his estate and made his wife, Burghley's daughter, miserable. He gave poor Lord Burghley much trouble, who in the end had to take his daughter and grand-daughters under his wing and provide for them. He could well afford to, and this young lady had an inheritance of £8500, when she was married to Francis, Lord Norris of Rycote – that lovely house of which a wing remains in the meadows outside Thame. Francis's grandfather had died for the sake of Anne Boleyn; it was in this house that Elizabeth used to stay with the family on her way to Oxford.

Like many Cecils, Lady Norris was a good deal of a hypochondriac, always worrying about her health, as we learn from letters from and about her to her uncle. Next year she was ill again and consulting Dr Paddy, who 'is peremptory that she hath taken mercury sublimate' – Forman had thought she was in danger of the pox, and this concoction was the recognised treatment. Evidently she liked dosing herself with medicines. 'My Lady was much afraid of death after they had showed her the basin, and called for . . . the truth from the doctors' mouths . . . and was after much distempered with heat.'[1]

We need not follow this tiresome young woman or her endless complaints about her health to Sir Robert Cecil, who had so many burdens to carry. Suffice it to say that, like her parents too, she was miserable in marriage, at length separated from her husband and lived long to survive him.

Another lady, to become far more important in public life, indeed the first lady in the land after James's Queen and daughter, was a devotee of Forman's. This was Frances Howard, daughter of Viscount Howard of Bindon. Perhaps her devotion was the less surprising when we see how remarkably Simon's forecast was fulfilled in her well-publicised career. She stands out, among all the characters in this book, a fantastic personality, with all the Howard family pride and ambition, with her credulity and snobbishness, her pertinacity and ultimate triumph – a figure that is a gift to any writer.

[1] *Salisbury Mss.*, IX. 256.

She first comes to Forman in May 1597, when she was nineteen: born 27 July 1578, 9.30 p.m., at Lytchett in Dorset, *'in a fortunate conjunction: she shall change her estate three times.* She hath a woman enemy, tall, long visage and ruddy.'[1] (Was this the Queen? There is no evidence that she took any notice of this Frances Howard, or did anything for her.) There were two more Frances Howards of the time: the Queen's maid-of-honour, who was the Earl of Hertford's second wife, and Lady Frances Howard, married to Essex's son, whom she detested, longed for Robert Carr and got him.

Our present Frances's father, the first Viscount, owned property at Marnhull in Dorset, where his second and third wives were buried.[2] It may be that this is where Forman came to know so much about his client from her early days. Her mother, the third wife, had been a mere Mabel Burton, a middle-class woman. But Frances was the grand-daughter of a duke: Howard blood boiled within her.

Left an orphan as a child of two, she made the best of her prospects, with great assiduity, all her life. At nineteen she was already married, beneath her, as she considered, to the son of a very rich Alderman, Henry Pranell, vintner. But she aspired to higher things. This summer of 1597, when Forman was making the acquaintance of Shakespeare's deleterious Dark Lady, other ladies were sighing for his patron Southampton, the young Earl still, as yet, unmarried. In June Frances put the question on behalf of Catherine Howard 'alias Nevill' [sc. Knyvet], wife of Thomas Howard, for Henry Wriothesley, Earl of Southampton'. This Catherine was the wife of Lord Thomas Howard, the naval commander, and mother of the desperate young poisoner of Overbury. A most designing woman, she made her husband rich at the state's expense – at least we have Audley End to show for it – and was said to have been Robert Cecil's mistress.

In July Frances Howard alias Pranell sent her urine. 'She hath taken some grief or discontent and cold; a rheumatic body, weak in the reins and a heat in the *Renus tenorea*' (sic). Next month 'she

---

[1] 226.

[2] *The Complete Peerage*, ed. G.E.C., VI. 583.

previous page Frances
Howard as Dowager
Duchess of Richmond
and Lennox

left Richard Napier
alias Sandy

below Richard
Sandy's Rectory,
Great Linford

Frances Howard, Countess of Essex and Somerset

DR SIMON FORMAN,

ASTROLOGER.

Engraved from the Original Drawing

in the Collection of the Right Honble

LORD MOUNTSTUART.

Publish'd July 1.1776 by F. Blyth N.º 87. Cornhill.

Simon Forman from an eighteenth-century engraving

supposes herself with child . . . she hath not had her course, *sed non est gravida*' (she is not pregnant). She remained childless – a great advantage in the re-marriage market.

In January 1598 Mrs Pranell is gunning for Southampton for herself: she asks 'whether he will be better friendly or not, and what will happen to her.' In June she puts the significant question 'whether she will be a widow or not' – such a happy consummation would open up better prospects. In July she received the consoling forecast: 'he [Southampton] leaves his old love – in time will marry Frances'. This was not to be. He was engaged in making Elizabeth Vernon pregnant – another frail maid-of-honour to anger the maiden Queen; when the job was done, Essex, who was her cousin, made the young man, with reluctance, marry her. Simon, as usual, is informative: we learn that Mistress Vernon was already twenty-nine years and two months when this came about, only a month or two before her baby was born. For her, a narrow squeak. Mrs Pranell was unwell: she sent her urine: she had taken grief and cold, and was suffering from a flux and rheumatic in her reins. In August 'Frances Howard alias Pranell' sent another specimen of her water: 'she supposeth herself with child.' But she was not.

In October she inquires 'whether her husband will come home from sea'. On 10 January 1599 she wants to know whether the Earl of Southampton – Simon has it in Latin to make secure – will love her better or no, and what will happen to her. The Earl is now married: Elizabeth Vernon has got her man. On 10 February Frances questions 'whether he doth bear her any good will, or did tell of the letter; whether she shall speed in the country, and whether the Earl will return'. The answer was, 'he bears her little good will and she will do ill in the country'. Southampton was on the eve of departure with Essex for Ireland. A further inquiry may relate to her husband: 'he will return about 23 May or Bartholomew-tide; he will have loss in his goods and want of money to spend. He bears her little good will now, or none.'

Whichever this relates to, Pranell disappears from view; presumably he did not return. This left her at twenty, a rich widow, with no hostages to fortune in the way of children, and very much available. In February 1600 she came to know 'what suitors she hath'.[1] In spite of Southampton's marriage she has not given up hopes of him. Forman has a note of 2 March 1600: 'I told her that she shall marry again once more before she enjoy her love Southampton . . . Stay unmarried till Midsummer be past, for it seemeth about the 22 May next she will contract or marry herself to somebody. Some fret [disagreeable] thing will fall out between Southampton and her [his wife]. He or his wife will be in peril of death before Midsummer. She [Frances] shall do well.' Then, in Latin, it seems that either he or his wife will die.[2]

There follows a letter, in a beautiful youthful Italian hand, from which we see the form in which his Court-clients who were women addressed him:

Father, how much I think myself beholding unto you I cannot express. Notwithstanding, I do exceedingly desire to speak with you concerning the conference I lately had with you, entreating you, as ever you will pleasure me, to deal as effectually in those things then mentioned as possibly you can – that at your coming to me (which I hope you will hasten with all convenient speed) I may be assured of the event of all things. Whether they will fall out sinisterly or prosperously I do not greatly care, so that I may be ascertained of the truth: the which, in regard of the great trust I repose in you, I doubt not but you will effect according to my desire. Thus, my kind considerations being remembered unto you, in haste I leave you.

Your loving daughter,
Frances.

To the signature Forman added Howard; and there is a post-script:

I pray you send me word by this bearer when your best leisure will serve you to come to me, and in the meantime use such means that I may at your coming be certified of everything at large.

We observe in this missive the lofty Howard tone characteristic of her, and also the complete dependence on Forman's occult

[1] 236.
[2] 208.

powers. The letter exemplifies the form he evidently exacted from his 'daughters': it is corroborated later in the notorious case of the younger Frances Howard, as we shall see.

What the 'things mentioned' between them were we learn from Forman's note: 'what wooers she hath, with whom and when she shall marry, and of her old love [Southampton] – what will become of him, whether she shall enjoy him or no; if yea, whether best to tarry for him, or no'.

Things did not fall out according to the lady's desire: Southampton's wife did not die, neither did he; they continued happily married. The widow Pranell had to look elsewhere.

In April a suitor turns up: young William Evers, Lord Eure's heir, inquires whether to marry Frances Pranell and what are his prospects in marriage, honour and wealth. 'He shall marry, it seems, a widow somewhat elderly; a kind, soft and honest woman, somewhat fat and very rich. But he shall not marry Frances.' One notes the familiar use of her Christian name.

Next day, his uncle Sir William Evers, now thirty, wants to know 'what good or bad fortune he shall have by the wars'. There follows a long and detailed forecast, which we need not go into: I do not know whether it was verified or not.

His nephew must have declared his suit, for in November Frances puts the question whether best to marry him: 'there be one she calleth son or child, a red beard; beware of treachery by him'. Again that month, whom shall she marry? Two days later: should she marry Lord Hertford, would she have any child by him? Would William Evers marry, and whom? 'It seems it may be a match, but hardly within seven days or seven weeks. Will Evers will come on Sunday night.' On 26 December, what ill is there towards her?

By this time many people were interested in the question upon whom the lot would fall: a rich young widow could make her own choice. John Chamberlain reports, 'Mistress Pranell is like to make a wide stride from that she was, to be Countess of Hertford; the world says they be assured already, if not married.'[1] The marriage took place secretly – understandably after the

[1] Chamberlain, I. 113, 116.

difficulties Hertford had encountered over his previous two marriages. Archbishop Whitgift suspended the prebendary of Westminster for performing the ceremony clandestinely, without banns or licence, and not in church. And one disappointed suitor, Sir George Rodney of Somerset, went clean off his head with chagrin: 'his brains were not able to bear the burden, but have played bankrupt and left him raving'. It was said that he wrote her 'a dying love-song with his blood, and ran himself on his sword'.[1]

The Earl of Hertford was hardly calculated to make a woman happy, but at least he could make Mrs Pranell a Countess. He had had dreadful trouble in his youth for his ambitious, and surreptitious, marriage with Henry VIII's niece, Lady Catherine Grey, with her near claim to the throne. He had spent some years in the Tower, and his marriage was declared invalid; he incurred the Queen's displeasure again when he tried to have this declaration set aside. To the stuck-up pride of the Seymours – simply because Jane Seymour had attracted Henry VIII's eye and her brother become Protector – the son added a querulousness all his own. He and Frances did not make a happy couple. Gossip said that, when his elevated bride got beyond herself, he would say, 'Frank, how long is it since thou wert married to Pranell?'[2] No one would allow her to forget that she had been married to a vintner.

In February she lost her ring – an omen, of course.[3] In November she twice put the question whether she was pregnant. No – merely sand in her back. But the figure indicated that she would be pregnant. She was not – and this much increased her value in the marriage market. She introduced Forman into the house in Canon Row; he tells us that in 1601, 'I came acquainted with my Lord of Hertford, and with my Lady Mary,' his sister.[4] One November night, as Simon and his man were coming away from the house they were 'like to have been both killed by Captain Hammond that was drunk'.

---

[1] *The Complete Peerage*, ed. G.E.C., VI. 505–6.
[2] q. E. Wingfield-Stratford, *The Lords of Cobham Hall*, 96.
[3] 411.
[4] v. later, Autobiography, p. 298–9.

To keep his treasure out of harm's way the Earl kept her a good deal down in the country. The rusticated Countess complained to Lady Mary, to whom her brother retorted, 'I have been told that you greatly pity the estate of my wife, that if she did there would be plots laid to entrap her . . . I cannot understand how my wife's estate is to be pitied, unless she does not discern her own happiness or acknowledge from whom, next under God, it came. Whatever she has been to me, I resolve to deal honourably with her.'[1] We hear of her rabbit-hunting in the warren at Old Sarum, but that in no way corresponded with the greatness of her mind.[2]

Her chance came when the Earl died, and she was free to change her estate a third time, as the stars had foretold many years before. For Hertford kept his word and left her now very rich indeed: 'better than £4000 jointure, besides his house in Canon Row, a fair house with a park and £300 or £400 a year belonging to it to her and the heirs of her body lawfully begotten, whereof there is no great danger'.[3]

With such wealth, and no children to share it, she could attract the greatest match in the kingdom, King James's cousin, Ludovic Stuart, Duke of Lennox. Not long after Hertford died she married the Duke, and at one bound entered the royal family. She at once gave herself regal airs and 'took state upon her', setting up a canopy of state, which people thought quite out of date.[4] The only duchess in the land, and a royal one, she became an intimate of the family and the rising Buckinghams. Next year she was dining in the King's Privy Chamber, though the King – who was very informal – was in bed. Intimacy did not prevent her from demanding £10,000 from the royal milch-cow to pay the Duke's debts, which she said had been promised before she would yield to the marriage.

She went round everywhere with the royal family: we find the King at beautiful Cobham to prevail on Lady Kildare to part with it to the Lennoxes – this is how they came by Cobham Hall, where

---

[1] *Bath Mss.*, IV. 161–2.
[2] *Cal. S.P. Dom.*, *1611–18*, 59.
[3] Chamberlain, II. 364.
[4] ibid., 375, 408, 434, 436.

they remained.[1] Rich Lady Hatton sold them her house in Hol-born.[2] When Prince Charles gave the French Ambassadress a parting jewel, the Duchess gave her one too, but embellished with her picture. The elevation of Buckingham to a dukedom – for what services? – was 'to the great disgust of the Duchess Lennox, who is said to labour all she can to reign still alone'. She had to be consoled by the creation of her husband Duke of Richmond, with its royal association; after which she was known as the Double Duchess, or, 'as some wags call her, the Duchess cut upon Duchess'. The couple now changed from Hertford's old house in Canon Row to the grander Ely House.

It is pleasant to record that the Duchess's niece married into trade, as she herself had so fortunately done: the girl married our old friend Sir Robert Napier's son, 'or Sandy as he was called when he was a merchant of this town'.[3] Nor did her curiosity or credulity fail in regard to the magical or merely wondrous. As a boy the poet and dramatist Sir William Davenant was her page: 'she sent him to a famous apothecary for some unicorn's horn, which he was resolved to try with a spider, which he encircled in it. But without the expected success: the spider would go over, and through and through, unconcerned.'[4]

But with the Duke's death in 1624 her brief reign was over – and unkind people laughed at the extreme show of passionate grief she put up, having already buried two husbands with equanimity. They put it down to the realisation that this was the end of her reign. Her presumption and her antics continued. People said that she might marry Lord Chancellor Bacon though fallen – anything to become prime courtier again.[5] When the Duke of Brunswick came over, she received him with the proviso that he must not offer to kiss her. At Ely House, in her retirement, she had as many Lenten sermons and chaplains to preach them as at Whitehall. And when she moved to Exeter House she did so in

[1] ibid., 441.
[2] ibid., 446, 477, 488, 498, 499.
[3] ibid., 495, 545, 551.
[4] Aubrey, I. 205.
[5] Chamberlain, II. 560, 594, 605, 612.

pomp, with a royal cortège of coaches, the young Duke, several earls and countesses and many peeresses following. There she set up her cloth of state as a royal widow.

We have a portrait of her from this time in her final widowhood, perhaps one of those she bequeathed in her will – it has fetched up at The Vyne, near Basingstoke. In it she proudly sports the letters FRL on the handkerchief she is holding, for everybody to see. She looks surprisingly young, fair flaxen hair, milk-white complexion, small head and a pretty pink mouth to kiss (or not to). She looks very pleased with herself, as she had reason to be. She is wearing a black mourning ring and two other wedding rings on the left hand, her right demonstratively carrying a staff. Her mourning garments are not exaggeratedly black, her pale breast is a good deal exposed, with a thick lace ruff around the little neck.

She did not change her estate a fourth time, that the prophecy might be fulfilled. She lived on until 1639, the threshold of the Civil War, devoting herself to raising an enormous monument in Henry vii's Chapel in Westminster Abbey, where she and her Duke rest – coronets, caryatids, black marble and bronze-gilt, crowned by the figure of Fame – just across from that king and his queen, Elizabeth of York.

Young Mrs Pranell had indeed made a success of things.

We have seen that Forman had been acquainted with old Lord Chamberlain Hunsdon's son, Sir George Carey, as far back as 1587, Simon's queasy Salisbury days, and we have profited from the extraordinary chance – though not unlikely in itself – that brought Hunsdon's ex-mistress to him as a client and so revealed to us the identity of Shakespeare's Dark Lady.

There are other traces that mark him on the margins of the Hunsdon family. We have seen Hunsdon's daughter Margaret, Lady Hoby, consulting him after a visit to Mrs Blague's in April 1601. She returned later that month, with gout in her hands and feet and swellings in her joints; she was only thirty-four, but the disease had been long upon her.[1] Now in May Lady Hoby is

[1] 411.

anxious for her brother, who is dangerously ill, and wants to know whether 'the Lord Chamberlain will live or die'. The answer: 'he is an enemy to himself, he doth hurt himself'.

This adds its own reverberation to the verses on him in the familiar Court-lampoon of this time:[1]

> Chamberlain, Chamberlain,
> He's of her Grace's kin:
> Fool hath he ever been
> With his Joan Silverpin.
> She makes his cockscomb thin
> And quake in every limb:
> Quicksilver is in his head,
> But his wit's dull as lead –
> > > Lord for thy pity.

Other Court-figures, too, are hit off with merciless precision in this last year of the Queen's reign, after Essex's rising:

> Little Cecil trips up and down,
> He rules both Court and Crown,
> With his brother Burghley, clown
> In his great fox-furred gown –
> With the long proclamation
> He swore he saved the town –
> > > Is it not likely?

Here is Ralegh:

> Ralegh doth time bestride;
> He sits twixt wind and tide,
> Yet uphill he cannot ride
> For all his bloody pride —

exactly: the thought maddened him. And here is the true story of Mary Fitton, as opposed to the rubbish written about her in this century, by people who know nothing about the time in which she lived. (So far from being a dark lady, she had auburn hair and

---

[1] The poem is quoted in full in C. C. Stopes, *Life of Henry, Third Earl of Southampton*, 235–7.

blue eyes – so much for all the nonsense written about her.) In the following verse she is the white doe, Pembroke the young Earl who undid her, the clown was Sir William Knollys who was besotted on her, the Reindeer the Queen, rendered furious (again):

> The Reindeer was embossed (i.e. foaming),
> The white doe she was lost:
> Pembroke struck her down
> And took her from the clown —
> Lord for thy pity.

The year before, in April 1600, the Lord Chamberlain – accompanied by his wife and Lady Hoby – had gone down to Bath for his disease,[1] as the playwright had done after his affair with the old Lord Chamberlain's mistress:

> I, sick withal, the help of Bath desired
> And thither hied, a sad distempered guest.[2]

For Hunsdon, evidently badly affected, it was to no avail: he died in 1603.

A further trace or two remain in the papers. Forman has a note that Lady Hoby's niece, who married Lord Berkeley's son and heir, was delivered of a son, 7 October 1601.[3] This was the second Hunsdon's only daughter. When she was left a widow, a mere Justice of King's Bench paid a pretty penny to marry such a noble lady: he made her a jointure of £1000 a year and was to leave her Berkeley son £10,000.[4]

We noticed Mrs Blague's concern to know what ailed Lord Scrope, brother-in-law of her friend Lady Hoby – and Forman's verdict, 'some discontent about his father'. The Queen had been very generous to her Hunsdon cousins and looked after them well all her life. Upon the old Chamberlain's death she made an outright gift of £400 to his widow, and renewed to her his

[1] *Sidney Papers*, ed. A. Collins, II. 187.
[2] Shakespeare's Sonnet 153.
[3] 411.
[4] Chamberlain, II. 424.

keepership of Somerset House (which Emilia Bassano would have known) – Lady Hoby had a room there.[1] The handsome sum of £800 was provided for the old lord's funeral, which enabled the family to give him the largest monument in Westminster Abbey.

Lady Hoby's sister, Philadelphia Lady Scrope, was a lady-in-waiting. She was not backward in claiming provision for herself. In 1606 she is writing to Lord Salisbury (who had made enormous provision for *him*self – we at least have Hatfield to show for it):

None knows better than yourself my services to my late Queen and dear mistress, and that my gain was small, considering the expectation of my place. By your directions I attended her Majesty that now is [Queen Anne] from Warwick hither, to my great charges and some pains. The rest of my fellows in that service have had satisfaction, and I only remain unrewarded. My dear mother had a pension of £200 a year during her life out of the Exchequer; and now it has pleased God to take her, my request is I may have the same pension.[2]

The state was a milch-cow for them all; there was a pretty scramble for the dugs.

Of other Court-ladies, public personages, we will name only a few. In 1601 came Catherine Bertie, daughter of Peregrine, Lord Willoughby – she was called after her grandmother, the dowager Duchess of Suffolk who married the handsome young Master of her Horse. The grand-daughter had been born on Whit Sunday 1586 at 4.40 a.m. Her horoscope said 'she shall contract herself twice, and twice be with child. Her portion shall fall into the hands of her brother'.[3] In fact she married only once, Lewis Watson, who became Lord Rockingham, and died in childbed. The horoscope was wrong – but that never matters with believers.

On 15 February 1600 Dorothy Brereton 'herself came'.[4] She was thirty-five; 'her husband deals hardly with her and loves one

[1] *Cal. S.P. Dom., 1595–7*, 309.
[2] *Salisbury Mss.*, XVIII. 444.
[3] 206.
[4] 236.

Joan Richards in Wood Street. He had £200 per annum with her; now keeps her like a drudge and loves her not.' Simon pasted in the information that she had been married 30 June 1596, between 4 and 5 p.m. and was now 35–6: evidently no chicken. A note is added, 'desiring you to make the plaster for my back against Friday or Saturday if possible you can, for I endure great pain. You may tell this bearer how I must use the oil for hearing which you gave me, whether I must take it hot or cold.'[1] Such a close-up is fascinating: I know no other such exchanges between patient and doctor.

This poor lady we can identify. She was the daughter of Sir Richard Egerton of Ridley, and half-sister of the famous Lord Chancellor Ellesmere, who was his father's bastard. The girl had been married when only twelve to Richard Brereton of Tatton, lord of the manor of Worsley near Manchester.[2] Their only child died, and there were no more children, we can understand why. However, in the end, her husband left her his Lancashire estate for life, and this – with her large jointure – made her a very good match.

A Cheshire neighbour, Sir Peter Legh of Lyme, a widower of her own age, had his eye on her, for an early codicil to his will bequeathed 'unto my cousin Dorothy Brereton of Worsley, in regard of her assured affection and true friendship, my best jewel of diamonds'.[3] Shortly after he married her, and her happiness was at length assured. Even her stepson, his father's heir, could not object; for, in addition to the wealth she brought to the family, she had no children to dispute it. The boy wrote her a priggish Cambridge letter: 'I have been informed by some kind friends, whose commendations of you together with the great love and care of my father towards his children showed in this match, doth much comfort me. And I do hereby promise to you, as his second self, all duty and obedience.'

All went well. Sir Peter was enabled to add to the Legh lands; Dorothy proved an excellent housekeeper managing her own

[1] 219.
[2] *Visitation of Cheshire*, ed. Sir G. J. Armytage and J. P. Rylands (*Harleian Soc.*), 142.
[3] Lady Newton, *The House of Lyme*, 77 foll.

estate, as well as the fine black-and-white house at Worsley where the couple spent part of each year. Two portraits of her at Lyme attest the change in her circumstances. In the first the younger-looking face is sad and numb; she is all in black, no jewellery, hand on the Book. The second shows a middle-aged lady bedizened with jewellery, chains of pearls down to her waist, jewels and ornaments in her hat, beneath which is a very wide-awake face; and, in place of the Bible, one of her special breed of monkeys. When she came to die, she scattered legacies around in every direction. Life had been a success after all.

This can hardly have been the case with Jane, Lady Clifford, wife of Vice-Admiral Sir Alexander Clifford, himself much away at sea. Forman says of her: 'she is unfortunate to herself, slow and ketchless [thoughtless]; negligent and will consume herself'.[1] In the last two years of his life Forman had a patient in the Catholic Lady Dormer of Peterley, in the country some five miles north-west of Amersham in Buckinghamshire. On 8 and again on 9 September Lady Dormer sent her water; it was pronounced 'good but thin, little hypost' (atis), which means excess of blood.[2] In the previous years 1609 and 1610 Forman had had patients from the household. Now in September 1611 he was within a few days of his end. A note of later prescriptions for Sir William and Lady Dormer at Bath in 1614 is probably by Sandy alias Napier, who took them on from Forman's practice.

[1] 206.
[2] 335.

Chapter XI

Last Years: Virginia; the Overbury Murder

For the last ten years of Forman's life, that is, after 1601, no Case-Books survive; whether he kept them up we do not know. It seems improbable, or they might have come down to us. Instead we have a number of jottings over the years, and something like brief diaries, particularly for 1607, 1608 and 1609. But there remains a mass of manuscripts, over and above all this; there are papers, medical and astrological, above all the 'books' he wrote and by which he set such store.[1] Pathetic as we may think this, it is no more so than in the case of the theologians who also covered such reams – the chief difference is only that these got theirs published, to encumber libraries.

Simon also wrote on these subjects, so weighty a part of the mental baggage of the age. We have his treatise on the Creation of the Earth, with his commentary on 1 Genesis; another on Adam and Eve, very orthodox and religious, with additions, such as that Grandsil, Adam's daughter, was 120 feet long, lived a hundred years and died without issue.[2] We have an attempt to construct a Chronology of the World gathered out of the Bible, which was precisely what the great Sir Walter Ralegh was struggling with contemporaneously in the Tower, trying to make sense of the ages of the Patriarchs, Noah begetting the first of his sons in his five hundredth year, and so on; or attempting to work out the measurements of the Ark.[3] It throws a flood of light on the futility of so much human thinking at all times; Forman was no less sensible, or more credulous, than his contemporaries in these respects.

[1] Most of them are among the *Ashmole Mss.* in the Bodleian, but there are a few also in the British Museum.

[2] 802.

[3] cf. my *The Elizabethan Renaissance: the Cultural Achievement*, 300–2.

In 1600 we find him writing out the two books of Appolonius Niger on the Art of Memory and four on Stenography. Among the mass we find Thomas of Saxony's Commentary on Alcabitius, which had been stolen from him and recovered. We must confine ourselves to what Forman wrote, on top of everything else – he displayed a manic energy. He wrote a 'book' on Cako, the mineral substance which he used in the attempt to transmute metals. We have a parchment book on the Cabbala or Magia Naturalis, quoting Solomon, Daniel, etc; a book of Astronomy, quoting Cardan, with a table from Cornelius Agrippa, and a Greek alphabet, which he used for purposes of secrecy, though he did not know Greek. He wrote Latin fluently, if inaccurately. A book is devoted to *De Arte Geomantica*, with directions how to reduce the geomantical to the astronomical figure. And there is his Discourse on the Plague, of some value for its authentic description of symptoms. These represent his major intellectual interests: astrology, alchemy, magic, medicine.

It does not differ essentially from Dr Dee, who is treated with respect – too much so – nowadays. The chief difference is that Dee was worthy of respect as mathematician and geographer. These practical interests, in Forman's case, took the form of medicine: chiefly herbal lore, but to it he added some knowledge of the new Paracelsan mineral treatments. We have a few traces of Forman's dealings with apothecaries – he fell out with one in Bucklersbury. He casts to know whether to buy Mr Havers's rhubarb, Mr Offley's man in St Laurence Pountney.' It is not good. There came more rhubarb presently.'[1] He made his own lozenges and pills, one kind of algaric aloes, another of turbith (turpentine), senna and sulphur of wine.[2] For the French pox – salves, a strict diet, purging. For raising milk in women's breasts – lettuce, parsley, radishes, as it might be for rabbits. I have come across only one suggestion of an aphrodisiac – artichokes with oil and vinegar, at the growing of the moon. One observes sympathetic magic again.

There was in addition Forman's immense experience of dis-

[1] 226.
[2] 1411.

ease, with an emphasis, perhaps, on women's ailments. His diagnoses are mainly astrological, though he had an eye – what an eye! – and his exceptional psychopathic intuition. So we find diagrams of the body, with the signs of the Zodiac influencing relevant parts; drawings of abscesses in face and neck, of his own hand with its indications as to the future. There are notes about the uses of herbs: both hemp and poppy are dangerous, increasing a patient's lethargy; how to prepare tobacco, which was now coming in, for medical use; sassafras, also from America, used in treating the pox. We have instructions how to set figures for a large number of purposes, covering an astrologer's whole practice: to recover theft, to know about the absent, about a ship at sea, about journeys, whether wives are honest, to compel the love of someone, how to procure revenge. We note everywhere Forman's obsessive concern with himself – like Boswell or Pepys, Rousseau or Proust; in that most profitable, for the ego is the most rewarding of studies.

Men's lives are so much more interesting than what they suppose themselves to think. In the realm of thought it is only the thinking of exceptional persons that has value – in this period, such people as Copernicus, Vesalius, Galileo; Erasmus, Fernel, Montaigne; Gilbert, Hariot, Bacon; or intelligent persons like the Queen, Sidney, Ralegh or Shakespeare.

I have been criticised by a fellow-historian for my inadequate sympathy with sympathetic magic. Does he believe in sympathetic magic himself? What such people really dislike is my insistence on the truth, and especially its implications, that most of what passes for thought with most people is nonsense. (This book is a marvellous exposure of it.) The realisation of this means an immense saving of time and energy – to devote to the real achievements of the human mind, in the arts and sciences, poetry, music, literature and the wonderful works of men's hands.

With his marriage to a young gentlewoman of family and his permanent establishment at Lambeth, Forman achieved social standing and respectability. The fact that we know every un-respectable detail of his private life is no disproof of this: other people had their affairs too. His standing is publicly recognised and attested. In the parish registers he is regularly described as 'gentleman', as Dean Blague's sons were, or a few other parishioners, Mr John Throckmorton, John Arden, Christopher Wormall.

Notices of him and his family corroborate his own notes. His wife's mother came to stay for two months in the summer of 1601, with her second husband, two children and a manservant. Simon had had his own manservant now for years and, what with wife and maids, it was a full household. In his prosperity other members of his family came to lend a hand, or just to batten on him: sister Jane was a help, brother John was sickly and died that year. We find his brother Robert consulting him whether to take a house – 'it was very good' – and his mother sending for his advice before her death. Though he had never cared for her, from her early neglect of him, he had evidently made it up with her as an old woman.

The parish registers give us some indication of the Lambeth background and of the crudities of the age. Often enough a 'foundling' is picked up and baptised; in October Edmund Wynder was 'slain in the Marshes', in July next year Ely Elston was 'slain in the fields at Lambeth Marsh', in August the year following Laurence Hill was 'slain in the field' – evidently a favourite place for fools to fight it out, or for duelling.[1] With more sympathy we note the same year, 'a poor man which died in the field'; in 1605 'Sybilla, a poor woman that died at Foxhall' (i.e. Vauxhall), another 'poor woman which died in the church porch'. Or there are drownings: 'one drowned at London Bridge', another at Foxhall Barn, a third 'in my Lord's ditch', i.e. the Archbishop's moat; but perhaps that victim was drunk.

In October 1603 'a manservant of Mr Forman's' was buried. On 27 July 1605 Dorothy, 'the daughter of Simon Forman, gent.' was baptised, proudly given the name of her grandmother, sister of Sir Edward Munnings, knight, of Waldershare, near Dover. Six months later the child was buried; the same year followed her uncle, plain John Forman. And so we come to the

[1] Lambeth Parish Register, vol. I, 1539–1669.

entry of his burial, 12 September 1611, 'Simon Forman, gent.' Too busy (and successful) to take on parochial duties, on the only occasion upon which he appears at the annual making of the accounts before the Rector, Dean Blague, Mr Forman's name comes first.[1]

Lambeth was on a regular highway for the Queen's moves from Whitehall to Greenwich; whenever she passed through, the newly cast bells were rung. Several times she 'took water' at Lambeth Bridge for Fulham Palace, to visit the Bishop of London, or went through the Archbishop's yard, or took horse at his gate. In 1601 she came to dine with Archbishop Whitgift, and again with the Lord Chamberlain, the second Lord Hunsdon.

Simon was vastly proud of his wife's connections and gives us their coats of arms in colour: Bakers, Munnings, Grinfords, Chiches, Lovelaces.[2] Some are founder's kin at Magdalen College – there is the pathetic sense of frustration once more at this late date. And they are related to the Cornish Arundells of Trerice, whose descent he cites several times. To keep pace with this he equips himself with 'the true arms of Sir William Forman, knight', Lord Mayor of London. It is a nice problem to know whether Elizabethans really believed in what they fabricated. We shall find him regularly making note of the cousinage into which he married, the Sandys, 'my cousin Marsh', 'my cousin Harrison', above all, 'my cousin Twyne.' This is Thomas Twyne, a well-known doctor and antiquary, a man after Simon's own heart.

He was not without the contemporary curiosity about antiquities, if only he had had the time to indulge it, in the hurry and bustle of his life. There are ancient prophecies of the Britons in a History of the Britons at New College – Oxford again. He has notes on Arthurian personages, King Mark of Cornwall, Sir Tristram and Sir Gawain; we are treated to three pages of Arthurian doggerel –

When Arthur first in Court began, [etc.]

He was fascinated by Gogmagog the Giant,

[1] *Lambeth Churchwardens' Accounts, 1504–1645*, ed. C. Drew, Pt. II. 237. *Surrey Record Soc.*, XLIII.
[2] 802.

with whom Corineus wrestled when Brute came first into this land; he was twelve cubits high, and of such strength he took an oak in his arms, plucked up by the root, [etc.]¹

After all, there were primitive giants carved on the hill-sides, like the Cerne Giant, or presumably one on the hill of the name outside Cambridge, as there was at that time a Gogmagog on Plymouth Hoe, to puzzle Elizabethan scholarship. Apart from the questionable dimensions, this kind of pre-history was equated with history by contemporary historians, Camden, Carew and others, and it appears as such in plays like *Lear* and *Cymbeline*.

In Thanet was found

the tooth of a man standing upright in the cleft of a rock, a mighty battle-axe by him: I judged to be an eye-tooth 3½ inches long. John Russell, a chirurgeon of Canterbury and father-in-law [i.e. stepfather] to my wife was there when found, 1596. About 1603 I myself at Cambridge saw the cheek-tooth of a giant in an apothecary's shop that weighed 8lb net. Another they said was 8½ lb, but I saw not that. They were found in digging a gravel pit in Cambridge.

– evidently mammoth-tusks.²

He was at Cambridge to acquire, in June, the licence granted him by the university to practice medicine, 'after long exercise and experience'.³ The sponsors on behalf of the faculty were two ancient doctors: William Ward of Eton and King's, and Thomas Grimston, physician to Queen Elizabeth and King James.⁴ Grimston was a Norfolk man, possibly related to Forman's clients.

His marriage widened for him his Kentish connections, for which he owed much to the Blagues. A number of them he had known before, like the St Legers. He once writes their name as Sellinger, which is the way it was pronounced – as in the old folk-dance, Sellinger's Round. He thought that Mr St Leger meant to take advantage of him over some property deal. But St Leger came to him to know 'whether he would succeed to his

¹ 236.
² 802.
³ 1763.
⁴ Venn, Pt. I, II. 269; IV. 335.

inheritance, and when'. Answer – 'the enemies are strong'.[1] We learn from further inquiries that Mr St Leger was catarrhous and fifty, 'an enemy to himself and easy to be deceived in fair words'.

At the end of 1598 a young Kent couple had consulted Forman over the wife's pregnancy. This was Peter Manwood and his wife Frances, daughter of Sir George Hart of Lullingstone.[2] Peter was the son and heir of Sir Roger Manwood, the Chief Baron of the Exchequer, before whom Christopher Marlowe had appeared in a case of manslaughter – and Marlowe wrote his Latin epitaph in St Stephens by Canterbury. The young couple lived there in the mansion which the Judge's wealth had enabled him to acquire. The wife was with child, and could not 'stand the pricking and gnawing in her body. – It is a species of the pox, the blood envenomed of some false conception.'[3] In December both husband and wife appear. 'Some thirty-two days hence she will die, or be in great peril. She is very weak and faint – the sickness is of God and also natural – according to the signs.' Nothing of the sort: the couple proceeded to have a large number of children. After this depressing prognostic they did not appear again.

Ann Carew of Stone Castle did – to receive another ominous forecast: 'she will die of her disease'.[4] But she was sixty-four, and perhaps did. Stone Castle was near Dartford, and had been the Bishop of Rochester's in pre-Reformation days.

It is more cheering to encounter the fair Mistress Flud again, of whom Forman gave so vivid a pen-portrait with her loves for so many, Sir Calisthenes Brooke, Sir Thomas Gates and other warriors – without neglecting men of the cloth. She is now a widow at twenty-six, in May 1600, and would like to know whether Vincent Randall will marry her.[5] Forman's account is no more friendly than before, positively disapproving.

It seems she shall marry, but not yet a great while. But, in the end, with a miserable, ungodly, untoward old fellow. It seems she desires

[1] 226.
[2] *Visitation of Kent, 1619–21*, ed. R. Hovenden (*Harleian Soc.*, vol. 42), 144.
[3] 195.
[4] 219.
[5] 236.

him [Randall] more than he desires her. She is not to be trusted, though she has a fair tongue, but will backbite and speak evil of her best friends. She professes virtue, loyalty, chastity – yet is full of vice, apt to be in love with many: hath loved men of worth and base fearing creatures, and some of the clergy. She spends much in pride and is in debt, poor in respect. She is wavering-minded, light of conditions and will overthrow her own estate.

In fact, she did not.

One observes the double standard usual with humans, especially with men in regard to women in earlier centuries. Partly for obvious biological reasons: women were supposed to be virtuous, on account of child-bearing. But Mistress Flud bore no children, to husband or lovers. This left her free. Vincent Randall may have been the son of a knight, but Sir Thomas May of opulent Mayfield was the real thing. We do not know whether he qualified for Simon's disparaging adjectives, 'miserable', 'ungodly', etc.; but at any rate she married him.[1]

We may resume Forman's brief entries of the more important people coming to consult him – no longer the full astrological figures, calculations, diagnoses. A new reign, something of a new age – in spite of the continuity in his activities, we cannot but feel the difference in the air.

In April 1603 there is an interesting question for 'the two pictures my wife lost out of her closet. These pictures her cousin Chiche Parke carried away. The Monday before they had them and looked on them; after we could not find them. I sent to her the Wednesday following, but they denied them absolutely. The women had them not, but Chiche Parke had them and she [Mrs Forman] had them again.'[2] The full story is rather revealing. She took an old acquaintance 'up into her chamber to a closet where hanged certain fine small pictures'. They took them out to look at them; the friend 'would have begged them, but she would not give them away for anything. A kinsman of hers, standing by, put them into his hose and, forgetting them, went away with

---

[1] *Visitation of Sussex*, ed. W. B. Bannerman (*Harleian Soc.*, vol. 53), 105.
[2] 354.

them.'[1] One wonders; it shows how minatures were displayed, and how much valued.

In September 1603 he is treating Sir Robert Lane of Horton, Northamptonshire, for an apoplexy.[2] Perhaps this may have been induced by the overcrowding at Whitehall, when, before the coronation, James I knighted people in droves, over four hundred of them. The mob included several old acquaintances, Mistress Flud's husband, Thomas May; Bishop Thornborough's son and heir; two Penruddocks from Wiltshire, a couple of gentlemen ushers, and no less than five Ropers in a row.[3] This was to cheapen the order of knighthood indeed. The late Queen had been very conservative of the social order; the first Stuart, in a bid for popularity, was already cheapening it – and of course, too easy-going, never acquired the popularity. In 1605 Forman is treating another of these knights, Sir Edward Tyrrell of Thornton, Bucks.; in 1609, the wife of another, Lady Fortescue of Saldon. On 5 July 1607 Forman notes, in familiar terms, 'this day Paul was knighted' – naturally, for Sir George Paul was a neighbour as comptroller of the Archbishop's household; he subsequently wrote Whitgift's biography.[4]

At New Year 1604 Forman notes, for the first time, the gifts he received – he must have received a very great number in the course of his practice. 'On New Year's Eve Frances Edmund gave me a chamber cushion and a tin ladle; another woman, two great wax candles, 6*d*; Goodwife Williams' boy, 7 or 8 apples, 6*d*; another 10 apples; Susan of Westminster, a pair of young [new?] gloves.'[5] We have hardly any indications of payments, though from gentry, like the Blagues, these must have been large. In June 1600 Mr Bertram Bulmer, twenty-one, 'must pay me £7; received £3, 10 June.'[6] This man may have been a brother of the well-known Bevis Bulmer, engaged at this time in a search for gold on the Scottish Border. Forman casts to know whether

[1] 389.
[2] 174.
[3] cf. Shaw, II. 113 foll.
[4] 802; Shaw, II. 142.
[5] 384.
[6] 236.

Bertram will marry Isabel Tempest, of that Border family – in itself a pointer.

At the end of the month we have a thumb-nail sketch of a life-story in Forman's old style.

Dorothy Delamot *pro marito suo* [for her husband]: he being gone for France, whether he will come again to her; because she was not his married wife but his concubine, she was in doubt of his return. – He came again to London, 7 March, but came not to her; 12 March she met him: he passed by her and would not speak to her. She came home sorrowful, and sent after 2 p.m. to speak with him, but it would not be. 17 March she went herself to him, and he made her stay all night.[1]

It would seem people just cannot help themselves.

In 1605 Mr Glover wanted to know 'whether he shall come to some dignity'. – 'He did obtain it with much ado. The King did knight him before he was chosen the Marches ambassadors,'[2] i.e. to the Marquis Spinola in the Netherlands. In fact he went further as ambassador to Constantinople; there were difficulties in the way, for the salary was supposed to be paid by the Turkey merchants. Glover was knighted at Hampton Court when on leave in 1606.[3] Two years before, Sir Thomas Shirley found himself at the end of his tether in the Middle East, his pretensions exploded and himself laid by the heels; he regarded Glover as 'a great author of his tragedy'.[4] In the event the ambassador was summoned home under a cloud. Forman gives us a bit of private information about him: 'this man was in love with my Lady Cheyney's kinswoman and did marry her; yet he had another wife in Poland or Turkey'. Chamberlain finishes him for us: in 1625 coming from Court on Algiers business, Glover, 'before he had spoken two words, fell down stark dead, and was so poor that the Turkey Company was fain to be at charge to bury him'.[5]

Forman's later Diaries carry what Halliwell-Phillips described

[1] 205.
[2] 1488.
[3] *Salisbury Mss.* XVIII. 238.
[4] ibid., XVI. 371.
[5] Chamberlain, II. 615.

curtly as 'many halek notes': we must cite them, or some of them, for their interest to doctors and psychologists. They are absolutely not pornographic: their importance to Forman was simply factual, to note down the exact time in case of conception, for casting a horoscope. His pet-name for his wife is 'tronco', presumably from the Latin word for body. So we find in 1607: '31 March, 3 a.m., halek tronco'; similarly 3 April, 9 p.m., and 6 April 6.15, when he confesses himself tired out, 'confatus fui'.[1]

Nevertheless, next day he rode to Swanthrop, in the delightful country between Farnham and Odiham. 'I came first to see Swanthrop House; that afternoon we bargained for it, in the parish of Crondall, and was Giles Paulet's.' There is still a monument in the church there to a previous Paulet, Sir George, of 1558. Forman 'took it of William West, came home 9 April'. He was becoming a man of property; several times he casts to know whether to take this or that house. From the days of his entanglement with Sefton he had been able to lend out money; in 1610 he casts to know 'whether Danson will pay me my money or stand to the uttermost of the law'.[2] On 12 April at 4.10 'halek tronco', two days later at 9 p.m., 21 at 5.45, 23 at 5.30.[3] That day he was at Mr Larkin's after appearing before the Lord Chief Justice; a week later he was discharged of his recognisance. I do not know if this relates to a renewed attempt on the part of the Doctors; if so they were defeated.

On 2 May he was with Sir Bernard Whetstone's steward – another coronation knight – about More's copyhold: 'I bought it for £6 more.' Next day, 'halek tronco, 5.30 a.m., four days after her course'; similarly on the 6th and 11th. May 12 he rode to Swindon, back two days later. Next day 'halek tronco', and on 18th, 23rd, 29th at 10 p.m. with great desire on her part, in Latin. So much for May: his sexual energy was slowing down compared with what it had been. Perhaps we may omit further entries of regular intercourse with his wife and include only those that occur with other women, for their exceptional character.

[1] 802.
[2] 205.
[3] 802.

On 5 June 'Mr Lancaster was here'; next day Forman's wife went to Greenwich 'to be gossip to Mrs Holmes', i.e. godmother at a christening. '12 June 9 p.m. Madam Hertford sent to me again to see me at the door and did it' – so relations with the Countess continued. The Hertfords owned Copt Hall at neighbouring Vauxhall, convenient for continuing consultations. Simon bought himself a new doublet and 'hose of black tufted canvas with birds' eyes' to go as a godfather to his 'cousin Twyne'. Thomas Twyne was the son of the well-known Canterbury schoolmaster, translator and antiquary, John Twyne. Thomas was a successful doctor, a Fellow of the Royal College of Physicians, who was interested in astrology; so now Forman had a cousin in the enemy's camp. Twyne wrote widely on Forman's range of interests, *The Wonderful Workmanship of the World*, *The Breviary of Britain* and *A New Counsel against the Plague*. They would have much to talk about as they went to Greenwich together.

His sister Jane and another woman brought up from Kent Forman's samphire, for medical purposes – we remember Shakespeare's contemporary description of the traffic from the cliffs:

> how fearful
> And dizzy 'tis to cast one's eyes so low!
> The crows and choughs that wing the midway air
> Show scarce so gross as beetles; half-way down
> Hangs one that gathers samphire, dreadful trade!
> Methinks he seems no bigger than his head.

One halek note is of interest: '9 July, halek 8 a.m. Hester Sharp, et halek at 3 p.m. Anne Wiseman, and 9 p.m. halek tronco.' '15 July, I began to cut and bush up the great garden of roses at Lambeth Marsh . . . made some dozen bushes or better. Also made an end of distilling my strong water . . . 25 July, Margery found the cuckoo on her gown . . . 27 July, my eyes began to be sore and continued worse till 8 August.'

At the beginning of August 'I cast my two images for my constellation', and the Doctors summoned him before them.

Secure in his Cambridge licence, he refused to come. '9 August, Anne Condwell came to lie at my house to be cured of her disease and leg'; they were old friends and this was a convenient arrangement: '11 August, 2.30 p.m. halek Anne Condwell'. For the rest of the month, beside his ordinary avocations and relaxations, he is engaged in setting the gillyflowers in the inner garden, dining at Pewterers' Hall – this was in Lime Street going up to Aldgate – supping with the respectable Mrs Stillingfleet from 6 to 8 p.m., and having his bees put into a new hive. September begins with 'halek Anne Cordray of the Bank 10 a.m.', and receiving his sassafras for medical use, when the note-book ends.

In April 1608 Mr Christopher Grimston 'made inquisition for his man who was old and trusty, whom he sent out with money to buy liveries'.[1] The man did not return, but Mr Grimston could not be persuaded he had run away. Nor had he: 'going over Moorfields he had been robbed and beaten with bastinados – brought to Redcross Street [leading out of Cripplegate] like to die. The Friday after he sent a message to his master.' Mr Grimston was of the Yorkshire family, not the better-known East Anglian one. He was Surveyor of the Duchy of Lancaster, and a neighbour in Lambeth, actually it was he who died there, this September.[2] A few stray notes this month show Forman in touch with the Dormers at Peterley, questing for his brother Robert and for Sir Richard Hawkins, who, after long imprisonment in Spain, was 'rattling in throat, spitting blood'.[3]

Towards the end of the year Forman was enthusiastically engaged in gardening – in accordance with Cicero's recommendation of it as a suitable occupation for declining years. Simon's operations were also in keeping with Thomas Tusser's contemporary advice.

29 November, I set the framboy [raspberry] trees under the west pale all along at Lambeth Marsh in Hanfield's garden. 7 December, I set the willows all along towards the lane, and afternoon the first rose-tree. 8 December, set the rest of the rose trees all along the bank towards the

[1] 205.
[2] Lambeth Parish Register, vol. I.
[3] 338.

lane. 9 December, all the other rose trees towards Davies' side, also set the filberts and two pecks . . . against the posts and towards the lane and the house. The camomile on the bank by the privy; and primroses set.

A week later rose-bushes and two apple trees by the pale, small roses and pinks under the pale; in January he set the beans in Hanfield's garden. 'They were watered twenty-four hours before, when the moon was full.'[1]

This was in accordance with the gardening lore of the time:

> In making or mending, as needeth thy ditch,
> Get set to quickset it, learn cunningly which.
> In hedging, where clay is, get stake as ye know
> Of poplar and willow, for fuel to grow.[2]

> Dig garden, stroy [destroy] mallow, now may ye at ease,
> And set as a dainty thy runcival pease.
> Go cut and set roses, choose aptly thy plot,
> The roots of the youngest are best to be got.

And plant of course – as Tusser says – at the growing of the moon: sympathetic magic again – one sees that there was nothing out of the ordinary in Forman's habit of thought.

In the entries in his pocket-book for 1609 we observe principally the ramifications of his cousinage through his marriage. This is a characteristic Elizabethan theme, but with Simon it was a matter of special pride to compensate for his ingrained sense of inferiority, the injuries he had received, to shore him up in social status. In the early months we have several entries about 'sister Sandys', who would be his wife's close relation. 'My sister Sandys sent to Elizabeth Hill . . . desirous of her service; she came not, but sent word she was not free.'[3] 'Sister Sandys sent a letter to tronco that Mary and Elizabeth be sickish'; he sets the figure to know how they will do. 'My cousin Elizabeth married at London with Sir Thomas Rotherham'; there were two of

[1] 240.

[2] T. Tusser, *Five Hundred Points of Good Husbandry*, ed. W.Payne and S.J.Herrtage (*English Dialect Soc.*), 77–8.

[3] 338.

them at this time when knighthoods were going so cheap: impossible to tell which one it was. A further indication of prosperity occurs with 'Francis came to be hind': in addition to his garden Simon must have had cattle on the marsh at Lambeth.

We have a vivid glimpse of Simon – we can almost see him – on 16 February 1609: 'I came into a stationer's shop in London and turned some books; the boy quarrelled much with me for tossing of his books and not setting them up in order.'[1]

A few entries denote earlier clients faithful to him over the years. The well-to-do merchant, Mr Hawes, wants to know how long his wife has gone with child. Mr Randall of London appears to have an imposthume, an abscess. Mistress Sybil Cornwallis puts the question 'when her lover, Mr Chandler, will come to her'.[2] A new patient is a Scotch lady, who has come south with the King and other Scots to graze richer pastures: the Lady Lovat of Lothbury. At the end of July 'the King of Denmark passed through London a little after noon' – on a visit to his sister, the Danish Queen Anne. (It was, indeed, a new world, much less English at the top.) A gentlewoman wants to know 'whether she should marry one forced to affect her'. This question was shortly to arise with the most flagrant publicity, at the summit of Jacobean society in the case of the Countess of Essex. It was to have the most damaging consequences for Forman's name with posterity.

The sea-folk continued to consult him about their chances and prospects, their goods, their missing husbands. Among these, in October 1609, Elizabeth Whitehead puts the question 'whether her husband will return from Virginia.' At the end of November 'we had letters from him by ship that came thence and sent certain things home'. A later note adds: 'he came not home'.[3]

This announces a new and most important theme. The year 1609 was filled with excitement about the colonisation of Virginia. The original settlement of Jamestown in 1607 was languishing and would never have taken root, if it had not been for the

[1] 338.
[2] 335.
[3] 205.

Second Charter put forth in 1609, by which English colonisation in North America became a national venture. National pride was involved, the greatest hopes entertained. A fleet was sent out with Sir Thomas Gates as governor of the colony. It is well known that his flagship was wrecked on Bermuda in a hurricane, that he and all the complement survived safely to spend the winter on that isle full of noises, and constructed two pinnaces in which they sailed on to Virginia in the spring. William Strachey's account of all this, coming back to Blackfriars, suggested Shakespeare's play, *The Tempest.*

In the context of this book we have met Sir Thomas Gates, another Cadiz knight, as one of the lovers of Mistress Flud, along with Sir Henry Wotton. In 1604 Wotton was recommending his friend to Secretary Winwood in the warmest terms: 'I entreat you to love him and to love me too, and to assure yourself that you cannot love two honester men.'[1] A stern and upright soldier, Gates gave the colonists some of the discipline they badly needed, if they were to survive. On his second journey, his wife died on the way over.

It is characteristic of Forman that what was uppermost in people's minds in London should have engaged his interest, alert and inquiring as he was. We find him gathering information about the New World with the keenest attention. Some of his notes may be taken to show what struck people at the time, particularly the strange flora and fauna. 'There is also in Virginia a kind of fruit called a maricock. They grow on the ground like a pompion, and such a flower cometh out first before the fruit, and as big as small cucumbers. They are full of seeds; the substance thereof is like a lemon and tasteth with a pleasant sharpness before they be ripe. Once ripe they are very sweet and luscious, very good to eat.'[2] Evidently, squash. Also a kind of plum, called a mutchumin, as big as an apricot, sweet and pulp sweet, thick like marmalade: it has a binding quality, helps any flux of blood, red and yellow, three or four kernels, they grow on a low tree.

---

[1] q. Alexander Brown, *The Genesis of the United States*, II. 894.

[2] 802; cf. W. Strachey, *The History of Travel into Virginia Britannia*, ed. L. B. Wright and V. Freund (*Hakluyt Soc.*), 119–21.

'The Indians do always in March boil the heart or pith of pine tree in water, strain it and drink the water – it purges up and downwards.' In India, i.e. the West Indies, there is 'a fruit called a plantain, grows up as a cabbage, spreads out in bushes, and on branches grow long and crooked like cucumbers, and are a very delicious meat'. We recognise the banana.

We are given a fairly accurate picture of Jamestown on 'low marshy ground, very unhealthful. And ever in May, June, July and August they are much troubled with a kind of burning fever and swelling in their bodies and face; many die thereof . . . But at the head of the river it is much more pleasant, not so full of woods nor nothing so thick; both the ground, country and air is more pleasant, healthful and more fertile.' At the mouth of the river they have sturgeon from April to the end of August; there follows an account of the fishes, animals and birds. Great store of wolves and black bear; 'snakes of divers colours, green, some red as blood, some speckled, some two yards long. In winter they have parakeets, also blackbirds with carnation pinions [i.e. redwinged blackbirds], birds all red as blood [i.e. cardinals.] In summer in the woods there are fireflies with lights in their tails like candles.'

There are lynxes speckled white and black, as big as a mastiff, their skins worth 20*s* or 30*s* apiece. There are beaver, otter, grey foxes; 'there is also a beast called an opossum, as big as an old cat, but a tail like a rat; his head is also like a rat. Also a racoon, some grey, some black, of the bigness of a little dog like a spaniel; and a musk rat that lives in the waters.'

There is more to the same effect, all very recognisable.

In these last two years of his life Forman was consulted by another Howard lady, Frances, the young Countess of Essex, in her trouble. The dragging of his name, after his death, into the shocking affair of the poisoning of Sir Thomas Overbury was responsible for the blackening of Forman's name posthumously. This was, like so much about him, very curious; for in fact he had nothing whatever to do with it. Forman died in 1611; it was not until two years later, in 1613, that the Countess had Overbury poisoned; the affair did not come into the light of day until the end of 1614, the Countess and her new husband were not sent to the Tower till a year later.

It is usually held that the Countess sought Forman's help through the intermediary of Mrs Turner, who later arranged the poisoning. There is nothing about her in his papers. The only Anne Turner who came to consult him, from Queenhithe, on 2 December 1600, was not the woman;[1] for she was born about 1562, where the pretty poisoner was fourteen years younger, born in 1576.[2] All that relates to the Countess and her friend has been abstracted from the papers, for the state-trials; all that we have are the letters quoted against them.

Lady Frances Howard was the daughter of the Earl of Suffolk, who, driven on by his rapacious wife, fetched up in the Tower later for (exceptional) embezzlement from the state. The girl was born 31 May 1590, and kindly King James found a suitable husband for her in Essex's son and heir.[3] They were married in January 1606, the girl being fifteen, the boy fourteen. The young Earl was abroad from the end of 1607 to 1609. On his return, when he expected to consummate the marriage – he was not in fact very good at it – his wife found that she could not stomach him. She was very beautiful, with an expression of child-like innocence, self-willed and determined, utterly spoiled. Moreover, to inflame her will, she had fallen for the masculine charms of King James's boy-friend, Robert Carr. From the confused and passionate letter the Countess wrote to her *confidante*, Mrs Turner, it is sometimes not easy to tell to which of her lords she is referring.

Anne Turner was the wife of George Turner, a successful doctor and Fellow of the Royal College of Physicians, who was also interested in alchemy; they were both Catholics. In her spare time – for the doctor was much older – Mrs Turner was the mistress of Sir Arthur Manwaring, a courtier, one of King James's cheap brand of knights. By him she is said to have had three children. The doctor seems to have been a *mari complaisant* for, when he died in 1610, he appointed Sir Arthur overseer of his will

---

[1] 236.
[2] cf. *D.N.B.*, under George Turner.
[3] *The Complete Peerage*, ed. G.E.C., XII. Pt. I. 68.

for the benefit of his wife, with £10 'to make him a ring with this posey *Fates junguntur Amantes*'.[1] It was very civil of him; but Manwaring did not marry the widow, in spite of her having promising resources of her own. She had a patent for making yellow starch to stiffen ladies' ruffs around their necks, and she used to supervise the catering at the supper-parties of Sir Thomas Monson (another Catholic), whom we have met before.

The young Countess kept her husband at bay, in spite of the pressure of her family; but with her infatuation for the handsome Carr she was becoming desperate. She sought help from her lower-class friend, though ordering her to burn her letter:

Sweet Turner, I am out of all hope of any good in this world, for my father, my mother and my brother said I should lie with him. And my brother Howard was here and said he [her husband] would not come forth from this place all winter. So that all comfort is gone and, which is worst of all, my Lord [her husband] hath complained that he hath not lain with me, and I would not suffer him to use me. My father and mother are angry, but I had rather die a thousand times over; for, besides the sufferings, I shall lose his [Carr's] love if I lie with him. I will never desire to see his [Carr's] face, if my Lord do that unto me.

My Lord is very well as ever he was, so as you may see in what a miserable case I am.[2]

So it goes on, distractedly. Mrs Turner had put her in touch with Forman, who was an authority in love-matters, not a poisoner.

You may send the party [Forman] word of all; he sent me word all shall be well, but I shall not be so happy as the lord to love me.

This means that she wishes to compel Carr's love, attract him to her; we have seen that this was usual enough in the case of Lady Essex's cousin, who had wanted to get Southampton. Forman had love philtres, incantations, figures – such things as silly humans believed in for such purposes.

The distraught Countess sought help from Forman, becoming his sworn 'daughter', writing to him as 'father', as her cousin had done ten years before over Southampton.

[1] P.C.C., Wingfield 37.
[2] q. Cobbett's *State Trials*, II. 931–3.

Sweet Father, I must still crave your love, although I hope I have it, and shall deserve it better hereafter. Remember the galls [obstacles] for I fear – though I have yet no cause but to be confident in you – yet I desire to have it as it is yet remaining well. So continue it still, if it be possible, and if you can you must send me some good fortune. Alas, I have need of it. Keep the Lord [Carr] still to me, for that I desire, and be careful you name me not to anybody, for we have so many spies that you must use all your wits.

My Lord [her husband] is merry and drinketh with his men; and all the content he gives me is to abuse me, and use me as doggedly as before. I think I shall never be happy in this world, because he hinders my good . . . Remember, I beg for God's sake, and get me from this vile place [i.e. Chartley]. Your affectionate, loving daughter,

Frances Essex.

This was how these great ladies wrote to their father-confessor. There follows a postscript:

Give Turner warning of all things, but not the Lord [Carr]. I would not have anything come out, for fear of the Lord Treasurer [Salisbury]; for so they may tell my father and mother, and fill their ears full of toys.

Forman was shortly beyond helping this forlorn young lady any further, and she was forced to look elsewhere; for on 8 September 1611 he died.[1] That he was an authority on love-matters, evident throughout this book, is corroborated by the last entry in his books. Within five weeks of his death he is casting, on 4 August 1611, to know 'whether love grows or declines between me and G. Cole'![2]

Forman's death is well known, from the account of it given by the astrologer William Lilly. On the Sunday before he was supping with his wife in their garden-house. She was teasing him on the subject, so familiar in this book, whether one could tell if man or wife should die first. 'Shall I bury you, or no?' she said. 'Oh, Tronco, thou wilt bury me, but thou wilt much repent it.' That sounds like him. 'Yea, but how long first?' 'I shall die ere Thursday night.'

---

[1] Not, as *D.N.B.* says, 12 September: that was the date of his burial.
[2] 205.

Monday came, all was well. Tuesday came, he was not sick. Wednesday came, and still he was well: with which his impertinent wife did much twit him in the teeth. Thursday came, and dinner was ended, he very well. He went down to the waterside, and took a pair of oars to go to some buildings he was in hand with in Puddle-dock. Being in the middle of the Thames, he presently fell down, only saying, 'An impost, an impost', and so died.[1]

His last diagnosis was certainly correct: straining at the oars burst an abscess. Lilly tells us that he was worth as much as £1200. He left a son by his wife, Clement born in 1606, to whom he reserved one of his books – a guide to herbs and their uses.[2] 'All his rarities, secret manuscripts, of what quality soever, Dr Napier of Lindford in Buckinghamshire had, who had been a long time his scholar.' And so they came to Ashmole, and down to us – with all they have to tell us of the secrets of the age, which no one has explored until this.

But this was not the end of Forman. His posthumous story made a great deal more of a sensation than anything in his life, and blackened his name.

Whether by his arts or no, the young Countess of Essex got her way with Carr and raised his latent heterosexual passion. Benevolent King James, a sugar-daddy to them all, was now as anxious to clear the way for a marriage between the Howard beauty and his favourite as he had been hitherto to marry her to Essex. This is not the place to tell the complicated story of the tortuous proceedings that followed.[3] The crucial point at issue was a sacramental one: was the Countess a virgin? She swore that her husband was impotent (his subsequent marriage proved that he was not), and a jury of matrons examining her under a cloud of veils, to spare her modesty, decided that she was a virgin. But the opposition said that Sir Thomas Monson's young daughter had been substituted for her. A jury of bishops spent a great deal of

---

[1] *Lives of . . . Elias Ashmole and William Lilly*, ed. 1774, 22–3.
[2] 1429.
[3] cf. my *The Tower of London*, chap. 8.

time on this important matter and had difficulty in coming to a clean decision.

Carr's friend, Overbury, knew too much about the relations of the infatuated favourite with the beautiful Countess. Her reptilian uncle, the Earl of Northampton, by a characteristic trick, got Overbury into the Tower, where she had him poisoned at leisure. The arrangements were made by Mrs Turner. When all this came out, it proved the ruin of Carr – who had been raised to the earldom of Somerset to make him worthy of the Countess – and his bride. Monson was imprisoned in the Tower; the governor, Sir Gervase Elwes, who had lent himself to these fell purposes, was condemned to death. Several of the lesser agents were hanged, including Mrs Turner; after which, yellow starched ruffs went out of fashion.

What had all this to do with Forman?

The fact that some of these people had been clients of his in love-matters had nothing to do with their misdeeds in regard to Overbury two years after Forman's death. Yet at the state trials his name was dragged up, his memory held up to execration by the horrid Lord Chief Justice Coke, just as he had abused and vilified Ralegh at his trial. Mrs Turner was described by him as 'daughter of the Devil Forman' – as if he were responsible for the poisoning! In consequence the notice of her in the *Dictionary of National Biography* absurdly concludes that she 'may have been one of his illegitimate children'.[1] In the absence of fact, people's imaginations run away with them; an aim of this book is to provide a foundation of fact in this hitherto unilluminated area.

The state trial of Mrs Turner throws a little more light simply on the techniques employed in that age and later – in all societies all over the world – to compel love. This is anthropology, with which we began. 'There was also showed in court certain pictures of a man and woman in copulation, made in lead; as also the mould of brass, wherein they were cast, a black scarf also full of white crosses.' When these things were being exhibited there was heard a great crack among the scaffolds, which threw the proceedings into utter confusion. Everybody thought the Devil 'had

[1] cf. *D.N.B.* under George Turner.

been present and grown angry to have his workmanship showed.'
Terror reigned for at least a quarter of an hour. It would be a
piece of vulgar rationalism, or perhaps of my well-known arrogance (with persons sympathetic to sympathetic magic) to
point out that naturally the scaffolds cracked when everybody
craned forward to have a better view of these exciting objects.

Other pieces shown in court were authentic enough: pieces of
parchment 'wherein were contained all the names of the blessed
Trinity mentioned in the scriptures . . . as also a figure in which
was written this word Corpus, upon the parchment was fastened
a little piece of the skin of a man.' These were aids to incline the
love of Carr to the Countess and of Sir Arthur Manwaring to Mrs
Turner. (When all this came out Carr's infatuation for his treasure
turned to hatred: she had ruined his life – he had had no part in
poisoning his friend.)

Mrs Forman came forward to help – and clear herself. Her
evidence, unfriendly to her husband, was such as we might
expect. Mrs Turner and he would 'be sometimes three or four
hours locked up in his study together'. After his death she had
been to demand certain images there: 'one picture in wax, very
sumptuously apparelled in silks and satins [was this of the
Countess?]; as also one other sitting in form of a naked woman,
spreading and laying forth her hair in a looking glass'. (We know
what St Paul thought of the temptations exposed by woman's
hair.) After the Overbury trouble burst Mrs Turner sent her
maid to burn all papers concerning the Countess and Carr.

A tell-tale note by Forman was exhibited, 'signifying what
ladies loved what lords in the Court'. Lord Chief Justice Coke
opened it, and then refused to have it read: he had seen that the
first name was his own wife's, Lady Hatton, whom he had married
for her money, who was herself no better than she should be, a
termagant and a scandal.

So what? – so far as Forman was concerned.

In this study there are two aspects to which I have paid hardly
any attention. The first Forman would have regarded as the most
important of all, the astrological. The second is the subculture of

the erotic and the priapian – a department of anthropology which has, at any rate, a real existence, though I am not competent to do justice to it. This exists at all times and in all places, though driven underground in England with the victory of Puritanism twice over, in the 17th century and with the Victorian Age. Relegated to holes and corners, it is perhaps emerging into the light of day again with the release from repression, which is sometimes described as permissiveness.

Much of what is regarded, ignorantly, as pornography is related to the cult of the generative powers, essential in earlier societies to the survival of the species. Vestigial relics of these cults are all round us, in graffiti and the like, though the 'educated' may not have the imagination or the knowledge to realise what they are. An 18th-century anthropologist of perception and scholarship, unhampered by Victorian prudery, understood very well. Payne Knight summed up, 'words are only the types and symbols of ideas, and therefore must be posterior to them, in the same manner as ideas are to their objects.'[1] In our time we should attach more importance to sub-conscious and unconscious urges in the phenomena so common still all round us – 'the propensity to draw phallic figures on the sides of vacant walls and in other places'; or the custom of nailing up a horse-shoe, which in origin represents the female organ, and hence its function, forgotten today, of protecting against witchcraft. People really do not know why they do what they do.

We cannot go into all this: suffice it to say that the material presented in this book offers a prime source for its study. To give one little example: the bundle of white crosses from Forman's study produced in court. Payne Knight instructs us as to their significance: they represent the male organ, 'a cross, in the form of the letter T., thus served as the emblem of creation and generation, before the church adopted it as the sign of salvation'.[2] And so with others of Forman's symbols and a great deal of his lore. We have several times noticed that cabbalistic names and signs occur, along with notes of images to be made at full moon,

[1] R. Payne Knight, *A Discourse on the Worship of Priapus* (ed. 1865), 23, 139.
[2] ibid., 28.

sometimes with the note, 'it was done just at the time'.[1] There is the specific historical point that he and his like were partially filling the gap left by the destruction of the cult-life so favoured by Catholicism at the hands of a rigid Protestantism. Catholic countries in the 16th century continued to allow popular devotion to these venerable cults, in some cases with no disguise of their sexual import: they were indeed supposed to be efficacious.[2] And it is, perhaps, not without significance that a considerable proportion of Forman's clients were Catholics or crypto-Catholics – though we have seen that his practice was so extensive that it included straight Anglicans like Dean Blague and Dr Dove as well as the puritanically inclined Hugh Broughton.

The psychological interest of Forman is very great, and I hope I have done better justice to it, while the medical interest is somewhat marginal. One gets an appalling picture of disease in Elizabethan life. Here one must keep a balance, and remember that it was the diseased who came largely for treatment. Freud can be legitimately criticised for erecting too dogmatic a theoretical structure upon the basis of his experience with Viennese neurasthenics. Similarly, one must not generalise too severely upon the basis of Forman's practice.

On the other hand, it was very wide and representative. Those who came not for medical treatment but simply for forecasts are evidence at least of the mentality of the time. And not restricted to that time, either, for such people we have always with us: they reveal themselves fully for what average humans are.

It is obvious, then, that the chief value of Forman's formidable mass of evidence to me is historical and social, in plumbing the depths of the society of the time – Shakespeare's Age – as never before, a revelation of social life in its most intimate and truth-telling recesses, without any disguises or illusions, any pretentions or hypocrisies, any vacuous theorising: just things *as they are*.

We have reason to be grateful for the new information Forman gives us at so many points, for his insatiable curiosity about

[1] 195.

[2] cf. the examples given in 'On the Worship of the Generative Powers', in Payne Knight, 140–1.

people, the facts he collected about them. Most of all are we indebted to him for solving for us the great mystery of Shakespeare's life, the Dark Lady of the Sonnets and of *Love's Labour's Lost*, who she was and what she was like – all completely corroborative of what he tells us himself about her. Nor need I refrain from pointing out that it finally confirms my previous findings with regard to these central and decisive years in Shakespeare's life. Corroboration, confirmation, completion have appropriately come, in A.E.Housman's phrase, from the arsenals of divine vengeance – if I may so describe the Bodleian Library.

That is only one shaft of light among many Forman throws into the surrounding darkness. What a portrait, in depth, of the time! – what an exposure of the underside usually covered up by conventions, pretences, humbug, social decorum; of the miseries and squalors, the ardours and passions, the fears and expectations, the sadnesses and tragedies!

And, of course, of the essential and inveterate foolery of men.

Part II

Forman's Autobiography

In Dei nomine, Amen.

This is the book of the life and generation of Simon, the son of William, the son of Richard, the son of Sir Thomas of Leeds, the son of Sir Thomas Forman of Furnival's and of Anne his wife, daughter of Sir Anthony Smith, etc.[1] Born in the year from the nativity of our Lord Jesus Christ, 1552, the 30th of December, being Saturday and New Year's Eve, at 45 minutes after 9 of the clock at night, of the natural body of Mary, wife of the said William Forman aforesaid, and daughter of John Foster, esquire, by Marian Hallam, his wife. In a village called Quidhampton in the county of Wilts, situate in the valley on the north side of the river between Wilton and Salisbury. Whose parents were well descended and of good reputation and fame, having many children and they disposed diversely.

He had by the said Mary six sons and two daughters, viz. William, the eldest; Joan, the second, which after married with William Hanham, gentleman, whose father was sometime mayor of Salisbury,[2] by whom she had no issue; after his death she married one William Brink and died without issue. The third child of the said William was Henry, that after took to wife Anne, the daughter of Thomas Hart, and had by her issue a daughter named Anne. The fourth was Richard, who took to wife Cecily Parlet, the sole heir of John Parlet; she died in childbed, and after he took to his second wife Joan Warham by whom he had three children, John, Dorothy, and Richard. And she also died.

The fifth child of the said William and Mary was this Simon, who in the forty-seventh year of his age took to wife, through the grace and will of God, Anne, the daughter of John Baker of Kent, and of Dorothy Munnings, the daughter of Sir Edward Munnings of Kent, knight. To whom was allied many houses of

---

[1] We do not need to take Forman's descent seriously beyond his grandfather.

[2] William Hanham was mayor in 1546. H. Hatcher, *Old and New Sarum*, 696 (R. C. Hoare, *Hist. of Modern Wiltshire*).

honour and worship, as the Cliffords, the Sondes, the Lovelaces, the Chiches, the Finches, the Ayliffes, the Grinfords, the Kemps, the Augers, and many knights and ladies, as the Earl of Cumberland, Sir James Clifford, Sir Michael Sondes, the Lady Lovelace, the Lady Ashenden, and divers others.

The sixth child of the said William and Mary was Robert, who took to wife Joan, the daughter of Stephen Poore, gentleman, of Dorsetshire; the said Robert died leaving his wife with child. The seventh child of the said William and Mary was a daughter, also named Joan. The last and youngest was John. Which two were not married after forty years of age. And this was specially to be noted in the children of the said William and Mary: there never was any of them did marry till they were at least thirty-four years of age. And it is recorded in ancient books that there are three things specially noted in the name of the Formans; that is, there was never any of them proud, covetous, nor a traitor. And that may well be seen to this day in the generation.

The father of this Simon died when he was but eleven years old; his mother lived after the death of his father forty years a widow. And when she was four score and twelve years old, she was a lusty woman. But we will leave them all and speak of the wonderful life of the said Simon.

OF VISIONS THAT THE SAID SIMON HAD, BEING YET A CHILD

Simon, being a child of six years old, his father loved him above all the rest, but his mother nor brethren loved him not. His father, for the affection he had to him, would always have him lie at his bed's foot in a little bed for the nonce. So soon as he was laid down to sleep he should see in visions many mighty mountains and hills come rolling against him. Although they would overrun him and fall on him and bruise him, yet he got up always to the top of them and with much ado went over them. Then he should see many great waters like to drown him, boiling and raging against him as though they would swallow him up, yet he thought he did overpass them. These dreams and visions he had every night continually for three or four years space.

These visions God did show him in his youth to signify unto him his troubles in his riper years. For the mighty mountains might signify the great and mighty potentates that he had controversy with afterwards. The waters might signify the great counsels that were holden against him to overthrow him. Yet God, the only defender of all that be his, would never let him to be overthrown, but continually gave him always in the end the victory of all his enemies. And he overpassed all with credit, by the help of God, to whom be praise for evermore! Amen.

HOW SIMON WAS SET TO SCHOOL, WITH WHOM AND WHERE

When Simon was almost eight years of age, in those days [before] the soldiers came from Newhaven [Le Havre], which was about the year of our Lord God 1563 that the plague began in Salisbury, there was a certain minister named William Rydout alias Rydar, that by his trade and occupation was a cobbler. But after Queen Mary's days when the law did turn, he was made a minister and so withal became a schoolmaster and teacher of children. He was a man of some fifty years, mean of stature, and a blackgrom Sir [a poor black parson]. He could read English well, but he could no Latin more than the single accidence, and that he learned of his two sons that went daily to a free school.

This parson, when the plague began, fled from Salisbury for fear thereof, and came to dwell at the priory of St Giles [at Wilton], near unto the father of this Simon: to whom this Simon was put to school at Michaelmas.[1] Where he learned his letters. When he came to learn 'In the name of the Father' etc., because his capacity could not understand the mystery of spelling, he prayed his master he might go to school no more, because he should never learn it. But his said master beat him for it, which made him the more diligent to his book. After some days, when he had pondered thereon well and had the reason thereof, he learned it. After that his master never beat him for his book again. He profited so well that in one year or little more he had learned his single accidence

---

[1] St Giles's was a small hospital at Wilton with a chapel, which continued after the suppression of the chantries as a school with a master. *V.C.H. Wilts.*, III. 362.

and his rules clean out. Boarding with this priest in the winter time he would make him lie always naked, which kept him in great fear.

After this he was put to the free school in the Close at Salisbury with one Doctor Bowles, which was a very furious man, with whom he went to school some two years.[1] Then did the said Simon board at one Mr Hawknight's, that sometime was Registrar to the bishop.[2] Near unto this Mr Hawknight dwelt a canon of the church named Mr Mintern, to whom many times this Simon went.[3] This canon seldom or never kept any fire in his house, but he had some load of faggots lying in a house. Always when he was a-cold, he would go and carry his faggots up into a loft till he was hot; when he had carried them all up, he would fetch them down again and burn none. So he made this Simon do many a time and oft to catch a heat, saying it was better to heat himself so than to sit by the fire.

So he went to school some two years with Doctor Bowles. Then about the year of our Lord God 1563, at Christmas his father had him. On the New Year's eve after, at night, the father of the said Simon died. He had kept a great Christmas, and on the day before New Year's eve he walked abroad to his ground with one of his men. There came a dove and alighted before him and always ran before him; many times they offered to catch it, and it would rise up and fall down again. So they followed it till it ran into a neighbour's woodbine. The same night, about midnight, after the dancing and sport was almost ended, going into his chamber to go to bed, one – as he thought – struck him in the neck. He took his bed, and died just twenty-four hours after.

[1] John Bowles (or Bold) was master of the chorister's school in 1563, and in 1565 was instructed by the Dean and Chapter to keep it as a free school and not to refuse any suitable boy. He was probably the Cambridge man, who matriculated from Clare College in 1546. J. and J. A. Venn, *Alumni Cantab.*, Pt. I, 1. 192.

[2] Forman is probably referring here to John Harding, notary public, active in the Bishop's courts at this time.

[3] Thomas Mintern was a prebendary from 1541 onwards; he had been a Fellow of New College, Oxford, from Sherborne. J. Foster, *Alumni Oxon., 1500-1714*, 1018.

HOW SIMON AFTER HIS FATHER'S DEATH WAS PUT TO SHIFT FOR HIMSELF

After the father of Simon was dead, his mother, who never loved him, grudged at his being at home, and what fault soever was committed by any of the rest he was beaten for it. She suffered him to go to school no longer, but set him to keep sheep and to plough, and gathering of sticks and suchlike. The boy, being but eleven years old just at the death of his father, yet having reasonable wit and discretion, was nimble spirited and apt to anything. Seeing the hatred of his mother and of the rest of his brethren and sisters towards him and that he could not follow his book nor be at quiet, he put himself an apprentice to one Matthew Commin of Salisbury at fourteen years, which used many occupations.

First he was a hosier, and thereby he learned to sew and to make a hose. Then he was a merchant of cloth and of all small wares, and sold hops, salt, oil, pitch, rosin, raisins, and all apothecary drugs and grocery. Whereby the said Simon learned the knowledge of all wares and drugs, and how to buy and sell; and grew so apt and had such good fortune that in short time his master committed all to his charge. But there fell out many controversies between his mistress and him, especially for one Jean Cole, her sister's daughter, which she kept.

HOW SIMON BEAT MARY ROBERTS, HIS MASTER'S MAID

Now Simon had put himself an apprentice for ten years with Matthew Commin, with condition that he should be three years at the grammar school. Which his master performed not –which was a part of the cause why he went from his master afterwards. Simon at first, being the youngest apprentice of four, was put to all the worst, and, being little and small of stature and young of years, everyone did triumph over him. Especially a kitchen-maid named Mary Roberts; oftentimes she would knock him that the blood should run about his ears.

It fell out, in tract of time, within the term of five years, all the other apprentices went away, and Simon served by it; and all things for the shop was committed to his charge. On a certain frosty morning his master and mistress were both gone to the garden and their kinswoman with them, leaving none at home but Simon and Mary, willing Mary to look into the shop and help, if occasion served. They being gone, so many customers came for ware that Simon could not attend them all. Whereupon he calls Mary to stand in the shop. She came forth, reviled him with many bitter words, and said she would anon have him by the ears; and so went her way again.

Simon put up all and said little, but made the best shift he could and rid them all away. He shut the shop door, took a yard and went into Mary, who, so soon as she saw him, was ready to have him by the ears. But Simon struck her on the hands with his yard, and belaboured her so, ere he went, that he made her black and blue all over. And bruised her head and hands that he laid her along crying and roaring like a bull. For he beat her thoroughly for all her knavery before to him done.

OF THE QUANDARY AND FEAR THAT SIMON WAS IN

When this combat was ended between Simon and Mary, and Simon had gotten the victory of Mary, he was much afeared. He thought, if his mistress should come home first, she would take the maid's part, and then should Simon be well beaten. But, if his master came first, then he thought it would be so much the better. And, as God would, his master came first, and, finding the maid crying and howling, demanded the cause; and she told him that Simon had beaten her.

'That's well like,' said he, 'but, if he had, he had served thee well enough, for thou hast beaten him full oft.'

With that, he asked Simon the cause.

'Sir,' said he, 'here came many customers that I could not serve them and look to the shop too; wherefore I called Mary to help to attend in the shop and see to things. She came forth and scolded at me, went in again and would not do it, that people might steal what they would for her. And because thereof I did give her three or four lambskins [soft strokes] with the yard.'

'Thou servedst her well enough,' said he, 'and if she be so obstinate, serve her so again.'

These words made the maid stark mad, for she thought he would have pitied her; but he took Simon's part. Then she cried the more till her mistress came, and demanded of her the cause; and she told her. Then she came into the shop with open mouth; but his master stopped her mouth and fury, and would not suffer her to beat Simon as she would have done. Whereupon she grudged at him much, and kept it in mind a long time after. But after this Simon and Mary agreed so well that they never were at square after, and Mary would do for him all that she could. Many a pound of butter she yielded in the bottom after for Simon's breakfast, which before that she would never do.

OF THE COMBAT BETWEEN SIMON AND THE TWO GODFREYS

In this process of time, while Simon dwelt with his said master, they kept a stannage [stall] at our Lady Fair. There were many knavish boys which were at play behind the stannage, threw stones against the stannage and often thrust down their ware. One Richard King, a journeyman [daily workman], come to his master to help at that fair, sent Simon out to see who made that quarrel. Among all the boys there were two of Godfrey's sons of the 'Swan', an innholder, which gave Simon hard words and said they would have him by the ears. He, being somewhat fearful, stood abashed, and the boys would not leave their knavery. At last out came King and, finding these boys to play the knave so with Simon and threatening him, hardened Simon to have them by the ears. So to buffets they went. Simon beat them both, and made them both give off. After that Simon would not shrink for a bloody nose with any boy, for he was then thoroughly fleshed by the means of King.

HOW SIMON WAS GIVEN TO HIS BOOK, AND LEARNED BY NIGHT
ALL THAT HENRY GIRD LEARNED IN THE DAY

Simon, thus being with his said master, was much given continually to his book, for he would never be idle. Many times his
master chid him that he was so much given to his book, and in the
end took all his Latin books from him, which troubled Simon's
mind much. So it chanced that a kersey man of Devonshire, one
Gird of Kirton [Crediton], boarded a son that he had with Simon's
master, that went every day to the free school. He was bedfellow
to Simon and, look, whatsoever he learned by day that did Simon
learn of him always at night. Whereby, though he profited himself
but little, yet he lost nothing of that he had before-time learned,
for his mind was most ardently set on his book.

HOW A.Y. LOVED SIMON

There was a man of good reputation and wealth that dwelt not
far from Simon's master, that had a proper fine maiden to his
only daughter: which, being younger than Simon, loved Simon
wonderful well and would surely see him once a day, or else she
would be sick. Often she would come to Simon's master and
entreat him very kindly on holy days that she might see him or
speak with him, and sometimes to go to pastimes with her. She
loved him so well that, if forty youth were at play before the
door, in a spacious place that there was, if Simon were not among
them she would not be there. But, if he were there, none could
keep her from thence. If Simon stood by his master or mistress
at the door, she would come and stand by him, and would not go
from him till necessity did compel.

Simon's master, well perceiving the great affection of the
gentlewoman towards Simon, would often say unto her, 'Mistress
Anne, ye love my boy well, methinks.' And she would answer,
'Yea, forsooth. If it will please you to give him leave to go run
with us, we shall give you thanks, sir.' Whereupon oftentimes he
would give him leave. As for Simon, he loved her not but in
kindness. But because she was so kind to Simon, he would do

anything he could do for her. And this love on her side lasted long, as hereafter shall be showed.[1]

HOW SIMON AND HIS MISTRESS FELL AT CONTROVERSY, WHEREUPON SIMON AT SEVENTEEN YEARS OLD AND A HALF WENT FROM HIS MASTER

When Simon had dwelt with his master some six years and a half, there fell out a controversy between Simon and his mistress – about a dozen of flax that his mistress lost from the stanning [stall] in Simon's absence, and then would have laid the blame on Simon and have beaten him for it. Of the which Simon thought great scorn, because he knew himself clear of the matter. When she would have beaten Simon, as she had wont to do, with a yard, Simon took the yard from his mistress, thrust her up behind a door and put the door on her. Whereupon she durst not meddle with Simon again, but with weeping tears complained to his master. Who, for so doing – although it was much against his will – beat Simon for it.

But he knew his wife to be a wicked, headstrong, and proud fantastical woman, a consumer and spender of his wealth. Oftentimes they two were also at square – insomuch that twice he had like to have killed her by casting a pair of tailor's shears at her. For once they went so near her that, as she was going in at a door, he nailed her clothes and smock at her buttocks to the door: the points of the shears went clean through the door, and she hung fast by the tail. Whereupon he swore in his wrath that, if ever he died before her, he would never give her anything.

These controversies were often between them, and many times when Simon and his master went to his farm together, some two miles off in the country, they would one complain to another of his mistress and her pride. His master would say to him, 'Simon,

---

[1] This was Anne Young, who died at Salisbury 8 May 1600. Perhaps daughter of William Young, of Market Ward, assessed at £5 goods, i.e. a well-to-do townsman. *Two Sixteenth Century Taxation Lists: 1545 and 1576*, ed. G.D. Ramsay (*Wilts. Arch. and Nat. Hist. Soc.*), 65.

thou must suffer as well as I myself. Thou seest we cannot remedy it as yet; but God will send a remedy one day.'

Now because Simon's master had beaten him for his mistress' sake, herself being in fault, Simon told his said master flat that he had not performed his covenants according to promise, therefore he would give off the trade and go to his book again. He wept sorely unto his master, and entreated him to have his good will. His master, seeing he would needs depart, consented thereunto and gave him his indenture. At the which his mistress took on mightily and they all wept, some for joy and some for madness and rage.

HOW SIMON, AFTER HE WAS GONE FROM HIS SAID MASTER, BECAME A SCHOLAR AGAIN AT THE FREE SCHOOL

Now when Simon was gone from his said master and was at his free liberty to serve elsewhere, he might have had many masters; but he would dwell with none, but provided and went to the free school every day for eight weeks' space, and followed his book hard. Then his mother would give him meat and drink no longer, nor any maintenance, whereupon he was driven to make many hard shifts. He was so greedy on his book that, if his master would not have beaten him if he could not say his lesson well, he would have wept and sobbed more than if he had been beaten. If his master gave him leave to play, that was death or a great punishment to him; for he would say, 'Play, play, here is nothing but play: I shall never be a good scholar.' When his fellows went to play he would go to his book, or into some secret place to muse and meditate, or into the church.

HOW SIMON BECAME A SCHOOLMASTER BEFORE HE WAS EIGHTEEN YEARS OLD

Simon, perceiving his mother would do nothing for him, was driven to great extremity and hunger, gave off to be a scholar any longer for lack of maintenance. At the priory of St Giles, where he himself was first a scholar, there he became a schoolmaster and taught some thirty boys. Their parents among them gave him most part of his diet, and the money he got he kept, to the sum of some 40*s*. When he had been schoolmaster some half year and had 40*s*. in his purse, he went to Oxford for to get more learning, and so left off from being schoolmaster.

HOW SIMON, WITH ONE OF HIS OLD SCHOOLFELLOWS, WOULD GO SEEK OUT OXFORD

Now it befell that in the year of our Lord God 1573, the 10th May, there was an ardent desire in Simon of farther learning and knowledge. Meeting with an old schoolfellow of his who before were always brought up together and love as brethren, whose father-in-law [i.e. stepfather] was as much against him as Simon's mother was against him. These two confederated together to go to Oxford, and did so. There they became both poor scholars: the one which was Thomas Rydar in Corpus Christi College, and Simon in Magdalen College.[1] Every day he went to the free school [i.e Magdalen College school] for a time, and followed his book hard always when he could have leisure.

Now there were two Bachelors of Arts that were two of his chief benefactors. The one of them was Sir Thornborough, that after was bishop of Limerick, and he was of Magdalen College; the other was Sir Pinckney, his cousin, of St Mary Hall.[2] These two loved him nothing well, and many times would make Simon to go forth to Loes, the keeper of Shotover, for his hounds to go on hunting from morning to night. They never studied nor gave themselves to their books, but to go to schools of fencing, to the dancing schools, to steal deer and conies, to hunt the hare, and to

---

[1] Thomas Rydar was probably a son of Forman's first schoolmaster, the cobbler turned minister.

[2] John Thornborough (1551–1641), b. Salisbury, became rector of Orcheston St Mary, 1575, of Chilmark, 1577, both in Wilts, of Marnhull, Dorset, 1578, prebendary of Salisbury, dean of York, bishop of Limerick, bishop of Bristol, bishop of Worcester. Foster, IV. 1479. Robert Pinckney, B.A. 1572, M.A. 1577, became rector of Lydiard Millicent 1577, Berwick St John 1579, Rushall 1580, all in Wilts. ibid., III. 1166.

wooing of wenches; to go to Dr Lawrence of Cowley, for he had two fair daughters, Bess and Martha.[1]

Sir Thornborough, he wooed Bess; Sir Pinckney, he wooed Martha, and in the end he married her. But Thornborough, he deceived Bess – as the mayor's daughter of Brackley, of which Euphues writes, deceived him. There was their ordinary haunt always, and thither must Simon run with the bottle and the bag early and late.

[1] Giles Lawrence, D.C.L., Fellow of All Souls College, Oxford, Regius Professor of Greek 1548–53, and 1559–85, Archdeacon of Wilts, 1564. ibid. ,II. 888.

Forman's Diary, 1564–1602

1564. The first day of January, between twelve and one in the morn, my father died and was buried the same day, being New Year's day. At which time I was just eleven years old. And the same day, seven years just, was Richard Forman, my grandfather, buried. This year, in the latter end of February, about the beginning of Lent, I was put to school to Peter Matthew to learn to write, continued with him a year, and boarded with my aunt Cockells.

Anno 1567, the 8th of February, being Friday, I went to Matthew Commin to dwell. I dwelt with him until the 24th of June, 1572, being Midsummer day. That day I went from him and travelled into the Isle of Wight to Newport. From thence I returned to Quidhampton. At Michaelmas after, I began to teach at Quidhampton, and I continued there till the 10th day of May, 1573. 1573, 10 May, I went first to Oxford. I continued there till the 12th day of September, 1574.

1574. Henry Evered, mayor [of Salisbury].[1] The 12th day of September, 1574, I came from Oxford to Quidhampton to make an oration before the Queen, being then at Wilton.[2] About Michaelmas I began to keep school at Wilton, and stayed there till the 19th of May, the which day I went to Mr Cox.

1575. This year in May, the 19th day, I went to be schoolmaster to the Dukes, of Ashgrove. I remained with him [them] till the 11th day of June, 1576. This year I had much trouble with Cox; he brought Parson Bref to see my books, and himself was like to kill me.

1576. This year in January, and till the 11th of June, I was schoolmaster to the Duke sons, of Ashgrove, till Midsummer.[3] At

---

[1] Forman got this name wrong, confusing it with that of a leading citizen who lived in St Martin's parish.

[2] Queen Elizabeth was entertained by the Earl of Pembroke at Wilton in September 1574, on her return from Bristol. J. Nichols, *The Progresses of Queen Elizabeth*, I. 409.

[3] The Dukes were prosperous clothiers with property in the parish of Wilsford near Amesbury.

Midsummer I went to Mr Combe's at Ashmore[1] and stayed there till Michaelmas, and taught. From thence went to Iwerne Minster and did teach there. And lay at the vicar's till the 2nd of January 1577;[2] then went to lodge at John Phillips'.

1577. I kept school at Iwerne Minster. I had much ado with the vicar, lived poorly, and did hunt much privily. This summer Mr Croutch and I became first acquainted.

1578. In February, in Lent or thereabout, I came to be usher of the free school in the Close at Salisbury: where I continued till Midsummer, and went from thence. In August I came to keep school at the Devizes. About Michaelmas I went from thence. Anthony and I travelled to Oxford and other places.

1579. In January, the 17th, I took the parsonage in Fisherton Anger, between 10 and 6 o'clock, and took the key at 12.[3] The 12th of June I was robbed and spoiled of all my goods and books first dwelling in Fisherton parsonage, and was committed to prison, where I lay sixty weeks before I was released. I had much trouble and defamation without desert by that cursed villain, Giles Estcourt.[4] And then was delivered by her Majesty and the Council.

I had much sickness, and could have no justice nor law, nor could not be heard, till a whole year was past – till I sent to the Council. This year I did prophesy the truth of many things which afterwards came to pass. The very spirits were subject unto me; what I spake was done. And I had a great name; yet I could do nothing but at adventure.

1580. All this year I was in prison till the 14th day of July. The which day about noon I was delivered on bail, where I had been sixty weeks before, and now by means of the Council's letters was delivered. The next day after I was out of prison, I went towards London poor and bare, with little money. The 18th day a cozening quean professed herself to be my sister.

---

[1] Ashmore is in Dorset, on the Wilts border, a few miles north-east from Iwerne Minster, both in the hilly country south of Shaftesbury.

[2] The vicar of Iwerne Minster was John Fry, instituted 1569.

[3] A tithing in the west of Salisbury; Fisherton Street still exists.

[4] Giles Estcourt, barrister of Lincoln's Inn, was city clerk of Salisbury and a leading J.P. until his death in 1587. He bought the former St Edmund's College of priests, and lived there in Bedwyn Street. *V.C.H.*, *Wilts*. VI. 84, 99, 104.

The 26th of July I went to Greenwich, and there wrought at carpenter's craft for my living. Where I was till the 16th August, at which time I came to London to cure Henry Johnson of a consumption. The 4th of September I went over with Henry Johnson into the Low Countries, into Zealand and Holland. We lay at the Hague some fortnight.

The 3rd of October I came to London again at 10 p.m. The 8th of October I went to Newbury, and lay at John Andrew's till the 16th of November. The 18th of November I came to Quidhampton, where I fell sick. And stayed there a year until the 23rd of October 1581, curing sick and lame folk. In the which time I cured the fellow of Chilhampton[1] of the King's Evil, which had twenty-four holes in his throat and neck. Out of the which in one morning I got eighty-six worms at one time like maggots. And, after, he was well. This year I began to live again.

1581. This year at Lent assizes I was bound over again. I lived at Quidhampton, and did many times thresh and dig and hedge for my living. The 26th of October I took a house in Salisbury on the ditch by the skinner. There I dwelt, practising physic and surgery. And I began again to live.

1582. The 24th of May I bought the leases of the two houses in Culver Street. In June I first came acquainted with A.Y. about the 12th day.[2] The 29th of August Robert Grey and I went to sea and to travel, and fell into the men-of-war's hands at Studland – we agreed on it the 29th of August, but went the 5th day of September. The 17th of October we came home from the Isle of Purbeck. The 23rd of October John Penruddock moved a question to me to be schoolmaster to his children, and I promised him.[3] The 2nd of November I came to London with Mistress Penruddock. The 28th of December I took a house in New Street.

---

[1] A hamlet in the parish of South Newton, a few miles north west of Wilton. In 1585 the manor here was purchased by Giles Estcourt for £360. Hoare, V. Addenda, 40.

[2] I think this means that Forman first became intimate with his boyhood friend, Anne Young.

[3] John Penruddock was head of the third generation in Wilts, retained as counsel for the city of Salisbury, several times M.P. R. Colt Hoare, *Hist. of Modern Wilts*, V. 80.

This year was the first time in sum that ever I did halek cum muher, and I dwelt on the ditch.[1] I became a schoolmaster to John Penruddock, took infinite pain and trouble, and had little profit.

1583. In February I travelled much in business for one and other, and in April, as to London, etc. The 24th day of April I first entered my house in New Street, when I came from London. The 9th of February I did halek cum two muher [with two women]. We went to London, and lay there till we had spent all.

The 6th of May I fell and hurt myself. The 22nd of July was a complaint made to the Bishop against me for using physic.[2] The 17th of December I had my ring made with the eagle's stone. This Christmas I was made lord of the revels, and had privy enemies, friendship of women. A fall in a tower, like to be killed, in catching of pigeons. Great expenses, profit by my pen. I changed my house, and came to dwell among mine enemies in New Street.

I overcame mine enemies with much ado, and by them I got an ill name. I lay fourteen weeks at London with my mistress,[3] spent much and got nothing in the beginning of the year.

1584. The 23rd of January I was first with Mrs Young to sweat her leg and to cure her. I dwelt in New Street. The 29th of February was the first time that ever I did halekekeros harescum tauro cum A.Y.[4] Jane Cole was married the next day. The 25th of April I rode to Marlock with Anne Parsons. The 2nd of June I bought my horse. The 1st of August I took the house in St Thomas's churchyard, and entered to dwell there the 7th of September. The 27th of September I first dressed Agnes Cole. The 23rd of October I redeemed Robin Grey out of the prison.

This year I had many things given me, many new friends, and much good of the woman whom I loved. I thrived reasonable

---

[1] 'Halek' is Forman's word for sexual intercourse. The phrase means 'intercourse with a woman'.

[2] John Piers was bishop of Salisbury 1577–89.

[3] This means Mrs Penruddock, his employer.

[4] This is Forman's full phrase for sexual intercourse, which appears more frequently and shortly as 'halek'. I do not know its derivation.

well. Profit by a woman's friendship both in meat, money, and apparel, for healing the sick. A reasonable good and quiet year. But I had certain brawls and slanders fell out against me about the detecting of one that had stolen certain things: whereby I was like to have been spoiled. Certain women became mine enemies. I departed from John Penruddock of my own accord about Michaelmas.

1585. The 15th of January I rode to Mendip and from thence to Wells and Glastonbury. The 1st of March I began to distil aqua vitae. The 2nd of March I sent to Mrs Commin for money. The 27th day of March A.Y. was delivered at 10 minutes past 7 a.m. of Joshua. The 29th of April I declared in the court against Agnes Commin for [his] healing of Anne Cole.[1] The 6th of May the Bishop's man, Dudgell, struck me. The 13th of May my sister Joan was married to William Hanham. The 16th day I served Jane Cole with a writ, and she fell out with me mightily. The 7th of June I arrested goodwife Commin. The 13th of July I arrested John Matthew. The 13th of July I was imprisoned, and swooned. The 14th day I came forth again. The 31st day I was imprisoned again. The 14th of August I was bailed. The 21st day I was committed to prison again. The 14th of September I engraved my sword. The 10th of October, Jane Bowles, I arrested her with process. The 11th day John Matthew made suit to me for agreement. The 28th day I arrested Mrs Commin with process. The 6th of December I had my silver cup given me. The 23rd December I arrested Prist.

This year was a year of much vexation, trouble, travail, enmity, and strife. I was much overborne, and had divers suits in law. My friends and I were set at variance. I lent money to my friends, and to Mrs Commin, and could not have it again; but was much slandered and infamed by her and her kinswoman, and they sought my life. I had much trouble by them and their false witness; was arrested and imprisoned; was beaten or struck by Dudgell unawares in the open street, 7th of June. The 1st of June I was set out of my house and imprisoned; swooned and was senseless eight

---

[1] Forman brought a case in Chancery against Agnes Commin and John and Jane Samways, Anne Cole's kin, for payment. C 2 Eliz., F10/53. cf. above p. 35–6.

hours. The 31st of July I was before the Bishop and Justices, and sent to prison, my house broke and robbed. The 21st of August I was committed to prison by the Bishop. The 19th December I gave my word for Prist, whereby I was endamaged and had much strife.

1586. This year I had much trouble and suits in law, and did travel and ride much. I got much and spent much, and had many new friends; was discharged from my former troubles and from the assizes (19 July). I had many enemies both secret and open. I had great power in making of friendship, and was bid godfather to a child. I did prosecute mine enemies in law. The 9th of August I first saw Eleanor Farwell, of Poole, for her disease. The 23rd August I returned to London. The 2nd of September I sickened. The Bishop and I were made friends by my Lord Anderson and Sir John Danvers. But I consumed and spent more than I got, and brought myself to beggar's state.

1587. The 1st of January at 7 p.m. A.Y. and I were like to have been betrayed. The 20th I rode to Poole. The 6th of March I was imprisoned 15 past 7 p.m. The 7th of April I had the Council's letters for my discharge. The 11th of May I began to distil many waters. The 10th of June I was discharged from bonds at the assizes contrary to the aspect of all men. The 29th day of August my books, which had been out of my hands long, were brought to John Penruddock's to be seen – where they lay long after, and many were lost. The 28th day I first called to John Goodridge, and he saw first the 4th of November. The 22nd of December I rode to Sir George Carey's.[1]

This year I had much trouble and imprisonments. I practised magic, and had much strife with divers that I had in suits of law; but I thrived reasonable well, yet I lost much. Thomas Eyre sent me to prison the 6th of March.

1588. In May, John Goodridge came to me to dwell, and I put him away the 7th of June. The 30th of June A.Y. and I fell out. In August Susan Farwell became my daughter. In August Stephen came to me first, and did see first the 21st of September.[2] The

[1] Sir George Carey was Governor of the Isle of Wight from 1582.
[2] This is Stephen Michell, Forman's step-brother.

14th of November the constable came for A.Y., and there followed much sorrow after it.

This year I did thrive sufficient well, and had many friends; many enemies and troubles towards the latter end of the year. My special friends and I were set at variance and put asunder; it was the beginning of much sorrow and strife. I began to practice necromancy, and to call angels and spirits.

1589, the 27th of January, being Monday, between 10 and 11 a.m., I was pressed a soldier to serve in the Portugal voyage. Whereupon I was constrained to forsake my country [i.e. neighbourhood] and dwelling, and all my friends. The 30th day I went away from thence to Hampton [i.e. Southampton] with the soldiers. The 10th day of February I was imprisoned at Hampton. The 12th day I came forth of prison again. The 17th day I hurt my thumb at Mr Basset's. The 28th of February I came to Salisbury again. The 3rd of March I went from Salisbury again to Newbury. The 5th day I was troubled with the stone in the yard. The 10th day the gonorrhea passio [pain] came on me. The 14th day I was at Quidhampton. The 26th day I was hurt in the leg with a hatchet. The 25th day of April I went from Newbury to Ash in Surrey,[1] and took Stephen's son in hand to cure; but it was an ill voyage. The 12th day of May I rode to Newbury, and from thence to Mr Basset. The 13th of May a slander was raised against me. The 18th of August I went from Stephen's to London. I took a chamber at Mrs Gott's the 20th day of August, and lay there. The 22nd day very poor, and without any penny; I took a chamber at James Ash's in Barbican.[2] The 26th day the infirmity took me again in my yard. I rode to Salisbury the 7th of November; came from thence the 13th day. Stephen was bound to me again the 21st day.

This year was a wonderful troublesome year to me. I went from place to place. I was glad to forsake all, and did change my lodging often. I got little; I spent and consumed all till Michaelmas. Then it began to mend with me. I practised again necromancy,

---

[1] Near Aldershot.
[2] Outside the City walls beyond Aldersgate.

magic and physic. My enemies prevailed against me, and I was like to have run into many mischiefs.

1590. The 23rd of January I came to my chamber at Mr Clover's, in Cow Lane, on Friday p.m.;[1] rode to Oxford the same day. The 19th of March I borrowed money, and came acquainted with Bess [Vaughan]. The 6th of April I came to lie at Mr Dale's. Stephen went from me to sea the 9th of May. The 28th of May Bess raised a slander by me; renewed again the 2nd of June, ended the 3rd of [June]. The 17th day I distilled my strong water for the stone. The 26th of July I was served with process to appear at the Star Chamber before the Council.[2] I went from Mr Dale's the 27th of July, Monday, and came to stay at Mr Parkes'. The 14th day of September I received Cudstean for my school. The 18th day of September I rode to Lewes to Mr Cumber's; he let unto me his house at Wickham.[3] The 15th of October I sickened in my belly. The 14th of November I was hurt in the face.

This year, 1590, from Christmas to our Lady day, the world went hard with me, and I wanted money and got little. Yet there was supplies and helps still at one time or other. But from our Lady day till fortnight after Midsummer, the world went very hard; I got little and spent much. I ran in debt much and, had not Mr Parkes been, I could not have told what to do. The 28th of May p.m. at 30 past 9, there rose a great brawl by Bess Vaughan against me: I was like to have come to much trouble by it, and to have been killed. I changed my lodging often. Between Easter and Whitsuntide I wrote a book of Necromancy. I lived hardly, yet found some small friends to help me sometimes. I was offered a wife many times this year between Easter ere Whitsuntide, and had the sight and choice of four or five maids and widows. From Midsummer till Michaelmas the world went hard, and I sold many things to make money. After Michaelmas I removed into Sussex, where I went to dwell at Wickham, and was at another man's finding. At All Hallow tide I entered the circle for necromantical

---

[1] Cow Lane led from Smithfield to Holborn bridge.

[2] Mrs Sweyland brought a case against Forman and others. Star Chamber 5, S79/33.

[3] On the border between Sussex and Surrey.

spells. And so lived hardly till our Lady day after, 1591. I spent much, and got nothing; but found good friendship, and William lent me money.[1]

1591, I lay at Cumber's.[2] The 20th of March I found two fishes. The 22nd day of March a.m. at 8, we heard music at circle. The 10th of April I put the longitude in question. The 21st day I rode to London, and lay at Molyneux' to teach him the longitude.[3] The 13th May I sent my chest to London from Cumber's. The 3rd of June I was at Oxford. The 6th of July I put my book of the Longitude to press. The 4th of August I came clean from Sussex and came to Mr Parkes'. The 20th of October I was sick in my back. The 22nd of November Mr Good's book came out against me. The 28th of November I borrowed money of Hugo. In December, 23rd, I borrowed more money of Ashley.

1592; the 13th of January, I received my books from Thomas Penruddock[4] at Salisbury – which had been out of my hands since my first trouble, which was some twenty-four years. The 8th day I did first dress Mrs Nicholls to cure her leg. This month of January I borrowed much money of Hugo, and did redeem my ring from John Kempton. The 8th of February Stephen was bound prentice to me. The 12th day the red mare was delivered to John Alwin. The 17th of March I entered first my chamber at Stone House, and came there first to dwell. The beginning of April I borrowed much money again of Hugo. The 7th of April I went first a-wooing to Anne Noke. I bought me much apparel, and began to come to credit; but it was but a bare year with me. The 11th of June I rode to Ipswich, and came home the 20th day. The 21st day I began to complain in my groin. The 6th of July I took my bed and had the plague in both my groins, and some month after I had the red tokens on my feet as broad as half-pence. It was twenty-two weeks before I was well again – the which did hinder me much. I was let blood the 10th of August.

[1] Presumably his brother William.
[2] i.e. at Lewes in Sussex.
[3] Evidently Emery Molyneux, the compass- and globe-maker; cf. E. G. R. Taylor, *The Mathematical Practitioners of Tudor and Stuart England*, 188.
[4] Son of John Penruddock.

The 27th of September I borrowed 20s of my sister Joan. The 26th of November I borrowed more money of Hugo.

This year I did many notable cures, and began to be known and come to credit.

1593, the 22nd of February, the Barber-Surgeons called me in question for my practice. The 5th of March, Stephen was bound to me again, and William Young came to me. Father Case and Alice Joyce this month were in my hand. The 2nd of April I bought Hugo's ring for 40s. The 14th of April I changed my chamber in the Stone House, and came into the lower chamber.[1] This month Undraths [Andrews?] was cured. In May I made my gown with velvet fur. The 11th of June I did halek Alice Blague, and the 15th of July. The 13th of August I redeemed my ring that was in pawn. The 8th day of October I went first a-wooing to Mrs Lodcaster. The 29th of November, Thursday at 3 p.m. Avis Allen and I first osculavimus [kissed]. She rose and came to me; et halek Avis Allen prius [first] the 15th of December, Saturday p.m. at 5.

This year I lost much money that I should have had for divers cures that I did; and was, besides that, slenderly paid for many cures that I did, because I did not bargain with them first. But my credit increased, and I got much. I cured Avis Allen. But if I did intend to do anything whatsoever, if I did tell anybody of it I was prevented and did not do it, or could have no power to proceed in it. Also, if I did take anyone in hand to cure and did [not] bargain with him first, then either I did not cure him, or else I was not paid for it when it was done. My knowledge in physic and in astronomy did increase; I began to come to credit and to get something about me. Gould overthrew Hugo Ashley in law for £7. I distilled my strong water, for the which I got much money.

1594, the 10th of January, at 30 past 5 p.m., I fell down the stairs. The 14th day (Feb) I was warned before the Doctors. The 16th of February William Buck, my man, came to me. The 8th of March I was before the Doctors. The 11th of March Alice Barker

---

[1] Forman notes that 'few lay in the lower rooms'. He took possession by carrying a book into the lower chamber: 'this was a profitable place'. Ashmole 205.

prorit [was pregnant], and on the 12th day she sent to me. The 21st day I was afore the Bench of Aldermen for Alice Barker. The 30th March paid the Doctors £5. The 4th of April I sickened. The 20th April Anne was christened. Then began the variance between Kate Nicholls and me and Nurse Dandly. Avis Allen forsook me. Mrs Braddedge thought I would have married her; but I intended it not, and she disliked me much till St John's tide [Midsummer]. The 22nd of September I sickened at night in my head. The 9th of December I fell down the stairs again at 5 p.m. The friendship between Avis Allen and I was renewed.

I got much and spent much, and had many brabbles and brawls. This summer, in July or thereabouts, I had the wet gout in my feet; it broke under the toe next the great toe in my left foot. I cured myself with the dregs of my strong water, through God's help.

1595. This 1st of January I was cozened by one of Greenwich, which made me go thither promising me 20s, but paid me nothing. The 2nd day I was cozened again almost, but I was deceived. About the 4th of January my throat began to be sore, and was sore till the 28th day. Mr Allen misliked of certain speeches I used, 31st of January, Friday p.m. at 8. The 1st of February, p.m. at 5, Saturday, his wife told me of his speeches. The 2nd of February, Sunday, at 5 Mr Allen came to me and had me home. On Monday the collectors came to me p.m. at 6. The 4th of February, Tuesday a.m., Mrs Flower and her cousin came to me. I and a gentleman were like to fall out for standing at the garden by a gentlewoman. The 5th day, Wednesday, then came at afternoon an old quent merchant unto me, that was the confederate with Mrs Flower. The 6th day, about 8 of the clock in the morning, came Hugh Fort to me from A.Y. Divers gentlewomen came to me that day. That afternoon at 4 came Mrs Johnson to me at the Red Cross in Watling Street to come and see her child. I went to her, et osculavi illam in domu sua [and kissed her in her home]. This 6th day at night Mrs Allen sent for me to supper, and I went not. Whereupon she took great grief and was sick; and sent to me the 11th day, etc. The 7th day Hugh Fort went away; at night came Mrs Taylor to me, at 6 p.m. the Northern man. The

11th day at 8 a.m. Mr Allen sent me a note of discourtesy for lifting up the cup.[1] The 15th day February, p.m. at 5, came one Christmas about a servant run away. The 25th of February, Tuesday a.m. at 15 past 8, halek cum Joan Wild.

The 12th of March, Wednesday p.m. at 4, Joan Wild: halek. The 13th day March, Thursday, Avis Allen and I went aboard my Lord Cumberland's ship, etc.[2] The 15th day, Saturday, at 9 a.m. came servants to seek for bran. At 3 at afternoon came Avis Allen unto me, and we were frayed again; we were half out afore; she told me how John Davies spake against me to her husband. The 28th of March, at 6 p.m., I was sent for to my Lady Hawkins, and went.[3] The 2nd of April, Wednesday a.m. between 8 and 9, my head and beard was cut. That day Allen took physic. I dreamed of John Barter and his wife, of Hinton St Mary, in the night.[4] I was forced to stay at Mr Allen's, because of Israel Johnson and Mrs Swayman [Sweyland], three hours longer than I wote [would]. I made syrups of violets that day. The 30th of April, Wednesday a.m. at 50 past 9, I began first to take my diet drink; that night my throat began to be sore.

In Lent I began the philosopher's stone, and before made my furnace and all for it – as in my other book it appears. I made many syrups and drugs, distilled many waters, and bought stills.

The 2nd of May a jar fell out between Avis Allen and myself: there was conceived some discourtesy, for that Joan [Wild] left her apron at my house, and she was sick about it. But we were friends again the next day. The 19th of May, Monday, Avis Allen took dislike of me pro halekeros [on account of intercourse], and in nowise would be firm with me again, nor come at me after but by great constraint, etc. The 26th of May we were friends again, p.m. at 30 past 2, being at garden, after we had related all matters between us. Deo gratias!

[1] This may refer to some magical use, perhaps the antimonial cup.

[2] This was a fine new ship which the Queen sententiously named the *Scourge o, Malice*. She made three voyages under Cumberland, and was bought by the East India Company. G. C. Williamson, *George Third Earl of Cumberland, 1558–1605*, 142.

[3] This was Margaret, 2nd wife of Sir John Hawkins.

[4] Near Sturminster in Dorset. Later that year, 25 September 'I dreamed I went awooing to John Barter's widow of Hinton Mary.'

The 2nd of June, p.m. at 8, the constable and others came with a warrant for me. The 3rd day, p.m. 30 past 12, I was with Sir Richard Martin, and bound to answer the next day at sises [sessions].[1] The 7th day of June, at 30 past 8, coming from the garden with Mrs Allen and her husband, I met with Mrs Wild just at our gate. Whereupon Avis Allen was sore angry. She went to the Fleet on Whitsunday [8 June];[2] she went to Walham Green the 11th June, Wednesday in Whitsun week, and she would not come at me. The 11th day, a.m. at 8, I put Anne to a new nurse, to Clemens the tailor's wife, of Great Bookham in Surrey.[3] The 12th day June, at 11 in the morning [Avis Allen] was with me, and Mr Allen came in the while. The 13 June, p.m. at 52 min. past 1, Friday, Avis Allen sent me her first letter, saying she would come no more at me. The 13th day, at 1 of the clock p.m., Friday, going down the stairs, I read John Ward's articles at stairfoot and, as I stood, a cat mewed twice. But I could not see her, which prophesied ill, and some hour after, the letter came. The 14th day of June, Saturday, in the morning at 12, I went to Mrs Allen to see her distilling, and came in a good time. We were reconciled, and made friends again between ourselves. And at 4 of the clock p.m., she came to me, and 30 minutes past 4 halekekeros harescum tauro. And at that instant time we renewed out friendship, and made a new league of friendship for ever to endure: God grant it may, and never break again.

The 18th of June I went from home, Wednesday, through William Fallowfield's words. And on Thursday I rode into Wiltshire to Salisbury, to see my friends, where I had not been in seven years before. The 30th day of June was a final conclusion and end of all our friendship between A.Y. and I; I received my rings and jewels again from her.

[1] Sir Richard Martin was an Alderman of London 1578–98, and took over as Lord Mayor 2 July 1594.

[2] This probably means the Fleet prison, perhaps visiting fellow-Catholics.

[3] Forman's acquaintance Elizabeth Slyfield (or Slyfford), daughter of a London citizen, was the wife of Henry Slyfield, who owned Slyfield in Great Bookham parish, where Forman had stayed with them. One sees the couple still on a brass in the church.

The 25th of July I was at Berwick St John's.[1] The 29th July I came to London again. This year I did lose many of my old friends, the most part. The 15th of September, at 3 p.m., I departed angry from Avis Allen. The 23rd of September, Tuesday at night, Mr Allen and his wife, Mrs Allen of the ship, and Mrs Roberts did sup with me. The 24th day, Wednesday, Avis Allen took physic and grief about Bridget Allen [i.e. 'of the ship']. The 25th day I took physic. Avis Allen came to me to end her league of friendship, and went from me in a fury. The 26th day, Friday, at 10 a.m., I went to Avis Allen: we conferred with her, and she would not be friends with me. We departed in ire. This day, p.m. at 55 past 3, I bought a pair of new black stockings, cost 12*s*. That morning I dreamt of three black rats and of my philosophical powder which I was distilling. That day came Mr Roche, the Queen's physician, to me to be acquainted with me.

The 23rd day (of October) I fell out with my man, like to put him away. The 24 October, Mother Parker told me that Wat was taken. The 30th of October my man and I fell out, and I put him away the same day at 4 p.m. The 31st October I was sick. The 1st November, Saturday, p.m. at 6, I sent word to Avis Allen that it would be a black day for her because she came not to me: I was marvellously fretted with it. Little doings in physic from Midsummer to Christmas. The 7th of November I was imprisoned by the Doctors. The 22nd, 23rd, 24th and 25th of November, a villain in prison urged me much and slandered me sorely to my great disgrace: Tutsham. I was delivered from prison the 25th of November.

The 4th of December, p.m. at 4, Thursday, Avis Allen and I fell out and parted, our friendship ended. The 7th day at 9 p.m. he [Mr Allen] misliked of me [that] I was there. The 8th day, Monday, 40 past 1, I was there, talked with her, and ended the matter never to use her more. The 12th day of December was a wonderful unlucky day to me. I brake two glasses and lost the water; many things framed evil in my hands, and I was very unfortunate, especially from 10 of the clock till night. At afternoon

[1] Near Tisbury in Wiltshire. Robert Pinckney was rector from 1579, so perhaps Forman visited him there.

I went to one to Chancery Lane sick; there came in Dr Wilkins the while, and he and I fell out about the sick body: one William Fulke. There was Mrs Starkie there. And always my ill fortunes fell out when the moon did [ascend] most commonly . . . The 27th of December Avis Allen and I were friends again perfectly, and halekekeros harescum tauro.

1596. The 2nd of January at 40 past 7 a.m., in halekekren Avis and I fell sick. Sunday, 11th January p.m. I was at Mr Bragg's at Tallis. The 11th of January, at night, I was first at Mrs Slyfford's; I supped at Mr Osborne's. I saw and conferred with many. The 14th of January, Wednesday, p.m. at 7, I fell down the stairs like to kill myself, hurt my left leg, and broke my shin. The 15th day at 8 a.m. I was warned to appear before Doctor Stamp of the Arches. The 18th January I went to visit Mr Chaloner. The 19th I was called to come before Dr Stamp and was warned to. The 20th day at 10 a.m. Sefton and I fell out. At that time I went to Avis Allen, and halek. Suspicion like to grow. That night I was at Mrs Allen's. The 23rd day, Friday, p.m. at 30 past 5, I went to Avis Allen. She and I fell out, for that she came not to me the day before, but made an excuse and went alone another way, which I suspected to Widops. She said she went, but I think she went to Kate's. The 24th day, I kept a feast, Mrs Osborne and Widow Slyfford. The 26th day, Monday, at 20 past 2, I went to Avis Allen and, after much talk, we were friends again. Deo gratias . . . [Three lines in cipher give details of her physical condition.] The 29th January p.m., Thursday, at 20 past 2, halek Julian in Seething Lane. At 4 I went first to see the 'Garden Katherine'. This 29th of January at 6 p.m. came one Mr Mosley, a physician, to talk with me about Elizabeth Watts at Billingsgate, to examine the medicine I gave her. The 30th January, Friday, in the morning I dined at Mr Bragg's. I went to speak with Mr Katherine for his garden, and I met Dr Jones. When I came home Henry Pepper came to me craftily to undercrop me, and told me he saw certain books of mine, as Cycatrix, etc. [More in cipher.] The 31 January, Saturday, Widow Sheffs was with me, and I went also. She was sick: Avis Allen sent me a note, and she dined with me.

The 1st of February she swooned at noon. The 8th of February I met Mrs Katherine as I came from Ratcliff; she told me of Mr Allen and of Avis Allen p.m. at 4. The 9th day at 10 halek cum Margaret App. The 9th at night my throat began to be sore. The 12th day at noon, I talked with Margery Sustbery at garden, and at 3 at afternoon with Mr Allen about our strife. The 18th February, Wednesday a.m. 30 past 10, halek Julian Clark. The 19th day, Thursday a.m., I was with Avis Allen, and she desired me to leave her company for ever. The 20th day, Friday, a.m. at 10, I cut the ring finger of my right hand almost off with my sword hanging by my bed. The 28th February, halek Anne Nurse at 3, Ankers p.m. at 6, and Judith.

The 1st March, strife with Pepper, about words. The 2nd March, halek Joan West. The 5th of March, Friday, I put on my new furred gown, a.m. 6. The 9th of March, I put on my velvet jerkin, a.m. at 9. The 12th of March, Friday p.m. 30 past 5, I went to garden, where I found Avis Allen; we became friends again and I did halek, etc., cum illa [with her]. The 29th of March, Avis Allen hit me in the mouth with her hand. The 5th of April, Monday, Avis Allen scratched me by the face that I bled. The 6th of April, Tuesday, I rode out to Maldon. The 10th day, I came home from Maldon. The 27th of April, in subliming, my pot and glass broke, and all my labour was lost pro lapide [for the philosopher's stone]. The 30th of April, Friday a.m. at 6, my throat within on the left side began to be sore, like the quinsy. The 26th of June, Avis Allen delivered of a man-child, named Alexander, that died shortly after.

The beginning of July, Sefton began his villainy, and slanderous speeches, and Atkins against me. The 25th of July, Allen and I fell out, and I came no more at him. In July Sefton and I fell out and Atkins, about their villainy. The 14th of August, Sefton filed his bill of covenants; Sefton's wife and I fell out for her lewd speeches. The 13th of August, I fetched my things from Mrs Clark's. The 16th August, Monday, Avis Allen sent me word she would not come at me, and took in dudgeon at my letter sent to her the night before; they brought me her 10s. But the 18th day August, I went to her and we were friends, and did halek. She promised me to come to me the next day; she came not, but delayed it from day to day. The 23rd day, p.m. at 20 past 6, I went to her; she and I fell out wonderfully, and departed not friends through her own folly. I went to the Clink . . .[1] [cipher]. The 26th August, at 30 past 2, she [i.e. Avis] sent for me, and I went home. We had conference, and became very good friends again; 30 past 3 I did halek Avis Allen, and at this time she was sick.

The 13th September I was arrested by Kate Whitehill for a blow. The 15th of September, a.m. at 8, I was sent to the Counter by my Lord Mayor at the Doctors' request.[2] The 29th of September, I came forth of prison. The 30th of September I was sent to prison again by the Doctors. The 12th of October I came forth of prison again. The 19th I came home to Kate's again. The 23rd of October, Jarvis stabbed Atkins in my chamber, and then began he his villainy against me with Sefton and Kyrwell. The 24th day they had out a warrant for me: I forsook my house and went to Kate's. The 27th of October at night, 30 past 6, my man went from me and put me away. The 31st day of October I went from London to Sandwich, and did travel and spent much.

1597. Avis Allen died 13th of June.

Between Michaelmas and Christmas I took Lambeth House, and entered it a month afore Christmas: Lambeth House at Westminster, nota.

1598. About Midsummer I came from Lambeth, and sold my house to James Bainton for £90 for five years and a half. At Christmas following, Bess went from me cum qua halek et fuit gravida [with whom intercourse and she was pregnant]. She came to me at Easter. Fardell lay at Lambeth at my house. My sister Joan lay at Lambeth Lane, and made much ado at Christmas in the beginning of the year – shut Margery out of door and Jane into the orchard. Robert Langley dwelt with me. John Good also dwelt with me then, and confessed to the robbing of my study. At

---

[1] The prison on the South Bank, in Southwark. Stow, II. 55–6.

[2] There were several Counters, for small offences, in London. Forman was several times confined in the Wood Street Counter, which pertained to the Lord Mayor and Sheriffs. Stowe, I. 296.

Midsummer I took the bail where I dwelt at London, but left not the Stone House. Alice came to me about Easter.

This year I got well [i.e. money], did spend much, and had good credit. The latter end of the year the Doctors arrested me, and I them, and went to law together. Mr Condwell and I came acquainted. I was in danger of killing by Bosgrove and Bainton, for my house of Lambeth.

1599. I left the Stone House at Christmas in the beginning of the year. I arrested Peter Sefton on his bond, and was bail for him myself on the action. Fennena, Bess Parker's child, was born the 9th of June, Saturday, some two months after she was married. I was married to Anne Baker, of Kent, Sir Edward Munnings' sister's daughter, the 22nd of July, Sunday, in the 47th year of my age.[1] I was quit from the Doctors from imprisonment; but I condemned them in law, and put them to silence for a whole year and a half after. At Michaelmas I was in Kent at Gravesend. At Whitsuntide I was at Parson Sandy's. I bought my gelding, cóst £18, and sent him to Mr Sandy's about Michaelmas.

This year was the great muster in August at St James's. I bought much harness and weapons for war, swords, daggers, muskets, corselet and furniture, staves, halberds, gauntlets, mails, etc. This year also I bought much linen.

1600. At Easter I put Peter Sefton's bond in suit. The 8th of May, Anne Young died of a dropsy. I wrote out the two books of *De arte memoratus* of Apollonius Niger, drawn with gold, of the seven liberal sciences.[2] Arthur came to dwell with me at Michaelmas. I copied out also the four books of Stenographia,[3] and divers

---

[1] In the Autobiography Forman says Sir Edward Munnings' daughter; perhaps father and son were both Sir Edward.

[2] cf. Frances A. Yates, *The Art of Memory*, 43: 'there was formed a tradition which, going underground for centuries . . . appeared in the Middle Ages as the *Ars Notoria*, a magical art of memory attributed to Apollonius or sometimes to Solomon. The practitioner of the *Ars Notoria* gazed at figures or diagrams curiously marked and called *notae* whilst reciting magical prayers. He hoped to gain in this way knowledge, or memory, of all the arts and sciences.'

[3] There was a marked growth of interest in stenography or shorthand at this time, from Timothy Bright's first attempt at a system with his 'Charactery', 1588 to John Willis' *Art of Stenography*, 'the foundation of all the later systems of shorthand'.

other books. I made many syrups, distilled many waters, and made many drugs. At Michaelmas I rode into Kent to Mr Webb's, and to Canterbury, much to my hindrance; we had an ill and unfortunate journey of it. About the latter end of November the Doctors sent for me to their Hall again; I went not, but wrote unto them. It cost me £40 this year in apparel, and better: almost £50 for my wife and for myself. Frances came to dwell with me after Bartholomew tide [August 24]. I bought many pictures about our Lady day. This summer I had my own picture drawn; and made my purple gown, my velvet cap, my velvet coat, my velvet breeches, my taffeta cloak, my hat, and many other things. And did let my hair and beard grow. Many slanderous speeches were by the Doctors and others used secretly against me; yet I thrived reasonable well, I thank God. I lent out much money on plate and jewels, had many trifles given me. I bought my swatchel [fencing] sword, and did the hangers [loops of the belt] with silver. Arthur came to dwell first with me about All Hallow tide [November 1st]. My brother John lay with me oftentimes. In the last end of this year or thereabout my brother Robert died.

1601. The 16th of January, Thursday a.m. at 9, halek Anne Condwell; a.m. at 12, Frances Hill. The 17th day at night, Friday, I supped at Mr Webb's. The 18th day, Saturday, I supped at Mr Baker's in Coleman Street. The 26th day of January, Sunday, at night towards Monday, my wife dreamed that she was with child, and Mrs Condwell the same night dreamed so also. The same 26th day, Sunday, in the morning, my throat began to be sore; at night it was very sore, and I was much troubled with the rheum. At 10 at night I did halek cum uxore mea [with my wife]. The 27th day, Monday, Dr Blague and his wife, and Mr Webb and his wife, dined with me. Halek Anne Condwell, p.m. at 30 past 3. The 28th day my throat was sore; Bess was with me, my wife's sister.

A week afore Whitsunday, I came again to Lambeth to dwell in Prat's house; and at Midsummer gave up London quite.[1] About

D.N.B. under Timothy Bright. Forman may have got hold of some earlier manuscript connected with the *Ars Notoria*.

[1] '16 March 1601, I took the house at Lambeth from Mr Prat, £20 p.a., received the key 26 March and sent a load of stuff thither from my house at London.' Ms. Ashmole 411.

Bartholomew tide I was at Mr Webb's. In September [a figure cast]: I shall be hurt of my servant unexpected and not mistrusting. In October my sister Joan and William Brink came to London to see me, and stayed a week. I came acquainted with my Lord of Hertford.

I rode three unprofitable voyages or journeys: the first, the week afore Bartholomew tide to Mr Webb's; the second, at Michaelmas to Malmesbury in North Wiltshire; the third, the 10th of November again to Malmesbury. In this voyage I lost the scabbard of my sword, and my stockings, nightcap-band and a towel, an ephemerides [astronomical almanac] and garters, and other things from my horse. My journey was in vain, and the parties were not confident [believing], but disappointed me when I came there. I came home again with much toil and travail, and spent much in vain.

The 2nd of November, Sunday, or thereabout, I and my man, coming from my Lord of Hertford's in Canon Row[1] at 8 at night and past, were like to have been both killed by Captain Hammond that was drunk. My wife's mother came in August, and lay with me some eight weeks, and her husband, Sybil and Will, and his man. The 23rd of November my wife and I fell out for her folly and negligence. My brother John died the 13th of December. He sickened the 5th day, and died the 12th day at night, and was buried the 13th day.

This year I thrived, thanks be to God, reasonable well. I bought much household stuff and provision for the house, and much apparel; and was at much charge in keeping of my horse, and my conies [rabbits]. Divers pigeons which were given me did not prosper with me, but were killed by rats and stolen; some pigeons flew away. My servants were very disobedient and negligent – carls. Stephen came to lie with me about the 24th of November, and tarried all Christmas [i.e. to Twelfth day]. Mr Horelstone [Hurleston], being sick, came to lie at my house about the 15th of December, Thursday p.m. I came acquainted with my

---

[1] Canon Row, leading from Westminster to Whitehall, was a fashionable quarter occupied by houses of the nobility. Stow, II. 102.

Lord of Hertford, and with my Lady Mary,[1] and divers other gentlemen.

1602. Accidents this year: the 1st of January, being New Year's day, at 4 p.m. I hit my right knee against the door-post going forth, which grieved me much. The 4th of January, p.m. at 4, I went to see Mr Short, sick at Giles in the Field, and saw there Sara Brewer. The 3rd, Sunday, I kept my Christmas dinner.

[1] This was the Earl's sister, Lady Mary Rogers.

Forman's Notes on his Family

There are three things generally recorded of the Formans from generation to generation: they were never covetous of honour nor of wealth, nor of other men's goods; never treacherous to any nor false of their word to any; nor never proud, but meek, merciful and pitiful. They never desire strife, but peace and quietness; they never desire hatred, but friendship; they never seek revenge of any notable injury. They always love justice and maintain the right, and are utter enemies to injury and oppression, apt to forgive. And have been always good commonwealth's men, as it appeared in old Richard my grandfather, in the time when the abbeys were suppressed in Henry VIII's days, which refused to have any of the abbey land when it was offered him; and in my father and divers others.

Richard Forman, son of William, took to wife Joan Wolsey, whom he stole out of Devonshire from Wolsey House, which lieth some six miles from Cullompton and Crediton. He brought her to Burford,[1] a mile from Salisbury south-east, and there he was married unto her – this Joan was sole heir to Wolsey house, and to all the lands and possessions of her father – about the year 1522. He had issue by her, William and Joan. This Joan was after married to Walter Hart, gentleman, of Netherhampton, and had issue a son named Walter and a daughter named Joan. Joan Wolsey deceased about 1551 and was buried at Fuggleston in the parish of Quidhampton, where she dwelled. Richard Forman deceased and was buried at Fuggleston, by his wife in the east end of the chancel, 1556, on New Year's day. This Richard was a courtier, governor of the abbey of Wilton before the suppression. After, the abbey and lands were given to William Herbert, Earl of Pembroke. [Richard] left all to William his son, who in his youth was brought up with my Lady Willoughby as her page.

William Forman was born at Quidhampton, 1524, and about the year 1544 he took to wife Mary Ratew, daughter of John Ratew

[1] Known more generally now as Britford.

and Margery Hallam,[1] born in Hampshire at Littleton, a mile from Andover. He had issue by the said Mary six sons and two daughters . . .

This William was sole heir and executor to his father. Because there were many accounts and reckonings depending between Richard Forman his father and William, Earl of Pembroke, about the abbey lands and goods and divers other matters – because he was steward after to the old earl – he procured a lawyer and a priest to make up all reckonings between them. Which was four years in doing, before William Forman could have his *quietus est* from the earl. In this time the said priest and lawyer, having the full use and possession of counting-house, books, writings and all deeds of land that were in the counting-house of the said Richard, stole away all the deeds and evidences of his lands. And the said William, mistrusting not, was deceived of all. Then, dying shortly after, Mary his wife – having many small children and being a woman full of care and heaviness, not knowing where much of the lands lay – knew not where to send for her rents. And to those places that she did know, sending for rent, they would pay her none, because she had not anything to show for it. The lawyer sold the lands, and so there was no recovery of it; because she, being a woman, knew not how to help herself in that behalf. And so was all the lands lost.

This William died, 1563 . . . when he had lived thirty-nine years. Mary Ratew, his wife, lived a widow forty-two years, and died 1604. She had lived ninety-seven years, and had her eyesight, limbs and memory very well – but a fortnight before she deceased she could walk alone two miles, thanks be to God. She left Richard Forman, her son, sole executor of all she had when she died. She was a widow when she was married to William Forman: she had two children before by another man, a man-child and a woman-child, Phyllis. The man child died, but the woman lived

[1] In the Autobiography Forman calls her Marian, and John Ratew is named John Foster, esquire – more probably John Ratew alias Foster. There are numerous variations in the spelling of names, and discrepancies in names, understandable in a world that went by ear – quite apart from lapses of memory or gaps in his knowledge. Not surprising when written records were the exception, and people relied on memory, tradition, gossip.

till she was sixty years old. She was married to one Henry Michell, by whom she had four children: Leonard, John, Sybil, and Stephen. Leonard went beyond sea at seventeen years old, and died without issue. Stephen was some twenty-seven years old [when] slain, 1601, in Sir William Monson's ship at sea by the Spaniards. Sybil married with a hatmaker, and she died 1607. John Michell married also.

Henry Forman, born 1547, took to wife Anne Hart, daughter of Thomas Hart, gentleman, brother to Walter Hart, which married Joan, daughter of Richard Forman and Joan Wolsey. This Henry had by this Anne Hart one only daughter named Agnes, born in Quidhampton about 1573, for he was married to Anne Hart 1572. His wife died 1574, 6 November, and was buried at Fuggleston. This Henry went beyond sea about 1580, being a widower, and was never more heard of. His daughter was living in Dorsetshire, 1604.

Forman's Account of four Shakespeare Plays: April 1611

'The Book of Plays and Notes thereof per Forman – for Common Policy.'

MACBETH AT THE 'GLOBE' 20 APRIL 1611

In *Macbeth* at the 'Globe', 1611 the 20th of April, Saturday, there was to be observed: first, how Macbeth and Banquo, two noblemen of Scotland, riding through a wood, there stood before them three women fairies or nymphs. And saluted Macbeth, saying three times unto him, 'Hail, Macbeth, king of Cawdor; for thou shalt be a king, but shalt beget no kings,' etc. Then said Banquo, 'What all to Macbeth, and nothing to me?' 'Yes,' said the nymphs. 'Hail to thee, Banquo; thou shalt beget kings, yet be no king.'

So they departed and came to the Court of Scotland to Duncan, King of Scots, and it was in the days of Edward the Confessor.

Duncan bade them both kindly welcome, and made Macbeth forth with the Prince of Northumberland, and sent him home to his own castle. And appointed Macbeth to provide for him, for he would sup with him the next day at night, and did so. Macbeth contrived to kill Duncan, and, through the persuasion of his wife, did that night murder the King in his own castle, being his guest. And there were many prodigies seen that night and the day before. When Macbeth had murdered the King the blood on his hands could not be washed off by any means, nor from his wife's hands, which handled the bloody daggers in hiding them. By which means they became both much amazed and affronted. The murder being known, Duncan's two sons fled: the one to England, the [other to] Wales, to save themselves. They being fled, they were supposed guilty of the murder of their father: which was nothing so.

Then was Macbeth crowned king. Then he, for fear of Banquo, his old companion, that he should beget kings but be no king himself, contrived the death of Banquo, and caused him to be murdered on the way as he rode. The next night, being at supper with his noblemen whom he had bid to the feast – to the which also Banquo should have come – he began to speak of noble Banquo and to wish that he were there. As he thus did, standing up to drink a carouse to him, the ghost of Banquo came and sat down in his chair behind him. He, turning about to sit down again, saw the ghost of Banquo: which affronted him so, that he fell into a great passion of fear and fury, uttering many words about his murder. By which, when they heard that Banquo was murdered, they suspected Macbeth.

Then Macduff fled to England to the King's son. So they raised an army, came into Scotland, and at Dunsinane overthrew Macbeth. In the meantime, while Macduff was in England, Macbeth slew Macduff's wife and children. And after, in the battle, Macduff slew Macbeth.

Observe also how Macbeth's queen did rise in the night in her sleep, and walked and talked and confessed all. And the doctor noted her words.

CYMBELINE

Remember also the story of Cymbeline, king of England, in Lucius' time. How Lucius came from Octavius Caesar for tribute; and, being denied, sent Lucius with a great army of soldiers, who landed at Milford Haven. And after were vanquished by Cymbeline, and Lucius taken prisoner. All by means of three outlaws: of which two of them were the sons of Cymbeline, stolen from him when they were but two years old by an old man whom Cymbeline banished. He kept them as his own sons twenty years with him in a cave.

And how [one] of them slew Cloten, the Queen's son, going to Milford Haven to seek the love of Imogen, the King's daughter, whom he had banished also for loving his daughter. How the Italian that came, from her love [i.e. from love of *her*], conveyed himself into a chest; and said it was a chest of plate sent, from her love and others, to be presented to the King. In the deepest of the night, she being asleep, he opened the chest and came forth of it. And viewed her in her bed and the marks of her body; took away her bracelet, and after accused her of adultery to her love. etc.

In the end, how he came with the Romans into England and was taken prisoner. And after revealed to Imogen, who had turned herself into man's apparel and fled to meet her love at Milford Haven and chanced to fall on the cave in the woods where her two brothers were. How by eating a sleeping dram they thought she had been dead, and laid her in the woods, the body of Cloten by her, in her love's apparel that he left behind him. And how she was found by Lucius, etc.

RICHARD II AT THE 'GLOBE', 20 APRIL 1611

Remember therein how Jack Straw [sc. Wat Tyler] by his over-much boldness, not being politic nor suspecting anything, was suddenly at Smithfield Bars stabbed by Walworth, the mayor of London. So he and his whole army was overthrown. Therefore, in such a case or the like, never admit any party without a bar between; for a man cannot be too wise, nor keep himself too safe.

Also remember how the duke of Gloucester, the earl of Arundel, Oxford and others, crossing the king in his humour about the duke of Ireland and Bushy, were glad to fly and raise an host of men. Being in his castle, how the duke of Ireland came by night to betray him with three hundred men; but having privy warning thereof kept his gates fast and would not suffer the enemy to enter. Which went back again with a flea in his ear, and after was slain by the earl of Arundel in the battle.

Remember also, when the duke [Gloucester] and Arundel came to London with their army, king Richard came forth to them, met them and gave them fair words; and promised them pardon and that all should be well if they would discharge their army. Upon whose promises and fair speeches they did it. And, after, the king bid them all to a banquet and so betrayed them and cut off their heads, etc., because they had not his pardon under his hand and seal before, but his word.

Remember therein also, how the duke of Lancaster privily contrived all villainy to set them all together by the ears; and to make the nobility to envy the king, and mislike of him and his government. By which means he made his own son king, which was Henry Bolingbroke.

Remember also how the duke of Lancaster asked a wise man whether himself should ever be king; and he told him No, but his son should be a king. When he had told him, he hanged him up for his labour, because he should not bruit it abroad or speak thereof to others.

This was a policy in the commonwealth's opinion, but I say it was a villain's part and a Judas kiss to hang the man for telling him the truth. Beware by this example of noblemen and of their fair words, and say little to them, lest they do the like by thee for thy goodwill.

THE WINTER'S TALE AT THE 'GLOBE': 15 MAY 1611

Observe there how Leontes, the king of Sicilia, was overcome with jealousy of his wife with the king of Bohemia, his friend, that came to see him. How he contrived his death, and would have had his cupbearer to have poisoned [him]: who gave the king of Bohemia warning thereof and fled with him to Bohemia.

Remember also how he sent to the oracle of Apollo, and the answer of Apollo – that she was guiltless and that the king was jealous, etc.; and how, except the child was found again that was lost, the king should die without issue. For the child was carried into Bohemia and there laid in a forest and brought up by a shepherd. The king of Bohemia's son married that wench. And how they fled into Sicilia to Leontes. The shepherd, having shown the letter of the nobleman by whom Leontes sent away that child and the jewels found about her, she was known to be Leontes' daughter, and was then sixteen years old.

Remember also the rogue that came in all tattered like Coll

Pixie; how he feigned him sick and to have been robbed of all that he had. How he cozened the poor man of all his money. And, after, came to the sheep-shearing with a pedlar's pack and there cozened them again of all their money. How he changed apparel with the king of Bohemia's son, and then how he turned courtier, etc.

Beware of trusting feigned beggars or fawning fellows.

Index

Adrian, Dr, 203
Alchemy, 160, 240
Alcock, Mary, trader, 173
Aleppo, 186, 191
Allen, Avis, Forman's mistress, 24–5, 50, 51–69, 288–95; William, husband of, 53–69, 91, 289–95; family, 182, 292
Allen, Thomas, mathematician and astrologer, 7
Anglesey, 121, 127
Anne, James I's Queen, 106, 107
Apothecaries, 87, 240
Archangel, 179
Archdell, Sarah, 77
Armada of 1588, 103, 164
Ashmole, Elias, scientist and astrologer, 8, 20, 41–2, 151
Aske, John, 166–7, 218
Aubrey, John, 26, 36, 195–6
Audley End, 226
Azores Expedition of 1597, 100, 166, 218

Bagley, 'Goodman', seaman, 173, 174–5
Bancroft, Richard, archbishop, 147
Barber-Surgeons, Company of, 9, 47, 83, 288
Barnsdale, Dr, 203
Bassano, Baptista, Queen's musician, 99, 102; see also Lanier
Bath, 235, 238
Bermuda, 254
Bertie, Catherine, 236
Berwick-on-Tweed, 103
Bible, 41, 146, 150, 239
Billingsley, Henry, translator of Euclid, 186
Blague, Thomas, Dean of Rochester, 49, 118–39, 243, 297; his wife, Alice, 92–3, 118–39,

288; Forman's character of her, 120–1; daughter, Frances, 140
Blood-letting, 9–10, 50, 203–4, 287
Bodleian Library, 129, 264
Bowles, Dr John, schoolmaster, 28, 157, 270
Braddedge, John, Forman's servant, 51–2, 90; his mother, 51, 289
Braxted, Essex, 119, 136–7
Brereton, Dorothy, later Lady Legh, 236–8
Brooke, Sir Calisthenes, soldier, 18–19
Brothels, 57, 59
Broughton, Hugh, divine, 17, 145–50
Burbage, Elizabeth and Humphry, 202
Burbage, James, actor, 99, 103
Burghley, William Cecil, Lord, 118, 121, 123, 147, 148–9, 157, 198, 218

Cadiz, 164, 184, 190
Cambridge, 9, 118, 136, 139–40, 146, 152, 205, 244
Canterbury, 92, 128, 245, 247
Cardan, Jerome, mathematician, 41
Carey, Sir George, second Lord Hunsdon, 38, 103, 183, 187, 233–5
Carey, William, 103
Caribbean, English ships in, 167, 173, 174, 177, 185, 187
Carmarden, Richard, Customs official, 198
Cecil, Sir Robert, 170, 176, 182, 234
Cezimbra, Sir William Monson's exploit at, 179
Chamberlain's Company, the Lord, 15, 79, 99, 103
Charles I, as Prince, 232

309